W. L. CHARLTON

THE MASQUES OF OTTAWA

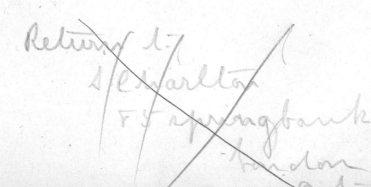

MARIA CHAPDELAINE

BY

W. H. BLAKE

From the original French of Louis Hemon

Cloth 12mo. : $1.50 net.

The Macmillans in Canada count it a high privilege to sponsor the very able translation by W. H. Blake of "Maria Chapdelaine." It is not too much to say that Louis Hemon's intimate view of the moods and manners and moments of the dwellers in French Canada is indeed an immortelle flowering in the somewhat straggling garden of Canadian literature. It may well be that "Maria Chapdelaine" will take its place in the undulating landscape of the literature of all time beside such classic stories as "The Vicar of Wakefield" and "Paul et Virginie."

TORONTO : THE MACMILLAN COMPANY OF CANADA, LIMITED

THE
MASQUES OF OTTAWA

BY

"DOMINO"

"Wherefore are these things hid?
. . . .
We will draw the curtain and show you the picture."
—SHAKESPEARE.

TORONTO : THE MACMILLAN COMPANY
OF CANADA, LTD., AT ST. MARTIN'S HOUSE.
MCMXXI.

THE PLAY-HOUSE CALLED OTTAWA.

Do not imagine that I spend much time at once in Ottawa.
I have never liked the kind of play-house that politicians
have made on that glorious plateau in a valley of wonder-
land with a river of dreams rolling past to the sea. Where
under heaven is any other Capital so favoured by the great
scenic artist? On what promontory do parliamentary
towers and gables so colossally arise to enchant the vision?
The Thames draws the ships of the world and crawls
muddily and lazily out to sea wondering what haphazard
of history ever concentrated so much commerce, politics
and human splendour on the banks of one large ditch.
Ottawa's house of political drama overlooks one of the
noblest rivers in the world, that takes its rise in everlasting
hills of granite and pines.

One, Laurier, used to dream that he would devote his
declining days to making Ottawa beautiful as a city as she
is for the site of a capital. To him as to others, Rome,
London, Paris, Vienna, Washington, should all in time be
rivalled by Ottawa the magnificent. But the saw-mill
surveyors of Ottawa spoiled that when they made no
approach to Parliament Hill to compare to the vista seen
from the river. Ottawa was built for convenience: for
opportunity : for expediency.

Parliament is its great show. Politicians are the actors.
Time has seen some interesting, almost baffling, dramas on
that hill. No other Parliament stands midway of so vast
a country. But there are people who prefer Hull, P.Q.,
to Ottawa, Ont. We have had some mild Mephistos of
strategy up there : some prophets of eloquence : some

7

dreamers of imagination : giants of creative energy scheming how to draw a young, vast country together into nationhood so that the show-men on Parliament Hill might have an audience.

But the Ottawa of to-day is a strange spectacle for the prophets. The great new Opera House is all but finished, when no seer can tell whether the plays to be put on there by the parties of the future will be as epical and worthwhile as those staged by the actors of the past. Imagination was not absent when Ottawa was created. But it needs more than common imagination to foresee whether these political playboys of the northern world are going to be worthy of the great audience soon to arise in the country that converges upon Ottawa.

Sometimes in Parliament you catch the vibration of big momentums in a nation's progress. Voices now and then arise in speech that reflect some greatness of vision. More often the actors are sitting indolently, hearing the clack of worn-out principals whose struts and grimaces and cadences are those of men whose cues should lead them to the dressing rooms, or to the wings, or somewhere into the maze of the back drop where nobody takes part in the show. Or they listen to men whose big informing idea constantly is that all we need to make economic happiness for everybody is to turn out the company now in and get another from the furrows. These latter believe that a nation is a condition of free trade—mainly on behalf of the farmer whose average idea of industry is a blacksmith shop on a farm.

One's head inclines to ache by reason of listening to the three-cornered claque on the Tariff as it was in the beginning, is now and ever shall be. Now and again we are inclined to study the men who are elected to Parliament and some of those who gravitate towards Ottawa without the bother of elections. They stimulate interest and challenge criticism, not less because the interest and the criticism come from a seat in the audience rather than from "behind the scenes"—which is not always a disadvantage. While the parliamentarians perform "Promises and Pie Crusts", the wives have their own play—"Petticoats and Power". The stage here is a triangle—Rideau Hall, Chateau Laurier, the Parliamentary Restaurant. At the cafe tables women from all the counties and electoral districts of Canada—many of them French—chatter about the great masquerade up at the Castle, the little-king show which at its best is worth more to Canada than the Senate. The homes of Ottawa are little shows whose players imitate the manners and the accents of the fine people in the Castle, the Restaurant and the Chateau.

"Nothing but a prinked-up panorama !" says the rugged Radical in a coonskin coat, member of a deputation with a railway ticket as long as his pocket. "Poor show ! What we want down here is more plain farmers' wives——"

He pauses. This man's first cousin broke away from the farm a generation ago because farmers' wives were too plain, and farmers did so little reading, and the big thinkers and doers all seemed to live in town. As he talks, up dashes a sleigh, jangling its bells and dangling its robes, and from behind the bearskinned driver alights a company that makes his coonskin coat feel clumsy and uncomfortable. He glances up at the great pile of walls on the hill. The hill is alive with fine people. In one of the sleighs a lady bows and smiles—at him ! He touches his cap and takes his pipe from his mouth.

"That lady ?" he replies to his sleeping-car mate. "Oh, that is the wife of a Senator, used to live in our town. Clever little woman she is, too. They tell me she's writing a novel and that Lady Byng is taking her up. Lady Byng —oh, yes, she writes novels. Good idea. Likely her books won't be quite so rough as some of our Canadian novels are. I like style in a book, all that fine manners stuff ; takes your mind off the humdrum of everyday life.

Byng—say, that was a wise appointment if ever there was one. My way of thinking, Lord Byng has 'em all beaten since Dufferin. Kings' and queens' uncles and cousins and brothers don't suit this democratic nation like a man who got acquainted with this country before ever he set eyes on it, through the boys he commanded out yonder. Great man ! Fit to be Governor-General of a great country, and I won't deny it. No snobbery. Seventh son of an earl, all his life a soldier and a worker. A real man, such as any of us could present to our constituents with pleasure and pride. Tell you what—listen !"

His sleeping-car mate feels a heavy clutch on his arm.

"Remember the old debate we used to have about 'The pen is mightier than the sword' ? Well, say—when you get the pen and the sword united in one outfit—what about it ? Oh, it's a great show, sure enough. I used to think government was a plain, plugshot business of trade statistics, card indexes and ledgers. But I've come to the conclusion that this old town has to make it a good bit of a social compromise and a show, or it can't be carried on, no matter who does it."

CONTENTS

THE MASQUES OF OTTAWA

THE UNELECTED PREMIER OF CANADA

RT. HON. ARTHUR MEIGHEN

ONCE only have I encountered Rt. Hon. Arthur Meighen, Premier of Canada by divine right, not as yet by election. I was the 347th person with whom he shook hands and whom he tried to recognize that afternoon. His weary but peculiarly winning smile had scarcely flickered to rest for a moment in an hour. For the eleven seconds that it was my privilege to be individually sociable with him, he did his best to say what might suit the case. He seemed much like a worn-out precocious boy, of great wisdom and much experience, suddenly prodded into an eminence which as yet he scarcely understood.

I was introduced as—say, Mr. Smith.

"Oh ?" he said, wearily. "Yes, I've read your articles. Er—Tom Smith, isn't it ?"

But Tom was not the name, I had scarcely time to say, and it made no difference. I should like to have shoo'd away the crowd and let him call me Jake just for a few minutes to get the point of feeling of this young man—though he is nearly 50—on how it feels to be Premier without a general election.

There may not be as much finality, but there is sometimes as much wisdom, in the choice of a leader by a small group as in his election by the people. Majorities frequently rule without wisdom. In accepting the gift of an almost worn-out Premiership and a year later entering the most significant general election ever held in Canada, at

13

least since 1878, Arthur Meighen falls back upon his courage without much comfort from ordinary ambition.   He faces a battle whose armies are new, pledged to hold what he has against two enemy groups, and to hold more than John A. Macdonald fought to get, without the sense of one great party against another such as Macdonald had.   No Premier ever went into a general election with so little intimate support from "the old party", with such a certainty that whichever party wins as against the others cannot win a working majority without coalition, and with the sensation that the party he leads is already what remains of a coalition.

Whenever I see Meighen I feel like hastening home to "cram" on citizenship for an examination.   I behold in him picnics neglected and even feminine society deferred for the sake of toiling up a political Parnassus.   In his veneration for constituted authority I can comprehend something of the Jap's banzais to the Mikado before he commits harikari.

Whatever there is, or is not, in the character of Arthur Meighen, he has a draw upon other men.   Any public task that he has in hand looks like a load that challenges other men to help him lift.   A really intelligent camera would show in his face a mixture of wholesome pugnacity, concentration of thought and feminine tenderness.   He feels like a big intellectual boy who unless mother looks after him will get indigestion or neurasthenia.   Sometimes men pity their leaders.   Meighen, with his intensity and his thought before action looks such a frail wisp of a man. The last time I saw him in public he was bare-headed on an open-air stage, a dusky, lean silhouette against a vast flare of water and sky.   On the same spot less than two hundred years ago, that singular, overbuilt top head and sharply tapering, elongated oval of a face might have been that of some aristocratic red man, deeply serious on the eve of a tribal war.

The little blank spots in Meighen's temperament are things that people like to talk about ; when the same idioms in an average man would be set down as mild insanity. Rumour says for instance that every now and then he must be watched for fear he go to Parliament without a hat. Why not ? It is only a British custom to wear a hat in the Commons except when making a speech. A bareheaded, even a bald-headed, Premier may be a great man. Meighen's negligence in the matter of a hat perhaps comes of the bother of finding the clothes-brush at the same time. Since Mackenzie Bowell, Canada has never had a Premier so naturally oblivious of sartorial style ; though his later appearances suggest that even he has fallen into the mode of well-dressed Premiers. In his early law days at Portage it is said that one evening when Mrs. Meighen was at a concert, he was given the first baby to mind, that when the baby cried he marked a paragraph in a law book he was reading, stole into the bedroom and took the baby over to a neighbour's house ; that when he was asked later where the infant was he gradually remembered that he had put the child somewhere—now where was it ? There is some other half forgotten tale of the strange garb in which he turned up at a friend's wedding, even before he was famous enough to be able to do that sort of thing with any degree of contempt for the conventional forms.

If Meighen remains Premier of Canada long enough, no doubt some really apocryphal yarns will arise out of these little idiosyncracies, just as legends wove themselves about John A. Macdonald, and Laurier. I remember that the clothes Meighen wore the day I shook hands with him were dingy brown that made him look like a moulting bobolink ; that he had not taken the trouble to shave because a sleeping car is such an awkward place for a razor, and it is much better for a Premier to wear bristles than court-plaster. Some one will be sure to remark that the Premier travels in a private car. Arthur Meighen never seems like that sort of Premier. One would almost expect him to choose an upper berth because some less lean and agile person might need the lower.

No doubt much of Meighen's democratic *gaucherie* about garments was abandoned at the Imperial Conference. He never could have worn a dingy brown suit when he got the freedom of London Upon some State occasion the Premier may have worn the Windsor uniform. Not without scruples. That uniform may not misbecome constricted Mr. Meighen more than it did the spare Mr. Foster, or the lean Mr. Rowell. But the Windsor uniform spells conformity, colonialism, Empire—not commonwealth. And Mr. Meighen went to London to represent the Commonwealth of Canada.

We were told by cable that the Premier took part in most of the sports on board ship, and of course lost most of the events. Well, there is no harm in a Premier beginning to be whimsically athletic near fifty. But, unless now and then he could manage to win something it was obviously only an attempt to make him interesting to the cables, on the principle that a polar bear is prodded in a cage to make him perform for the "lidy".

Weeks before he went the Premier foreshadowed the attitude he would take at the Conference. Again and again it was repeated as he slowly left the country, even pausing at Quebec to say it again ; and thereafter the cables took it up, repeating it over and over, until the people of Canada began to suspect that the correspondents were almost as hard up for news as some of them were during the war. Mr. Grattan O'Leary knew he had a difficult character to popularize on the cable ; a man who until he became Premier, outside of Parliament was as diffident as the hero in "She Stoops to Conquer"; at High School in the little stone town of St. Mary's, Ont., so studious that he never could catch a baseball that wanted to drop into his pocket ; at college immersed in mathematics, at

Osgoode in law ; as a young man opening a forlorn office in Portage, still a sort of lariat town, when Meighen was shy of even a family saddle-horse.

In Portage Meighen lived in a weather-boarded frame house, during the time when in bigger Western towns other politicians were putting up little palaces, causing their electoral enemies to wonder where they got the money. In Ottawa when he became Premier he lived in one of the plainest houses, with no decorative fads, no celebrated pictures, not much music, but plenty of room for the juveniles ; described by a political writer who was there the evening of the appointment as "just comfortable." He was at home that evening, discussing simply a number of public matters, but not a word about the Premiership, till as the visitor was rising to go and said, "Oh, by the way—permit me to congratulate you," Meighen broke into his bewildered smile and said bluntly, "Thanks !" He was not outwardly impressed by the least impressive Premiership that ever happened. The nation had nothing to do with it. Meighen had not been elected. He had drafted no platform before he became Premier. He did it afterwards. All that happened was a change of captains on a ship.

Meighen had been spiritual adviser to Borden in other remakings of his Cabinet. This time he was not consulted. Sir Robert never had such a predicament. In the words of the old song, "There were three crows sat on a tree." The names of the crows were—White, Meighen, Rowell. Their common name was Barkis. Which should it be ? White echoed—Which ? So did they all. Great affairs are sometimes so childlike. Meighen was willing to accept White as Premier. White had been for years in the spotlight. Did he hope, or expect, that Sir Thomas would refuse ? We are not told. But he must have surmised. In any case White was off the ship.

The choice came down to two. Here again it was a

spotlight man—or Meighen. Rowell had become famous when Meighen had not ; but he was a converted Liberal, and of only three years' experience. The necessity was obvious. Sir Thomas, declining the leadership, must have recommended Meighen, much to the Premier's joy.

Yes, it was time for a leader. Mr. Rowell was out—and off the ship. Happily there were no more crows on the tree, or Meighen would have been forced to hold an election in order to get a Cabinet.

However, the three of them consented to remain in the crew, until further notice. Thus much was settled. Meighen should lead,—but what ? As yet little more than a hyphenated and quite stupid name, which had never yet resolved inself into a platform. But the name and the platform were both as clear as the constitution of the party, in which, under the political microscope, there was clearly discernible a Unionist Centre, a Tory Right and a Liberal left.

"Lacks solidarity," mutters Meighen. "Looks like tick-tack-toe. But wait."

The third disturbing feature was the condition of the country. From his wheel-house Meighen could see many clouds. The Reds, whom he had ruthlessly handled in the Winnipeg Strike ; the rather pink-looking Agrarians ; the Drury Lane coalition of farmers and labourites in Ontario ; Quebec almost solid Liberal behind Lapointe ; Liberals angling for alliance with Agrarians ; Lenin poisoning the Empire wells of India with Bolshevism ; League of Nations every now and then sending out an S.O.S., interrupted in transit by Lord Cecil or Sir Herbert Ames; and—not least threatening of storms but if properly negotiated favourable to this country on the Pacific issue—Mr. Harding busy on a "just-as-good" substitute for the League of Nations with Washington as a new-world centre when Mr. Meighen had hitherto neglected to advocate a Canadian envoy to that Capital.

Having scanned all these weather signals, Mr. Meighen decided that diplomacy for the present was dangerous and that boldness was better. In his programme speech at Stirling he divided the nation into two groups—that of authority and order to which he belonged, and the heterogeneous group of incipient anarchism to which belonged all those who did not agree with him.

Having done this with such further definition of his programme as might be necessary, the Premier took a trip to the West to prepare the way for Sir Henry Drayton's tariff tour. He went to that land of minor revolutions as a representative of government by authority, high tariff, conscription during the war, the Wartime Elections Act, and a minimum of centrality in the Empire as opposed to a maximum of autonomy. It was a disquieting outlook. But Westerners love to hear a man hit hard when he talks. Meighen has often been bold both in speech and action. In the Commons last session he paid his respects to Mr. Crerar by calling the National Progressives "a dilapidated annex to the Liberal party." Which adroit play to the gallery with a paradox came back in the shape of a boomerang from a Westerner who called the Government party "an exploded blister." On a previous occasion talking to the boot manufacturers in convention at Quebec he took a leap into the Agrarian trench with this pack of muddled metaphors. "I see the Agrarians a full-fledged army on the march to submarine our fiscal system."

Epigrams like these do not make great Premiers. But they are the kind of schooling that Meighen had. In his young parliament days he was an outrageously tiresome speaker. He heaped up metaphors and hyperboles, paraded lumbering predicates and hurled out epithets, foaming and floundering. He had started so many things in a speech that he scarce knew when or how to stop. Commons, both sides, rather liked to hear him struggle with his verbiage. Later he developed the rapier thrust,

some snatches of humor, a trifle of contempt. He learned
the value of playing with a rhetorical period that he might
later leap upon a climax. Frank B. Carvell was periodi-
cally egged on to bait the member of Portage. He did it
well. I recall once when the member for Carleton was
spluttering vitriolic abuse at the member for Portage that
Meighen muttered, "Oh, you wait. I'll get you." Which
he did—immediately. Young Cicero had his Catiline.

One of Meighen's best speeches now will rank with the
best in any country where dignity has not quite deserted
the art of parliamentary oration. But he is rather too
fond of picturesque language to make a really great speech.
He has a strong intellectual grasp of what he wants to say
and a high moral measure of its significance to the nation ;
but for a Premier he is too prone to lapse into the lingo of
partisan debate which in Canada—since the battering days
of the giants that followed Confederation—has not been
on a very high level. Meighen's best speeches are temperamentally big, but he has yet made no great speech
which will live, either in whole or in part, as a glorification of
his country. It takes a Lincoln or a Roosevelt to be in
high office and say things that palpitate in the heart of a
crowd. Wilson did ; but he was dangerous. You judge
a man in high office by words and deeds. Lincoln was
great in both. Lloyd George is great in either, but not
always in both at once. Macdonald could thrill a crowd
with a homely epigram and turn his hand to a vastly
national piece of work. We have yet to be sure that Meighen
can be as big in action as he has sometimes been in speech.

Unless one is too easily mistaken, the Imperial Conference imparted a steady sense of responsibility to Arthur
Meighen that he rather lacked when he took office. He
found himself in a very uncomfortable spotlight. He had
not been used to measuring his words to suit such momen-
tous occasions ; nor accustomed to realizing how small the
greatest men and the most impressive human arrangements

are when you get to the centre and no longer have the perspective. He represented the oldest self-governing Dominion. A word misplaced might make a vast difference. He realized the significance of the event—especially before an election. He was never able to keep out of his mind what might be happening at home in such places as Medicine Hat. The issues which he discussed were big. He handled them worthily, with a due admixture of boldness and caution.

It was no time for mere sentiment, but for careful deliberation of matters that lay beyond Canada, beyond the Empire, in the danger zones of world politics, more especially of the Orient. The status of Canada as a nation north of the United States depended in that case vastly more upon a definition of Japanese and Pacific policy than upon any heroic allusion to the Great War. No man could have traversed this precarious business with more insight into the probable effect of what he had to say upon the Empire, the United States, and his own electoral prospect in Canada. The day after his announcement of a general election this year the Premier spoke to an open-air crowd at the Canadian National Exhibition. He chose the Imperial Conference, and mainly the Pacific issue, as his theme. In twenty minutes of unrelieved, almost solemn seriousness, he made that weighty business interesting to a crowd not too friendly in politics, with scarcely a gesture, speaking direct to the people instead of using the amplifier tube, making himself heard and understood with the clarity of studious conviction and straight mastery of all the links in his logic.

And Meighen knows how to lead. His bewildered smile is a prelude often to a strong move in action. Older and wiser men learn to love this lean wildcat who knows the strategic spots in the anatomy of the foe ; who can spit scorn at the Agrarians and venomous contempt at the Liberals; who dares to glorify a government of authority

and of force as though it were a democracy ; who can hold
the allegiance of some Liberals and lose that of few old
Tories.   He has earned that allegiance.   He carried his
load in the war.   Long enough he lay up as the handy
instrument of a clumsy Coalition, as before that he had
been dog-whip for the Tories.   When Premier Borden
wanted a hard job well done he gave it to Meighen, who
seldom wanted to go to Europe when he could be slaving
at home.

Fortunately for Meighen he had been but a year in
office when Opportunity came to him with a large blank
scroll upon which he might write for the consideration of
other people his views about, "What I Think of Canada
as a Part of the Empire."

No law examiner at Osgoode ever offered him such a
chance to say the right thing wrongly or the wrong thing
first.   It was a fascinating topic.   Other Premiers had
done such things off-hand, almost impromptu as it seemed,
and inspired by merely patriotic sentiment.   This was a
notice that the Premier of Canada could speak his mind
in advance, or if he so preferred, wait till the Conference
of Premiers opened and spring a surprise.   Meighen lost
no time in deciding to prepare for the N.L.C. party a brief
on Imperial relations.   Here was a thing out of which he
could make capital—for Canada and the party and the
coming elections.   And if ever Meighen had delved for
material he did it now.   He was going to the Imperial
Conference of Premiers with a mandate—to help define
Canada's position in the great Commonwealth about
which Mr. Lionel Curtis had written two large books and
the Round Table had published forty-four numbers since
1910 ; when nobody had as yet issued the one clear call
for Canada.   Foster, Borden, Rowell—since Laurier and
Macdonald—had all taken a hand in this.   But there was
some new way to state the case that would—or might—
seem as large and strong for Canada at the Imperial Con-

ference as the voice of either Borden or Rowell had been
at the Peace Conference or the Geneva Assembly.

The Premier could picture Sir Robert scanning his
manifesto to the British press ; Sir George, his old mentor
of speechmaking in the House, comparing it to what he
used to say for Joe Chamberlain ; more clearly than all,
Mr. Rowell himself, who for two years in the Cabinet had a
monoply of that great subject to which he had devoted
clear thinking, concise language, and some diplomacy.

The author of "Polly Masson" might have drawn
from the new Premier on this subject some such confessions
as are suggested in the following imaginary, but not improb-
able interview.

Mr. Meighen, intensely revising his manifesto for the
cables looks up and says :

"Er—what did you remark ?"

"That you were about to say——"

"Was I ? Oh, yes—about the Round Table. On three
legs. Hasn't even as much stability as the Canada First
minority—most of whom are not in Quebec. These are
the negligible but uncomfortable extremists."

"Ah ! Then you are of the moderate majority ?"

"You mean I used not to be. Well, events move fast.
Men change with them. I have been called a Tory."

"Yes, a tariff Tory."

"A moderately high tariff—sufficient unto the day."

"Quite so. But not a tariffite in sentiment."

"Tariffs are not properly sentiment. They are business."

"But Joe Chamberlain sentimentalized the tariff. He
was even willing to have free trade in the Empire to get an
Imperial zollverein against the rest of the world."

"Why mention Chamberlain ? Are you—twitting me?"

"Because he afterwards wanted an Imperial Cabinet.
And if I'm not mistaken you began to learn parliamentary

speeches from one George Eulas Foster only a few years after he stumped England for the Chamberlain idea."

Meighen smiles ; that wan but wholesome illumination of a thought-harassed face.

"Hasn't the old flag been some sort of issue in every Federal election since Confederation ?" he is asked.

"Of course. No Federal election can be held in this nation, except by virtue of the B.N.A. Act, and every election carries with it an inferential challenge to amend the Act. Macdonald settled that—by a grand compromise with Quebec."

"But—as a Canadian first."

"Granted. But he also said in 1891—mm—now what did he say ?"

"A British subject I was born——"

"And a British subject I will die. In his day——well said."

"You will not say that in 1922 ?"

"Probably not. Subjects do not vote in true democracies. Events change men——"

"And parties. Even Premiers ?"

He turns his spindling anatomy about in the chair, suddenly rises and darts to a bookshelf, seizes a book and flicks over the pages.

"After all," with a yawn, "we have now and then to go back to Laurier, the biggest if not the greatest autonomist of all Premiers—though Sir Robert Borden years ago spoke at Peterborough quite as broadly, if less eloquently. Here it is—spoken during the war by Laurier. 'We are a free people, absolutely free. The charter under which we live has put it into our power to say whether we should take part in such a war or not. It is for the Canadian people, the Canadian Parliament and the Canadian Government alone to decide. This freedom is at once the glory and the honour of Britain which granted it and of Canada which used it to assist Britain. Freedom is the keynote of all British institutions ?' "

The clock ticks louder. It is time to go.

"'Tell me, Mr. Meighen, i it not after all the mandate of Canada's part in the war that stands behind the attitude you are bound to take at this Conference ?"

"You mean that if Canada had not gone to war magnificently as she did, the war—might have been lost ?"

"Essentially that. Hence the new nationhood of Canada born of the war. You, or any other leader, even as Tory or as clear Grit, would not foist upon this free nation any issue which does not do justice to the sense of nationhood begotten by the war. Would you ?"

"I will say—no."

"Then as to the Anglo-Japanese Alliance ?"

"Canada must be free, because she has a vital interest in the American aspect of such an Alliance that even Britain has not. This nation is the electric transmission transformer between Britain and the United States There is a Pacific zone of policy in which Canada has a big stake."

"I see. Now as to the next election ?"

The Premier rises : now thinner and more intense than ever.

"My friend—just this. The solidarity of the British Commonwealth League of Nations is at the root of the welfare of the civilized world. In every nation of this League, no matter by what party label the Unionist cause is identified in the baggage room, it is a matter of vital importance to the solidarity of the League that such party should remain or go into power. So—I hope to get from the Conference such a reasonable endorsation of Canada's stand on the main issues that our party here——"

He pauses and gazes fixedly at a large map of Western Canada. The visitor imagines that he is looking at Portage, his home town.

"Er—you were saying, Mr. Meighen ?"

"Medicine Hat," he answered vacantly. "Somehow, you know—I wish Kipling had never made that remark about Medicine Hat,—'all hell for a basement.' "

"You don't worry about the Hat just because there's going to be a bye-election while you're away ?"

"No,—for I know pretty well that I won't hold that seat. What worries me is the fool use that some people will make of a freak election as a forerunner of doom. However, as I was saying about the Conference—I hope to get such a reasonable endorsation of Canada's stand on the main issues that our party here can work to victory advantage in the next election. I may as well be honest. Arthur Meighen, Premier, has not yet been elected. But he intends to be, because he ought to be, because the party he leads can do this country more good for the next few years than anything else in sight ; because the party which carried the war and the re-establishment has been given a new lease of life, at least some vision, and a vast deal of experience which Canada is going to need from now on more than she can ever need the wholesale patent nostrums of millennial doctors who think the plough-handles are a sign manual of a new efficiency in government. We all know what is happening to Russia. I'll be perfectly frank, and say that I fear this young nation may be induced to scrap experience for experiment—which above all times would at present be the inauguration of an economic system for which the nation is not prepared, for which it has not been educated, and because of which it cannot afford to take for its education the bitter experience which too often succeeds glittering experiment. What the world needs to-day is economic justice, not economic revolution. No nation in the world has a better chance than Canada for sound economic justice to all that makes her the world's young leading democracy. But economics isn't everything. Good-night."

THE PERFECT GENTLEMAN PREMIER

RT. HON. SIR ROBERT BORDEN

HERE is a modest, honourable man who saw his duty to the nation and the emergency never more clearly than he knew his own defects. Canada never before had a mediocrity of such eminence ; a man who without a spark of genius devoted a high talent to a nation's work so well that he just about wins a niche in our Valhalla—if we have one. It was the war that almost finished Borden ; and it was the war that made him.

Canada has been governed by strategy, imagination, and common sense. We have had Macdonald, Laurier, and Borden. The first finished his work, the second wanted to, and the third had finished his work two years before he resigned office.

Sir Robert Borden was the only man in the world Premier both when the war began and when it ended. Of all Premiers of Canada he was the least like a Canadian, and he achieved European fame with less title to personal greatness than either Laurier or Macdonald. For the crowd there never was an inspired moment in Sir Robert's life, nor ever one when he did not try to do his whole duty. He never interested the people and did not always hold the profound allegiance of his party. Yet there never was a public man in Canada to whom the average politician would as soon take off his hat in absolute respect for his moral purpose, integrity, fair-mindedness and sense of honour. There was enough morality wasted in the equipment of R. L. Borden to have supplied the lack of it in some of his heterogeneous followers. But it was morality that he could not transmit except by silent influence.

Other celebrated Premiers had governed by the personal method. The moral law was written all over Borden. He was a walking decalogue. He worked for the good of the country without detriment to the Conservative party. But there never was any Borden Mount of Transfiguration. He never could lead except when he was considered by the Majority to be right. In the war he took refuge in the nation, and its patriotism. But for the war one doubts that Sir Robert would ever have won any title to fame.

The man's whole makeup is a sort of righteousness. He had no use for the mirror more than to adjust his necktie and his hair, of which a woman writer said :

"That wonderful hair of his must have brought the unctuous fingers of many masters, spiritual and otherwise, down upon it in commendatory pats. . . . . I daresay that it was his mother's pleasure in it and the way she enjoyed running her fingers through it that made him realize—subconsciously at least—that his hair was a very magnificent asset." The writer also described the garden of the Premier —his wonderful roses ; how he talked about the personalities of the wild flowers so dear to his soul, and the perversities of the wild cucumber—but amiably declined to say a word about the destinies of nations.

Laurier had his flute. Borden should not be denied his wild garden. I used to think, watching the Premier in the House, that he would make a splendid bronze bust of an Egyptian god.

But the man never could dress for the part of leader. He needed too much grooming. He must always be immaculate. A trifle of neglige would have ruined his career.

We never heard of his "iron hand within the velvet glove." He had neither the hand nor the glove. He was an influence ; never a power. Even when the stage was all set for a show Sir Robert could not take the spot-light.

He did not abhor the calcium ; he merely did not know what to do when it was on.   During the tour which preceded the triumphal election of 1911 he was strong enough to win the country and weak enough to pose for oratorical photographs of Sir Robert swaying a crowd—on the roof of a Toronto hotel.   Those photographs were published as authentic pictures of the Premier in action.

But real action seldom happened to Premier Borden. He never could invent occasions.   He had no craft to play the game, no intuition to penetrate into the conscience of a lukewarm supporter or of a man whose policies and programmes might bedevil the union of the party.   On his tour in 1915 when, after seeing and hearing more of the realism of war than any other man in the country, he undertook to translate his emotions to crowds of people here, he was compelled to use the tomtom-on-the-Midway performances of R. B. Bennett, at a time when dominating men of both parties put their political makeups into their pockets in order to do honour to the tragic cause of which on behalf of the nation he was the spokesman.

Political history is very largely a chronicle of stupendous noises, of pageants and tumults and shoutings, of strategies and manœuvres, secret conclaves and cabals, of sinister intrigues and specious platitudes in parliament to cover them up, and of occasional great episodes when the leader feels called to vindicate himself and his followers.   Most of these emotional experiences seem to have been denied to Sir Robert.

I daresay it was mainly his lack of imagination.   Borden must, "work for the night is coming."   The day's work was often bigger than the man.

His advent to the leadership was a moral makeshift. His defeat of Laurier in 1911 was not a triumph for anything that might be called Bordenism.   His conduct of the political side of the war was creditable, at times splendid, never consummately wise, never heroic.   His exit was as uneventful as his advent. Sir Robert had more than finished his work.

The Conservative party as such carries no indelible imprint from the man who for nearly a quarter of a century led it. He led it by going alongside. He was not a great partisan. He had no overwhelming and audacious bigotries.

Borden was the first Conservative leader of note who never could play the ace of Quebec. The Laurier Cabinet knew how to play politics by imagination. Borden had nothing but a demoralized remnant, which the Liberals pillaged when they discarded Free Trade, helped themselves to a high, virtually protective, tariff for revenue only, took a reef out of the Tory "old flag" monopoly by establishing the British Preference and sent a contingent to the South African War in the name of Empire. Laurier was master in Quebec, in the new West whose two new Provinces he created, in immigration, in great railways, in a deeper St. Lawrence, in flamboyant adventures with great harbours, in the Quebec Bridge. Borden as yet was master of nothing. Such brilliance and success had never been confronted by such a demoralized party and so much drab common sense in a leader.

Sir Robert's Premiership was a desperate inheritance. The direct plunge into the Naval Aid Bill was a badly staged attempt to capitalize the reaction against restricted reciprocity. That first session of the Borden Parliament goes on record as the most complete one-act farce ever inflicted upon a patient country. The Imperial issue was a play to the gallery, and it is the one clear issue that seems to remain of all the Borden idea.

Sir Robert in his whole life never constructed an epigram. His two great predecessors had made several. Epigrams sometimes outlive policies. He never delivered a great passionate speech. He had opportunities but could not meet them. Fine speeches enough, to be sure ; many of them instinct with a sort of ethical nobility ; but a great palpitating speech, never.

It is not likely that if left to the logic of ordinary evolution Sir Robert ever would have recreated his party even on Imperial issues ; or convinced the West that Conservatism was not merely anti-agrarian ; or shewn Quebec that Conservatives in the second decade of the twentieth century are better Laurentians than the Liberals by preserving better the anti-continental idea. Such things call for leadership by imagination and a Cabinet of strong men. Sir Robert had neither. Even in the House he was not the party leader. Conservatism established by Macdonald as a great system of damnation to the Grits, was on the low road to extinction. It was not in the power of Robert Borden to save it. The country was swept by a new Liberalism that by astute manipulation had kept sympathetic both manufacturers and radicals.

Long before the war came, Canada recognized in Mr. Borden a Premier who knew the meaning of moral caution so well that he knew not boldness at all except that his cause was right. Borden had the ethical stolidity of Asquith without the latter's personal weaknesses or his powers of oratory. He needed somebody with him as stage manager and makeup artist. Even his virtues might have been advertised with effect—though as a rule, except in characters like Lincoln, it takes the perspective of time to put those into a poster. So eminently respectable ; so high in honour ; so fair in judgment ; so irresolute in action ; so defective in imagination ; so content to be overshadowed by lesser men in his own party even though he never was intimidated by bigger men in the Opposition : such, so far as we could see him before the war, was Sir Robert Borden.

Platitudes lay in wait for the Premier to utter **them.** Only by an effort of will could he lift them to a plane of high interest. He could sketch great issues with the solemn hand of a great preacher pronouncing a benediction ; but he never could utter an aside, or crack a joke, or tell a story, or forget that once upon a time Fate had picked him to be a leader and so help him he would go through the motions of shepherding while the other men were the real collie dogs of the flock. If only Borden could have broken some bucking broncho, or worn some new kind of bouquet, or invented some imitation of a brazen serpent to hold up, the people and the party might have got hold of him and followed him.

Such was Premier Borden before the war, and so he remained, but under a magnifying glass, afterwards. The war was a godsend to the Government. It drove out alleged dissension in the Cabinet and gave the party which had met defeat in the Naval Aid Bill a chance to perpetrate something which no Parliament would dare try to defeat. Sometimes I almost think Borden was for short periods in the war a truly great man—in the eyes of the angels. He had known the war was coming ; he had said so. There was a secret plan of action on file in the Archives months before it came. Not his to exult in I-told-you-sos to the leader opposite who had mitigated the menace. He rose to his programme of duty. He did not even wait till Britain declared war, but cabled assurances of aid on August 2nd, 1914. Special Parliament was assembled. The hour had struck. A Halifax writer present at the Khaki Parliament says :

"Sir Wilfrid easily bore off the honours in oratory. It was a great occasion and he rose to it. . . . . Sir Robert is no orator, but he spoke in straight man-fashion of the great crisis. The climax of his speech was a solemn warning of the dark days to come 'when our endurance will be tried.' "

Had the Premier issued a referendum in that first month of Canada's going to war he would have wept at the amazing number of Noes from the Province in which Laurier was born, and the provinces in the Far West which

he had created ; in the one, obvious indifference whatever
the cause ; in the other enmity from the Nationals whom
Laurier had imported to make Liberal voters. Even in
the rural areas, traditionally the stronghold of Liberalism,
indifferentism was the rule ; and in the city of Kitchener
where Laurier had politically baptized Mackenzie King,
his successor, there was almost a state of civil war.

But the fervour of the Hughes programme prevented
the Premier from taking stock of the nation. He permitted Hughes to treat Quebec as an automatic part of
Canada at war—which it was not ; and he failed to use
even the Machiavellian energies of Bob Rogers in getting
a line on the psychology of the West, supposed to be useful
only in elections. Sir Robert had long known of the
menace of Germany, and his Naval Aid Bill was one proof
that he knew. But he did not understand the menace of
disunited Canada. There never was in Ottawa any informing vision of Canada at war. Canada, in fact, was not at
war. Political feuds were indeed forgotten ; thanks to
a noble-minded Premier that was natural enough. But
had there been a national poet then big enough to translate
into great verse the true spiritual state of Canada, he
would have written with poignant sadness about Quebec ;
perhaps a few verses on the overwhelming British-born
majority in the First Contingent. He would have explained that being a native son of Canada, whether you
were English or French by extraction, did not of itself
lead to enlistment in the ranks. The Premier should have
known whether Sam Hughes was awarding patronage by
making officers from the Conservative party or whether
according to his own statement he was doing just the
opposite. In fact it was the Premier's business to see that
the Minister of War pursued neither policy.

But with the Hughes flares all about him it was hard
for the Premier to see the nation ; most of all Quebec. In
this matter of the two Canadas, Sam Hughes saw his

c

opportune duty and he did it. Sir Robert saw his and shrank from it, not weakly but blindly. Quebec should have been the instant objective of all the wisdom in Canada's Cabinet. Except for one or two grand battalions and a minority of broad-minded French-Canadians, Quebec was not at war, as part of united Canada. Banging the drum and blowing the bugle in Quebec was as wrong in strategy as to send Bob Rogers down to exorcise, as he did in 1915, the phantom of conscription. Sir Robert knew that even in civil times his Government was electorally ignored on the St. Lawrence. How much more in a time of unpopular war ? Was it not clear that every hurrah for the Empire in Ontario, every fresh battalion mustered and drilled in Toronto, every troopship down the St. Lawrence, was a nail in the coffin of Quebec's potentiality in the war ?

Yes, Sir Robert Borden knew that. He knew that Laurier was sulking like Cassius in his tent ; that he was gnawing himself over the failure of his own predictions about the peace welfare of the world as well as for his own defeat in the election of 1911 ; that the man of the "sunny ways" was becoming a reactionary and a cynic, an old leader of great power, which he was willing to use to the utmost for the prosecution of the war had he been in office, but in opposition was manacled by a sense of futility against forces in Quebec which he understood and feared far more than did the Premier.

No doubt the Premier traversed all this, many a time and in great concern. And it may be that he saw so sharply into the sad hopelessness of it all that he decided not to ask Laurier for advice, or even suggestion. Such is lack of imagination.

Laurier had his day in the grand expansion of the country. Borden would have his, in the sacrifices and moral energies of the dark days to come. It was a greater thing to be Premier in war than ever it had been in peace.

Canada was a greater land in action on the West front
than ever she had been stringing railways, settling farms
and building towns on the frontiers. The more Canada
went to the front of her own free will, the greater she seemed
abroad. The credit of this nation at war went up in
London and Paris much faster than its investment credit
had ever gone on the exchanges. The further one got
from Ottawa the greater the country seemed. A Canadian
Cabinet Minister meeting a British Minister in London
could talk for an hour on the wonderful war character of
this country. London was the centre of gravity of the
west front, and of Canadian Ministers. The Premier
spent almost half his time in or near London, whenever
summoned, or whenever politic to go—to a place where
the rancours of Ottawa were all buried in the grand cause.
The Premier of Canada sometimes went to London when
he would rather have stayed at home ; more often when he
felt that it was emotionally bigger to be Premier in London
than in Ottawa.   He was more honoured in war than
Laurier had been in peace. He would have been a better
Canadian had he stayed in Ottawa more.   But there were
many Canadians who were more concerned about how to
help Foch and Lloyd George win the war in Europe than
about how to knuckle down to common business at home.
The trek to England and to Europe became a fad.   The
nations went world crazy. Premiers neglected to "saw
wood." It was a matter for gratitude that they did not
parade in khaki.

Premier Borden's lingering objection to Coalition here,
even after it was established in London, did him no credit.
He was displeased when the Chairman of the Imperial
Munitions Board, back from a business conference in
London, asked if the Premier had any objection to his
stating the case for the need of Coalition at a public dinner.
Of course the Chairman was out of order. But he was
talking business, not politics.

The war was not going well. The British part of it was badly enough bedevilled by distance and differences of opinion between various Dominions without the distraction of party politics.

But for the great services of win-the-war Liberals the Military Service Act might have disrupted the Coalition even when it came. It was an extreme measure ; much more hazardous here than in Britain—except for Ireland, of which we wanted no imitation in Quebec. There were times when Sir Robert longed for the wings of a dove. His offer of Coalition came at a time when he knew Laurier would refuse it. Conscription he carried out as a necessity. He never wanted it. No Premier of a free-will nation would. There were bigoted anti-Quebeckers who would have had compulsion from the first to show the French that Canada was greater than Quebec. But if Canada had sent conscripts in 1915 what would have become of the glory of the Canadian army ? The argument that it was the best men who were killed, thereby robbing the nation of its flower, is thoroughly ignoble. Canada has never regretted that her best men died first, or that the Premier delayed conscription until it was inevitable. Canada does regret that the Government did not until too late, attempt to make any national register of the strength of this nation as had been done in England before conscription came as the final result. To have applied conscription before the United States went to war would have driven thousands of slackers across the border. Enough went as it was in the fear that conscription was coming.

The bilingual bungle in the Commons was even worse than the bad feeling over conscription. In this debate the angry French element in the House were a bad commentary on the still hopeful minority of broadminded French-Canadians who wanted to carry on the honour of Courcellette. The controversy over titles was no feather in the cap of the Premier, who made a bad fist of defending a practice the most glaring instance of which was the creation of hereditary titles in a democratic country.

Canada's "dark days" were fast coming. The resignation of Hughes was due before it came. The Premier's patience was scarcely any longer a virtue in this case, when four months after the declaration of war he had been compelled to make a diplomatic visit to Toronto's war camp in order to smooth out the troubles created by his "Chief of Staff."

From that time on to the end of his career we had the spectacle of a Premier overburdened and weary in his office, bewildered by the insistent advices of other men and sad over the failure of even conscription, in the face of such wastage, to get Canada's 5th Division into the field without weakening the four divisions we had. The Union Government was too heavy a load for so weary a man to carry. It had done its work, most of it well, some of it too late. The head of it was worn out. He was away much for his health, more for service in Europe, coming back to reconstruct his Cabinet, with the aid of Meighen, then away again. He had lost Hughes, Rogers, Crerar, Cochrane.

The strong men he had left, except Meighen, White and Foster, were Union Liberals.

Why did the Premier not himself resign? His work was done. His Union Government had finished the work which the nation gave it a mandate to do.

The answer must be in Sir Robert's own conviction that as a Premier of Canada he still had a great work to do in Europe in the settlement of peace. That work he did, some of it much more ably than much he had done at home. We had to read the headlines diligently to see where next Canada's mobile Premier would be needed in the adjustments of peace. More of the answer might be found in the doubt as to whether any man in Canada clearly knew what the Government's work, and therefore its mandate, would be. It was a time of upheavals when any nation with a Government carrying on its work constructively according to programme might have been glad to escape the further upheaval of a general election. But political parties have usually been profiteers in the emergency of a nation. Did the Premier fear that his resignation would force an election before the new party was ready ? We are not told. Under pressure he called a caucus in 1919 to determine the programme of whatever party he had in the Union. The caucus determined nothing. Did he hope to carry on until the legal expiry of his term in 1922, thereby evening up with the Liberals who wanted to bring on an election in 1916 ?

This also we do not know. Sir Robert was a weary and baffled Premier. He did not know how to let go. Once even his faltering hand was off, who was to succeed him ? There were three men to consider.

The man's work was done. He knew it. Much of it had been nobly done. He knew that the nation was sure of this. And he now understands that even with the failures and the weaknesses of his administration, both as Conservative and Unionist Premier, we cordially concede to this high mediocrity a place in our critical affairs only second to the credit that he gained in England and in Europe as the head of a nation that had gloriously fought and magnificently won—in the war.

Canada never had as great and noble a servant, who failed so conspicuously on personal grounds to be the nation's master. But there were elements in the patriotic servant-hood of R. L. Borden, higher than the political masteries of more brilliant men.

A POLITICAL SOLAR SYSTEM

Rt. Hon. Sir Wilfrid Laurier

Fifty years from now some Canadian Drinkwater, charmed by the eloquent perspectives of time, may write an "Abraham Lincoln" string of personal scenes from the lives of Wilfrid Laurier and John A. Macdonald. The narrative will thus begin in the very year that the story of Lincoln ends, and it will carry on down just fifty years in our national history to the time when Wilfrid Laurier, passionate student of the Civil War, reached the end of his climax in the affairs of Canada and the Empire. But the poet who does this must be inspired ; because no young country at that period of time in the world had had two such remarkable men as contemporaries, and political foes, and lucky is the nation which at any period has such a man as Laurier.

Outwardly Laurier's political career was complex where Macdonald's was simple. John A. was as great a Canadian as Laurier ; but in the simpler times in which he lived he had less cause to be puzzled by the web of fate and of political cross-currents at home and abroad, even though he was immensely more baffled by politicians and party emergencies.

Laurier swung in a great romantic orbit of political sentiment, vaster than that of any other statesman we ever had. For the fifteen years up till about 1906, he seemed like the greatest man ever born a citizen of Canada. Before that period he was a romance. After it he was a national hallucination. The last three years of his life he was a tragedy.

Yet the tragedy kept on smiling. Half a century of smiles. We never had a statesman who could smile so potently. Never one with such mellifluous music in his voice, such easy grace in his style, such a cardinal's hauteur when he wanted to be alone, and such a fascinating urbanity when he wanted to impress a company, a caucus or a crowd. The Romist whom Orangemen admired, the Frenchman who made an intellectual hobby of British democracy, the poetic statesman who read Dickens and re-read in two languages Uncle Tom's Cabin and sometimes played the flute, and the Premier of a bilingual country who had a passion for the study of the war which emancipated the negro, was the kaleidoscopic enigma of Canadian public life.

Laurier was nearly all things to all men. He was sometimes many things to himself. He idolized himself and laughed at himself. He venerated British institutions and passionately loved Quebec. He came to his flowering period in a party of Free Trade and went to seed in a party committed to a species of protection. He spoke English as fluently as Bach wrote fugues, and with more passion and beauty of utterance than any of our English-Canadian orators. One moment he could be as debonair as Beau Brummel, the next as forbidding and repellent as a modern Caesar. He was consistently the best-dressed public man in Canada. A misfitting coat to him was as grievous as a misplaced verb in a peroration. He superficially loved many things. Life was to him, even apart from politics, a gracious delight. He knew how to pose, to feign affability and to be sincere. With more culture Laurier would have been the most exquisite dilettante of his age. But he cared little for poetry in verse, not much for fine music, had small taste for *objets d'art* or the precious in anything. His greatest affection was in his home, his greatest charm in fine manners, his master passion in speech, and in managing Cabinets to win elections for the party which to him meant a greater and more inspiring Canada. We have had better debaters ; but never a man except himself who in the House could make a sort of grand music out of an apologetic oration on National Transcontinental grades.

A writer who at various periods of time was very intimate with Laurier thinks he was a man of deep emotions. This may be doubted. A man who talked so easily and was so exquisitely conscious of himself could scarcely be considered spiritually profound. Other men and events played upon him like the wind on an Aeolian harp. He was tremendously impressionable ; and by turns grandly impressive. A personal friend relates how a man with some experience as a critic of drama—probably himself— went to see Laurier by request for a talk on the political situation ; how Laurier invited him to a chair and immediately took one beside him an inch or two lower so that his own face was on a level with the visitor's ; how for some minutes he sat feeling the power of this actor who tried to persuade him to run as a Liberal candidate, and when he rose again seemed taller and more aloof than ever.

That is acting. Some other man might have done the same thing and made no impression. Laurier could perform obvious tricks with a consummate grace. And he performed many. There never was a moment of his waking life when he could not have been lifted into a play. His movements, his words, his accent, his clothes, his facial lineaments were never commonplace, even when his motives often may have been. He was Debussy's Afternoon of a Faun ; poetry and charm all the days of his life.

During the ridiculous deadlock on the Naval Aid Bill, when his supporters went so grotesquely far as to read the Bible to talk out the Bill, he was away from the House for a week, reported as quite ill, in reality having a very delicious time at home reading light literature. The day he came back the news of his coming was heralded to the Commons. The benches were packed. Not till they

were all full, every Minister in his place, every page at
attention and the House like a pent-up Sabbath congregation, did the then leader of the Opposition make his
grand, swift entry, bowing with courtly dignity to the
Speaker and taking his seat amid a claque from his supporters, in which even the Tories felt like joining.

Sir Wilfrid Laurier had the infallible knack of adjusting
his makeup, not always himself—to any occasion from
which he could extract profitable publicity, or upon which
he could do some charming thing for somebody else.   He
is reputed once to have worn overalls among a gang of
timber-jammers, but he felt rather ridiculous and soon
took them off.   Interviewed abed in his private car at a
railway station by a political friend, he suddenly became
conscious of his pyjamas and rolled back into the bed-
clothes with a smile.   He was not happy in *deshabille*.
Entertained at an arts luncheon in 1913, he made the
most of a very Spartan meal, consented with much dignity
to exchange his plate of cold beef for another man's cold
mutton, listened with great gravity to a short programme of music, asked the names of the composers
and the players and spent most of his brief speech
denying that he was anything but a philistine in art,
and pledging himself if ever he was Premier again to do
more for Canadian art than had ever been done before.
In conversation at a friend's house with a stranger he
claimed that at college he was always a "lazy dog." Visited
once by an agent who tried to sell him a phonograph, he
consented to play the flute for a record ; after listening to
the record and being assured that it was a faithful replica
of his own performance and asked if now he would not buy
the machine, he answered gravely, "No, I think I will sell
the flute."   This story may be apocryphal, but it is delight-
fully true to character.

On one of the thousands of "occasions" in a career that
was almost perpetual drama he was buttonholed in his

office by an American reporter who, having been warned that the Premier of Canada never gave interviews, boasted that he would break the rule. After half an hour the American reporter came out to his confreres of the press gallery, sat down at a typewriter, lighted three or four cigarettes, nervously aware that he was being watched for the forthcoming article, and after spoiling a number of sheets and tearing them all up he confessed, "Well, boys, I thought I was pumping Laurier, but it's a cinch he spent most of my time pumping me."

To the Liberal press gallery men he was as much a captain as he was to his followers in the House. He gave them daily audience during the Session, very often in a group, and at such times he usually asked, "Well, boys, what's the news?" He wanted good news; and many a reporter tricked up the truth now and then to give it to him. Informed once that "Bob" Rogers had vehemently in his office denied any cabal in the Cabinet against the Premier he swiftly replied, with that splendid, satirical smile, "Well, the fact that Bob Rogers says there is none would convince me that there probably is."

Laurier was the kind of man to whom other people naturally happened. He was a human solar system in which many kinds of people wanted to gravitate, even to the ragged little girl on the prairie who picked him the wild flowers that he wore in his coat as far as she could see him on the train platform. He discovered early in life that he could interest other people much as some men find out they can juggle or sing. It was a fatal gift. Laurier was far too long in this country, much too interesting. Women in Ottawa could make delirious conversation out of how this man at 72 got into a taxi. He was more phenomenal to English than to French. He never cultivated Paris and would not have been at home there. At Imperial Conferences and Coronations he was an Imperial matinee idol in London. In Ontario he was regarded with much the same awe as the small boy views the long-haired medicine man. To the Quebecker he was the grand magic ; until Bourassa came, irresistible, incomparable on stage. But Laurier had no great intensity ; no Savonarola gift to sway a crowd ; he just charmed them ; when they came to remember his song—what was it ? Earlier in life he was a sort of Ulysses, led by magic. He loved the *petit ville* of Lin where he was born. But it was too small for him. He was lured into studies, to college, to the bilingual university McGill, to law, to discourse with learned Anglo-Saxons, to the study of British Government by democracy, to the translation of himself into English. The translation, which was almost a masterpiece, made him the first and perhaps the last French Premier of Canada, and in many respects the greatest Premier we ever had.

This alone was something. Speaking their own tongue, Laurier could impress the English. He could tour Ontario and feel grandly at home in the Liberal shires, among the men of the Maple Leaf. He could follow one of his two transcontinentals up the Saskatchewan, and to multitudes of many nations led from Europe by his own immigration policy conduct a Pentecost for the two new Provinces. He could fling magic over Manitoba, and on the Pacific he had power. But in Nova Scotia he could never equal the memory of Joseph Howe, a greater orator than Laurier.

What this man's sensations were as he studied himself in the art of politics may be compared to what an English Canadian of similar temperament would feel like if he could fling a spell over Quebec. Laurier made a second conquest of Canada. He took a great Cobden party from Edward Blake and made it almost protectionist, Imperial and his own. He grafted a sort of Liberalism on to polyglot nationalities. In about the same tenure of power he created a personal ascendancy the equal of Macdonald's, in a nation almost twice as big and much more complex.

In ten years he changed the face of Canada as no Premier had ever done before or ever can do again. He was looked at in Imperial London as though he were the joint picturesque descendant of Wolfe and Montcalm, with a mandate to make Canadian Liberalism an instrument of Empire, a bi-racial Government a final proof of the eternal wisdom of the British North America Act, and a measure of reciprocity a safeguard of Anglo-American entente

So the son of the village surveyor from the tin-spired parish of St. Lin had made himself very nearly monarch of all he surveyed, with the notion that his right there was none to dispute Sprung from the most backward province in Confederation, he pushed Canada forward with hectic speed, not counting the cost, nor caring what the end might be, so long as he died Premier of a prosperous nation and therefore happy.

At about the age of sixty a reaction came over Laurier ; first noticeable in less enthusiasm and more reticence at the Imperial Conferences. The French-Canadian who had lost a segment of his idolatrous following in Quebec because of clashes with the clergy and the sending of a contingent to the South African War, began to resist the cold machinations of the Chamberlain group. He began to see Empire, not as a commonwealth of democracies, but as domination from Downing Street. At home he was shrewd to observe that the Canada of his own domination was a complex of many "nationals," only a few of which were historically rooted in the Anglo-Saxon idea. He saw that the bigger half of this Canada was arising in the West, which he believed he had truly because politically created ; and the West had but a slender minority of people to whom the Maple Leaf meant anything.

If the party which he also had recreated into a Laurier Liberal party was to continue dominating Canada until white-plumed Laurier had finished his work, it must be by a stronger leverage than Imperialism. He had managed

to hold Quebec, which now thanks to himself and Lomer
Gouin, was almost solidly Liberal. The prairie farmers
he must not lose. And the grain growers were not keen
about an England which bought their wheat at open
world prices in competition with cheap wheat countries
like Russia, and their cattle at prices dictated by the
Argentine ; when both cattle and wheat were cheapened
to the producer by the long-haul railways which Laurier
and the Tories had built.

And although the "Old Man" had scant knowledge of
business, he had the wisdom of the serpent to translate the
signs of the times ; yet lacking somehow the vision to
foresee that a play for the western vote by a measure of
reciprocity would resolve itself into a boomerang at the
polls. Laurier had a wonderful Canadian vision. In
1904 he refused a Liberal M.P. from the Pacific Federal
interference in the Oriental problem, saying, "The day
will come when we shall be glad of Japanese warships on
our Pacific coast."   Yet in 1912, in a letter to a friend, he
gravely minimized the German menace. He understood
America and Asia better than Europe. His vision was
keener in power than in defeat.

And then the war, which in a few strokes finished the
almost complete picture of Laurier. His support of the
Government in going to the aid of Britain was at first a
flash of the old generously impulsive Laurier who loved
England. That love he never lost. He expressed it in
the House down near to the end of the war. He loved
England a thousand times better than some Englishmen
do. For the Empire it is doubtful if he was ever profoundly
enthusiastic except as he saw in it the glorious evolution
of self-governing democracies such as Canada, his first love.
He understood this country. It is not remarkable that he
did. Any public man of Canada should. But Laurier's
love for his own country was of an especially intense character, because it was for a long while so deeply romantic.

As he grew older the original veneration he had for England as the mother of democracy was more and more transferred to Canada as an experiment in that form of government. The more he won elections, the greater grew his passion for democracy and for interpreting his native land. The pity is that a man cannot go on winning and losing elections without suffering some damage to his clear love of country. The highest patriot is he who knows best how to lose himself and his election, all but his conscience and his cause, for the sake of the land he loves. Laurier did not remain till the end of his life the highest patriot. Weary as he is said to have been of public life as far back as 1905, he was lured into winning more elections by the adulation of his followers and his own love of swaying men as a master, until elections with him became a habit and the loss of one a tragedy.

And even the war which shook so many men's love of country to the depths—some of them over the precipice of profits, others to the passionate heights of sacrifice—did not obliterate in Laurier the fatal desire to win elections. One has almost to cease thinking to remember that Wilfrid Laurier did hope that an election would yet be held during the war that would return him to power. The failure of the Government in the war would be largely the fault of Quebec which he still in large measure controlled. He held that ace. And when the time came he would play it. The Premier wanted no advice from him. Laurier offered him none.

When the bilingual dispute was transferred to the Commons, Laurier took the only side consistent with his character and his career. He avowed his belief, as always, in Provincial rights, but he asked Ontario to use its strength with clemency. Even with an element of bitterness he did not lose his dignity. But the fine sparkle of the Laurier we all knew was gone. He was beset with complexities and contradictions. The one simple thing about him was his hope to finish his work by winning another election. In the debate on the Nickle motion for the abolition of any further king-made aristocracy in Canada, he was an acidulous old cynic, offering to go and burn his title in the market place if certain others would do likewise. Those photographs of Laurier in the Windsor Uniform, making him look like a refulgent relique of the court of Louis XIV. were no longer prized in the family album. Away with them !

Poor, splendid old man ! Even in his crotchets and quavers he was charming. To the very last he could rise in the Commons and with a voice as thick as wool make members opposite fancy they were hearing great music.

In 1916 an artist painted a portrait of Laurier to hang in the Legislative halls of Quebec, where the sound of his magic voice had first been heard in parliamentary speech. The artist began to paint the Laurier of "the sunny ways." The old man corrected him. "No, if you please," he said gravely, "paint me as a ruler of men."

It was the Cardinal speaking ; the man who had disciplined more Cabinet politicians than even Macdonald, the master of Cabinets ; the old man who remembered the power of an earlier day.

Early in 1917 he was offered coalition by the Premier. He refused. Laurier knew that coalition meant conscription, and conscription meant dragooning Quebec.

It came home vividly to the old leader in Opposition, whatever it may have done had he been in power, that to advocate conscription would drive Quebec into the camp of Bourassa from which he and Lomer Gouin had between them managed to save a large majority of French-Cnadians. The struggle of Bourassa to oust Laurier began with the Boer War. It was fated not to end until either leader or the other should quit. Before the war Bourassa was flamboyant and defiant. After it began he was openly and brazenly disloyal, when the doctrines he preached were inflammably acceptable to people uneducated to citizenship in so conglomerate a thing as Empire. The easiest thing in the world is for a high wind to sweep a prairie fire. The war and Bourassa together had the power to sweep Quebec, had Laurier and Gouin shown signs of yielding to the demand for conscription. I am told that Laurier personally believed in conscription but saw this terrible danger of disrupting the nation over Quebec. The war only had staved off the Irish question, a conference on which was in session when war was declared. Laurier dreaded the spectre of a second Ireland in Quebec. He knew all the forces and how they would operate. By his own methods, mistaken or otherwise, he had spent most of his life to achieve unity. He dreaded to see that unity imperilled. I think he would have been glad to see Quebec enlist as Ontario and other Provinces had done. That was impossible. Conscription was a menace in Quebec to the man who had failed to estimate the jack-boot menace in Germany, but who had not failed to oppose the idea that navalism in England was as bad as militarism anywhere.

No judgment of Laurier, when it comes to be adequately made by the historian, can fail to take account of this sentiment in an old leader to whom the unity of Canada had become an obsession far transcending his original passion for the solidarity of Empire.

The Winnipeg convention of 1917 was a piece of almost calculated cruelty on the part of men who should have known that the old chief's day was politically done. His party which for years he had penetrated with his personality was slipping into disunion. Vaguely he knew that the western wing of it was almost gone over to Radicalism such as he could not control. But in Ottawa there was an even more direct split. There, conscriptionist Liberals called the Convention for the purpose of proclaiming win-the-war independence of Laurier and considering Coalition on its merits. But the western Liberal machine captured it by a fluke. For a few days the old chief dreamed that

D

the West had rallied to his standards.   Then he awoke to the reality that even in the east he was head of a divided house.

The man who in 1916 had been painted as a ruler of men found in that summer of 1917 the Win-the-War Liberals deserting him, some of them with sobs.   They loved him well.   He was the old king.   Conscription was now the issue.   The Government had decided upon it late in 1916.   In 1917 the Military Service Act was brought down in the House.   Laurier knew at what it was most directly aimed—Quebec.   He fell back on the ruse of invoking the Militia Act whch called for defence only. There was no defence.   He knew it.   He moved for a Referendum, knowing that in the West, sore over the Wartime Elections Act, and in Quebec, and in the absence of the soldier vote it might carry by a majority sufficient to defeat the Government, to force an election and send him back to power.   He was beaten.   Conscription became the law.   To enforce it came the Coalition.   The election was held.   The Liberals were again beaten— partly by men from their own ranks.

Still the old king hung on.   He was now too old to let go.   Even the Coalition might fail.   Or the war might be ended   And then——?   The last fighting act of his life was to call the Ottawa Liberal Convention, of the men who had not abandoned his colours ; the men for whom he was not still holding the open door.   But a few months before he died here he was "up on his toes," as George Graham said of him, sending out battle calls for some election that must come now.   The war was over ; the army coming home.   The Coalition's day was "done." Those stalwarts must return to the fold.

But most of them came not.   There was still work for them to do, and surely no haste for an election.

What ?   No more elections for Laurier ?   Not one more chance, after all the waiting, for him to finish his work ? Poor old infatuate ! splendid even in his illusions. There was no work for Laurier to do now. There was no room for him to do it if there had been. There were few to follow him except in Quebec—for in his dotage he would not believe that the West had so forsaken him.

In a few months he was dead. And when dead, once again men forgot their political opinions and for a brief while somehow worshipped the memory of the man whose life was almost the coming true of a dream, whose work was never done, whose evening of life was a tragedy. And case-hardened politicians who had borne the burden and the heat of the day with Laurier, wept.

But the power of Laurier is not dead. In the long perspective of history the figure of this great Canadian, with his "sunny ways" and his bewildering Atlas load, will stand out vividly when many of his successors will be scarcely visible in the haze.

THE GRANDSON OF A PATRIOT

HON. WILLIAM LYON MACKENZIE KING

IN December, 1913, there was a Literary Society dinner in the University of Toronto at which Sir Wilfrid Laurier was the guest of honour and speaker on "Democracy." My own seat at a table was next to a restless, thick-bodied, sparse-haired man who seemed younger than his years and to whom I had not been introduced. During the hour that Laurier spoke this man continued to lean over the table so as to catch a view of his fascinating face. He interested me almost as much as did the speaker. I had never sat beside such an irrepressible vitality. Like a bird to a succession of swinging boughs, he hung upon the golden utterances of his old chieftain and political mentor concerning a subject so poignantly dear to the experiences of one and the imagination of the other.

First impressions are sometimes reversed on closer acquaintance. I was uncomfortable beside Mackenzie King, but interested. On a latter occasion I was still more interested, and rather more uncomfortable. The early impression remained, that he had very little faculty of restraint—what scientists call inhibition.

That occasion will not soon fade from memory. Often I can hear in imagination a thousand students singing "Vive le roi ! vive le compagnie !" before the fine old leader spoke, and that earnest, hectic disciple joining in. When I discovered who he was I ran back in fancy to the time when Mackenzie King was a student at that same university. At that time William Mulock was Vice-Chancellor and became keenly interested in the brilliant young student of economics with whose father he had attended law school.

52

King entered the University the year that the chief author of the National Policy died. He graduated one year before Laurier became Premier, in the golden age of Liberalism triumphant, when "freer" trade was emerging as a symbol of that brand of democracy in opposition to free trade in a minority. How we have fallen upon evil days ! Farmers' sons at college no longer regard free trade as the forerunner of political absorption by the United States, but as the vindication of the farmer as a group in government.

Mackenzie King is a man about whom nobody ever could have a lukewarm conviction. He is either cordially liked or disliked. More than most other men in public life he has become the victim of violent opinions. For this he is temperamentally responsible. People consistently decline to reason about him. They speak of him vehemently. His dominant note of character is rampant enthusiasm. King is always intensely in love with whatever interests him. His enthusiasms are not so much on the surface for many people, as underneath for causes—and for a few men. Gifted with an uncommon capacity for absorbing impressions and collecting data for research, he has made himself a sort of pathological study to other people. In mastering economics he has himself been enthralled by his own enthusiasm.

At the time of Laurier's speech on democracy King was peculiarly enthusiastic about John D. Rockefeller, Jr., head of the Rockefeller Foundation. But he had lost no jot of his fervent admiration for Laurier in Ottawa and was still passionately devoted—as he remains—to Sir William Mulock, his political godfather. Nobody has ever criticized him for his ardent discipleship to the two older Canadians. There is an old-fashioned spontaneity about this mutual regard much above the common commercial admiration of one man for another in business. Many have blamed King for his attachment to Rockefeller, and have used that connection to his detriment as Liberal leader.

In April, 1920, he was flatly accused of having been an absentee from Canada during the war, employed by the Rockefeller interests and so "entangled in the octopus" that as leader of the Liberal party he would become a menace to Canada. It was the old bogey of continentalism in a new setting, and it took Mackenzie King twelve pages of Hansard to make his defence in the House. The incident forms a hinge to a career which is worth a brief survey.

King was born in Berlin, Ontario. son of a subsequent lecturer in law at Osgoode Hall and of a daughter of William Lyon Mackenzie. At the University of Toronto he was one of the '95 group that included also Hamar Greenwood, Arthur Stringer, and the late Norman Duncan and James Tucker. There was a rebellion during that period in which there is no record of the grandson of a glorious rebel having taken part. At college he displayed a passion for pardonable egotism in which there were elements of a desire for public service. The Family Compact at Ottawa must have interested him. Liberalism, as understood by the Laurier group, was emerging from the disreputable mess known as continentalism, fathered by Goldwin Smith, who was beginning to be estimated for what he really was, a brilliant philosophical pamphleteer bent upon the obliteration of Canadian nationality.

After graduation King went for a brief term on the staff of the *Toronto Globe*. In that year the Liberals came into power. King was engaged by Sir William Mulock, Postmaster-General, to inquire into sweatshop methods in contracts for postoffice uniforms. No man could have done it better. He had a native appetite for that sort of investigation, and he was helping to establish the new Liberalism.

For the next four years King was out of the country. Had he followed the academic fashion of that period he would have been in training to become a citizen of the

United States. Chicago University, built by John D. Rockefeller, attracted him first; Harvard next. He was still studying economics. No other Canadian had ever spent so much time and talent on this subject. At Harvard he became a Lecturer, and was sent to Europe to investigate economic conditions. While there he got a cable from the Postmaster-General of Canada, who had created the Department of Labour as an adjunct to the postal department, and established the *Labour Gazette*, and wanted a deputy who should edit the *Gazette* and look after the details of the office. King courteously declined, saying that he could not accept until the expiry of his contract with Harvard. The salary of the Deputy-Minister of Labour was $2,500 under a man whom he tremendously admired, and as yet with no clear ambition to become a member of the House led by the man whom he was afterwards to worship, and to succeed.

There is no proof that Laurier took any uncommon interest at this time, as he afterwards did, in the Deputy-Minister of Labour, though he noticed that the young man was making a great success of his work. Much if not most of King's tuition in politics at this stage came from William Mulock, who as a member of the Commons in Opposition, had fathered the fair trade resolution in Convention and did much to convert the Liberal party from free to "freer" trade.

In the eight years up till 1908, by experience with conditions,, King made himself master of the subject which was later to appear in his book, "Industry and Humanity." He was repeatedly made chairman of this or that mission, board, and commission at home or abroad, to get the true facts about labour, immigration and employment. By a sort of genius for conciliating groups, even when he antagonized individuals, he became for a time the world's most successful mediator in labour disputes. Industrial warfare had not as yet adopted the trench system. Direct action, the One Big Union, the sympathetic strike and collective bargaining were scarcely dreamed of, though anticipated in the philosophy of Karl Marx, as yet not transplanted to America. Socialism, as expressed by Henry George, whose "Progress and Poverty" was a classic in King's college days, was the most radical element with which the young Deputy had to deal. But the Government's policy of foreign labour nationals being gradually absorbed into labour unions made Canada, in proportion to population, a very difficult country in which to act as conciliator.

During his eight years as Deputy, King was made two offers, each of which illuminates the criticism that in the war he was only a nominal citizen of Canada. A group of Canadian employers, recognizing his success as a mediator, offered him $8,000 a year to act on their behalf with the heads of labour. Without consulting his chief, King declined the offer. He said that he preferred the $2,500 from the Labour Department, where he could be independent of either one side or the other. Later President Eliot, of Harvard, on the death of the man who occupied the chair of political economy, offered King the post, pointing out that his duties would keep him but six months a year in Boston. The salary was at least twice what he was getting in Ottawa. Again without consulting his chief, King declined, on the pretext that he had no desire to leave the useful work he was doing for the Ottawa Government to become a citizen, even of eminence, in the United States. During the same period he was asked to act as conciliator in a great mining strike in Colorado, when violence and murder were the law, and when the result of his action led to the enactment of a successful arbitration measure by the Government of Colorado.

All this was prior to King's election as member of the House of Commons. Eight years as Deputy in the Department of Labour, he stepped into the Commons and the

Ministry of Labour with exceptional qualities to succeed. His record as Minister was the natural but uncommon sequel to his experience as Deputy. King was so long the one man whose whole time was spent in the effort to reconcile industry and humanity in Canada that it seems hard to recollect that he spent but three years as Minister. During that time, as well as before it, he became the ardent disciple of Laurier. While there was great advantage in having spent so many years as Deputy, it is a pity for the sake of the young leader's subsequent elevation that he did not come under the spell of the old chieftain as a candidate before Laurier had begun to grow cynical in office. In 1908 Laurier had been at least three years tired of public life when there was no man to succeed him, and when, as often as he expressed his weariness of trying to govern a nation so temperamentally difficult as Canada, he was tempted by the adulation of his supporters to try again, until winning elections for the sake of remaining in power became a habit.

Admiration such as King felt for Laurier made criticism impossible. He worshipped Laurier. In this he was not alone. Older men than King, among his colleagues, shared the same spell-binding sentiment. And there was no member of the Cabinet who grieved more than King at the defeat of Laurier in 1911.

Here begins the Standard Oil story. The *Montreal Gazette*, in a report of two speeches made at a certain club, published an accusation that King had "deserted Canada in her hour of crisis in search of Standard Oil millions."

As similar statements may be made during the election campaign, it is fair to know the facts. King was employed by the Rockefeller Foundation, not by Standard Oil. The connection is merely one of cause and effect. The Foundation spends on the wholesale betterment of humanity the multi-millions which Standard Oil accumulated from the people. The theory of justification here is that the people

would have spent these millions foolishly, whereas the
Foundation spends them well.   There is some truth in the
theory.   King was engaged solely upon the industrial
relations programme of the Foundation, with special
reference later to industries of war, and with permission
according to his own stipulation to conduct his researches
in Ottawa from which in the ten years between 1911 and
1921 he has been absent only upon special occasions.   He
was in the unusual position of working in Canada and
being paid in the United States, for researches of benefit
to the cause of American industrial relations during the
war.   His book, Industry and Humanity, which is the
literary form of those researches, was all written in Ottawa.

These are respectable facts ; the only objection to
which is that the full statement of the apologia occupies
twelve pages of Hansard and must have taken at least two
hours of Parliamentary time.   The original accusation
was a malicious stupidity.   The vindication was a confessional in which the Liberal leader told the House every
iten that he knew.   Half the number of words would have
been twice as effective.

This introduces my second impression of the Liberal
leader, two years after the outbreak of war, at midnight
in a baronial farmhouse in North York, Ont.   He had
been addressing a political meeting in a school-house some
miles away.   There was a golden harvest moon and the
scene from the spacious piazza overlooking the hills of
York was a dream of pastoral poetry.   Suddenly motor
headlights flared out of the avenue and from the car alighted
the same restless man whom 'I had met three years before
at the dinner to democracy.   In a very little while we both
became so interested in what he had to say that neither of
us cared to go to bed.

Next day I found him still more interesting.   He spoke
with bubbling frankness and uncontrolled fervour about
many things and certain people, chief among whom

was John D. Rockefeller, Jr. He described the young magnate's trip into Colorado during a recent great strike, an itinerary planned on purpose that the son of John D. Rockefeller might get a first-hand knowledge of what conditions actually were, what the labour leaders thought, and what sort of people they might be. With graphic interest he described the young financier's reception by the miners, the speech he made, the big dance in which he took part, the camps and mines he visited ; a picture of capital conciliating labour such as seldom comes to notice outside the pages of a novel. He made no effort to eulogize himself. He was absorbed in generous admiration for the other man and with enthusiasm for the glorious chance that Rockefeller seemed to have to make a new Magna Charta of brotherhood between Capital and Labour. In this he was a tremendous idealist. In many respects one was forced to regret that the world somehow did not seem quite so full of brotherly intention as Mr. King said that it was.

"The common ground of both capital and labour is humanity," he said over and over in various form. "The antagonism of each will be forgotten when both unite in an effort to forward the interests of the whole community without which neither can prosper."

"Right !" I felt like screaming, had there been a moment to do so. "Bravo !"

The idea found expression in his book which he was then engaged in writing. And it is doubtful if any book on the subject of political economy was ever the source of greater happiness to its author than "Industry and Humanity" was to Mackenzie King. On the merits of democratic statesmanship as revealed in that book, Mackenzie King should be Premier of Canada in 1922. Alas ! men are often greater in what they say than in much they are able to do. Mackenzie King is a species of rather emotional idealist. He has studied economic humanity somewhat at the expense of his perception of human nature.

During the evening King talked with equal gusto upon his intimate knowledge of a certain popular song writer in Chicago, the story of whose life he told with vivid strokes of descriptive pathos ; and upon his still more intimate acquaintance with the late William Wilfred Campbell, poet, whom he had seen in the same moment feed his pigs in a near suburb of Ottawa, and create a line of poetry— which King quoted—"The wild witchery of the winter woods." He was seized with the idea that a Foundation such as the Rockefeller should subsidize poets and song-writers. The pity of it always is that the world is far too desperately cynical in high places to accommodate such generous impulses. Mackenzie King's fervent advocacy of a reform sometimes creates more antagonism than the cold attacks of an adversary. His passion for the better-ment of humanity often outruns his judgment. His statements smack of exaggeration even when they are absolutely true. He lacks a sense of proportion and a capacity for restraint. "Better is he that ruleth his spirit than he that taketh a city." But a political leader must do both.

Had he expected the Liberal leadership, the close of the war and almost the end of Laurier should have found the member for Prince ready for action or advice. But there is no record that, at this time, his counsels were sought by the Liberal party, or that he thrust himself into the limelight. Three months after the Armistice, Laurier was dead. Even then King was not mentioned as his successor. Four months later he was chosen, when not even he quite understood how it was done. King did nothing to reform his party along new lines, or publicly to state what he considered its reasonable position to be as between the Union party and the Agrarians. A broad manifesto from the new leader at such a time would have been useful. Never had a political leader in Canada such a duty of broad revision within his party. King neglected the opportunity. The *Toronto Globe* realizes what a squeezed lemon the Liberal party has become between the other two groups and calls for a working alliance between the Liberals and Agrarians to upset the Government. The *Mail and Empire* paternally points out that it is the duty of Liberals to enlist, Quebec included, under the hegemony of the party which has already incorporated Liberals and is ready to save that party from obliteration by the free-trade group.

Beneath the conventional assurance displayed in each of these organs of public opinion one detects an under-current of uneasiness, by no means mitigated by the farmer victory for the Commons in Medicine Hat, which the *Globe* construed as a triumph on parade, and the Agrarian turnover in Alberta which the *Mail and Empire* with all its sturdy protestations cannot honestly interpret as other than a calamity. Each of the historic parties feels itself confronted by a new sort of menace comparable to nothing in the history of Canadian politics. Two parties which ten years ago were in opposition are now flung together by the fear of a common danger and refuse to admit it. *The Globe's* hope is that Farmerism will become the new Liberalism. *The Globe* is right. But the captains may not be of *The Globe's* choosing and the planks in its platform are not those which *The Globe* in its days of sanity would have accepted for the good of the people. It is the intention of Farmerism to absorb all there is of Liberalism. Mackenzie King knows it. He knows that the Liberals will suffer more than the Government from the plough movement. Yet he is invited by *The Globe* to try the trick of the bird swallowing the snake !

The essence of Liberalism has always been liberation ; emancipation. But the farmers are out to smite all the shackles from all of us. They intend to stop short only of Bolshevism. An ex-Cabinet Minister of Alberta predicts that the farmers will sweep the country at the next election and steer it down the rapids of economic ruin. He cites Drury and Co. as examples of a certain sort of cunning whereby they did not at first show their real hand, in order to get people to feel that Agrarianism is not half so bad as painted and then—the broadening out into the People's party. The farmers are not notorious for sheer cunning; neither for stupidity. They are naturally hesitant about being as radical in office as they were on the stump. As an economic group they are no different from the old Free Trade Liberals, except that they seek to govern as a class on behalf of that particular group. Meanwhile the nation more or less opposed to farmerism is disintegrating itself into more groups. Labour is out for a species of self-determination; a Labour Party. A veteran Liberal statesman recently asked me this question:

"Suppose that in industrial centres like Montreal, Toronto, Hamilton and Winnipeg, Labour puts a candidate into every constituency; that in smaller factory centres which dominate essentially rural ridings they do the same. In each of these more or less labour-dominated fields suppose we have the possible four candidates. Is the Labour-Unionist in doubt over his own candidate going to vote Liberal, Liberal-Conservative, or Farmer?"

"As a man of long experience in elections—suppose you answer that?" I suggested.

He did not, but went on:

"I know what I should say to a labour elector under such circumstances. I should say to him · 'You had better not touch the farmer candidate with a ten-foot pole because—the farmer wants dear food and you want cheap food; he wants long hours and you want short hours; he wants imported manufactures and you want employment in your home town; he wants free trade and you depend upon a measure of protection.'"

Nobody has ever more pithily stated the case. There is no basic mutuality between the farm and the labour union. The farmer is as much a capitalist as he is a labourer.

I asked the Liberal statesman bluntly :

"Don't you think that in order to avoid political devastation by splitting the vote into three opposition groups each fighting the other, it is the immediate business of the two historic parties to unite against all parties of experiment, especially against the emancipating farmer ?"

He gave this evasive but shrewd reply :

"I am a lifelong Liberal. I have been in the habit of reading newspapers on both sides of politics. I am now driven to take the Conservative organ for my daily political food."

I commend that answer to Hon. Mackenzie King. If the Liberal leader is now as anxious to serve the nation of his birth as he was when he twice refused large salaries and comparative ease for the sake of continuing to do Canada's work, would it be high treason either to himself or to his party to call a Liberal convention out of which he would father a resolution of federation of historic parties based upon such a compromise as Macdonald created in the federation of provinces ?

The answer is obvious : "Fantastic ! Absurd ! Impossible !"

Mackenzie King will put up a smoke screen to hide the defection of the West from historic Liberalism. He will insist that the Liberals want only a reasonable tariff for revenue while the Government want protection—when Heaven knows each of them wants substantially the same thing in opposition to the farmer who wants everything. He will point with confident pride to the solid Liberal *bloc* Quebec, when he knows Quebec is dominated by Lapointe who can demand from him just what he wants as the price of Quebec's solidarity ; and he knows equally well that Quebec is as much opposed to continentalism as the Liberal-Conservative Government can ever be. The man who wears the mantle of Laurier without his Orphean magic cannot lead Quebec.

However, Mackenzie King was put where he is to lead, and he intends to keep on doing it. If he can regulate a few of his enthusiasms and so adjust his personality as to make Liberalism as led by him powerful enough to be the dog that wags the Agrarian tail, he should be set down as one of the most remarkable men in the history of Canadian politics. He legitimately chuckles over Quebec. One can fancy him matching that race-group against the Agrarian *bloc* and the Government industrial centres group, and saying to himself :

"Labour may lop a few from the Government; Michael Clark a few from the farmers—enough to make my friend Mr. Crerar a most excellent colleague in my Coalition. Excellent fellow, Crerar !"

A low-tariff group, of whom 75 per cent. are Quebeckers, amalgamated with a no-tariff group who are near-Continentalists, is at least entitled to serious regard as a fantastic experiment in administration. But we may trust Hon. Mackenzie King to simulate a vast moving-picture smile of high benevolence and great sagacity as he contemplates such a fantasia—with himself as the chief tight-rope performer and Niagara roaring below.

NUMBER ONE HARD

Hon. T. A. Crerar

Some Frank Norris such as wrote "The Pit" and "The Octopus" should arise in Canada and write a Wheat-Politics novel about T. A. Crerar. This man's photograph was once published squatting Big-Chief-wise in the front row of 300 farmers on a raid to Ottawa—I think early in the war about prices. It was a second to the last delegation which the farmers intend to send to Ottawa. The next one was in 1918, when the farmers went to protest against conscription. If you ask T. A. Crerar to-day, he will predict that in days not far to come manufacturers will petition a farmer government in Ottawa. Because the farmers in the West regard Crerar as almost a geological process, which sometimes results in a volcano.

Crerar was projected into public affairs by 50-cent wheat, monopolistic elevator companies, discriminating railways and protected manufacturers ; all of which, while he was still a young man who should have been going to dances and arguing about the genesis of sin, he concluded were into a dark conspiracy to make a downtrodden helot of the prairie farmer. To-day Crerar is at the apex of a movement. He embodies the politically and commercially organized campaign of the biggest interest in Canada against all other merely "big" interests. He is willing to let himself be talked about as the next Premier of industrial and agricultural Canada on behalf of all the farmers whom he can persuade to elect him a majority minority in the next Parliament. And the prospect does not even dazzle him, or awe his colleagues of the coonskin coats and the truculent whiskers.

Crerar began responsible life as a farm boy in Manitoba, taught school, and managed a small elevator company ; he became President of the United Grain Growers and of the Canadian Council of Agriculture—and the next obvious thing to say is that he entered politics as Minister of Agriculture in the Union Government. But T. A. Crerar had been in politics a long while before that, though he had never even run for Parliament or legislature. Unusual, unprofessional politics. Hear what the present Secretary of the Canadian Council of Agriculture has to say about the parliaments of the Grain-Growers in 1916 :

"Their annual conventions are parliaments of the Middle Western Provinces. Resolutions and recommendations of all sorts and description are debated and decided upon. Questions of far-reaching influence, socially and morally, have their beginning, so far as Western Canada is concerned, in the Grain Growers' Conventions. Records of these Associations show that besides recommending the establishment of co-operative elevators, co-operative banks, co-operative dairies, free trade, single tax and a dozen other economics reform, the Grain Growers in convention fathered Prohibition long before it was adopted, advised and urged woman suffrage many years before that measure was generally favoured, and were the first sponsors of the idea of direct legislation. The Grain Growers' Association and their annual conventions are the source and inspiration of all the commercial activities, and social and political reforms with which one finds the name of Grain Grower connected so often in Western Canada !"

This is the reforming political school that has trained the man now openly discussed as the next Premier of Canada. And for the benefit of any Canadian Norris who dreams of writing a problem novel about Crerar, it may be said that he is the most drab and unpicturesque personality that ever stood in line for any such office in this country. In the triangle of leaders at Ottawa he is the angle of lowest personal, though by no means lowest human, interest. Meighen is impressive ; King brilliant. Crerar—is business. He would be a hard nut for a novelist to crack. A man like Smillie impresses the imagination. Crerar, who is to the Canadian farmer what Smillie was to the British miner, invites only judgment.

The first time I met Crerar—at lunch in a small eastern club—he impressed me as a man enormously capable in business, tersely direct in his judgments, somewhat satirical and inordinately sensitive. He seemed wary, almost cryptic in his remarks. Recently sworn in as Unionist Minister of Agriculture, he had turned his back on Winnipeg, where he was a sort of agrarian king, and taken his first dip into the cynical waters of Ottawa, where he was but one of a Ministerial group some of whom were abler and more interesting than himself. He had not yet appeared in Parliament. He dreaded the ordeal. He had no knowledge of just to what programme he would be expected to adhere, except the general one of winning the war. He had little enthusiasm for the Premier, probably less for most of his colleagues. So far as he had been able to survey Ottawa, he considered it an administrative mess. His direct ways of doing business were menaced by a sense of muddle and officialdom. He missed the breezy, open ways of "the Peg" and the sensation of being general manager of the biggest commercial concern west of the lakes, the Grain Growers' Grain Co. Crerar could not business-manage Ottawa. When he opened his Agriculture door he saw no box cars trailing in from the elevator pyramids on the skyline ; he smelled no wheat ; he saw no "horny-handed" farmers writing checks to cover their speculative investments in grain which they had not yet sown. No wheat-mining comrade motoring in from the plains came to thrust his boots up on the general manager's desk and say, "Believe me, Tom, I paid thirteen-ninety for those protected articles. What a shame !"

Crerar complained of indigestion. I think his nerves were on edge. I asked him if he expected to co-relate Agriculture with Food Control and Trade and Commerce.

"Oh, I suppose so," he said wearily. "Nobody in Union Government knows what he will do yet. I don't like Ottawa. Its whole atmosphere is foreign to me."

He seemed almost contemptuous. He had made the patriotic plunge in order to put his particular brand of radical Liberalism at the service of a Tory-Unionist Government. He did not like it. Of all the Liberals who entered the Union Cabinet he was the sworn Radical. Both Calder and Sifton were machine men from governments that still had Liberal labels on their luggage. Crerar represented the great inter-prairie group of no compromise and of economic enmity to the Tories. He was rather looking for trouble ; thinking rather hard of how he could get through with such an uncomfortable job, do it well and get back uncontaminated to his own dear land of the wheat and his fine office in the most handsome suite of offices in the Grain Exchange at Winnipeg. The Ottawa that he hated was the Capital that old line politicians had created. He was looking forward to some Ottawa of the future which like Canberra, the new dream Capital of Australia, might be vacuum-cleaned and disinfected of all the old partisan microbes.

Crerar made his success in a country where the visible signs of getting on in the world are a bigger factor than anywhere else in Canada. The prairies are mysterious and sublime. The West is plain big business. Crerar represents the West rather than the prairies. He is temperamentally a man of Ontario, where he was born ; solidly businesslike and persistent. He glorifies hard work. And he went West at a time when the law of hard work was just coming to replace the old-timer's creed of hanging on and waiting for something—usually a railway—to turn up. He came up with the farmer of 60-cent wheat in a part of the country where everything that the farmer had to buy in order to produce that kind of wheat was high in cost. Cheap wheat and dear wherewithals have been to T. A.

Crerar and his kind Number One Hard experience. His axioms began with the plough made under a high tariff. His code of ethics was evolved from the self-binder, rail-roaded the long haul by systems that thrive on the tariff. His community religion—not his personal, which one believes has been pretty devoutly established—is embodied in the emotions of the skyline elevator following the trail of the steel and the twist of the box car.

One cannot mention these rudimentary western things without a species of enthusiasm for the Westerner, and a consequent precarious sympathy with the views of Mr. Crerar. Transplant yourself even for a year, as the writer did twenty years ago, to the far northwest, and you begin in spite of all your previously inrooted sentiments, to share the beliefs and talk the language that lie at the basis of even so arrogant an organization as the Grain Growers' Association and so inordinate an oligarchy as the Canadian Council of Agriculture. A man cannot fight the paralyzing combination of drouth, wet, early frost, rust, weevil, grasshoppers, eastern manufacturers, high tariffs, centralized banks and bankrupt octopean railways in the production of under-dollar wheat, without losing much of his faith in the smug laws of economy laid down by men who buy and sell close to the centres of production.

Now begins the work of the novelist, making *precis* notes for his Crerar masterpiece ; investigating the prairie farm of 1900, anywhere between the main line and the skyline. For the sake of space we copy his notes, hastily sketched :

> Low hill—General aspect, poplar bluffs, billowy landscape— Log and mudchink shack ; pole and sod roof—stable and shed ditto—Three or four cattle and lashions of grass—Broncho team and new high-painted wagon—No family—Dash churn—Lucky to have a wife—Some hens—Sod-breaking plough, long snout, breaks odd fields twixt bluffs—Coal-black loam, strong—Wheat and oats, wonderful early growth—Drouth first year—Second year, pole fences, more fields, and wet season—More crops but

half spoiled by wet—Sacks on trail to cars, toiling across prairie
to elevator—Smudge of train, bit of a town and a tank—No cars
to load grain—Must sell to elevator—Monopoly—Low price—
Grading wheat to No. 2 Northern—55 cents, used to be 40—Lien
note to pay on wagon and binder—Goes to indignation meeting—
Lots of that—Farmer revolutionaries—Want Gov't. to pass
acts compelling Rys. to supply farmers cars to break low-price
monoply of elevators—Act passed, but roads in league with elevators—Same old trouble—Rise of radical leaders—Organization of
farmers into group to fight interests—Helots on prairies—Helpless
unless organized—Only partial relief from Gov't.—Two new provinces in 1905—Grits make great splash, promising Utopia along
with newer trunk lines and big towns, etc.—Farmer grins, goes on
organizing, in each province association of grain growers (G.G.)—
Every few towns some fiery evangel—Great on conventions,
regular convenanters, old style—Schools of debate and Utopian
legislation—Gov'ts. wear goggles and organize elections—Farmer
organizes group ideas, to oppose old line politics—Say Eastern old
parties effete in West—Townsmen league with farmers, common
interest ; low price wheat means lean purchases and laggard towns
—By this time young man Crerar in Wpg., taken from managing
small elevator company to be general manager G.G. Grain Co.—
Co-op. movement develops in all associations, for buying and
selling—G.G.G. Co. give farmer equal rights with city man in
speculation on what farmer grows—Horn into Grain Exchange,
little office—Under Crerar Co. grows to much the biggest corporation in Exchange ; whole ground floor offices of G.G.G. Co. which
as commercial organization focuses the buying and selling end of
whole agrarian movement—Head of this, naturally chief of movement—All remedial and legislative programmes merged in economics of G.G.G. Co.—Crerar wiry, quiet executive, now fuse plug
to a real agrarian party with a programme which through Canadian
Council of Agriculture, members from all over Canada, constitutes
itself a parliament of farmers telling old parties to go to the devil—
Liberal gov'ts in prairie province mere annexes of new radical
group which is now bigger nationalist force than Quebec ever was,
ready to march upon Ottawa——

On this basis the novelist builds his political fabric of
Crerar, who began life as a Laurier Liberal, became a Free
Trader of the Michael Clark school, and ten years ago gave
symptoms of pushing the economic side of the agrarian

movement to a point where it aimed to become the new Liberalism of the prairies. He was the business head of a revolutionary movement of which other men became the ardent, flaming crusaders, both in and out of Ottawa. Crerar calmly evolved his practical evangelism out of the ledger of exports and imports. Nothing excited him so deeply as comparative statistics. He never trusted to the moral or emotional side of the case. His crusade was in the national ledger. His church was the elevator ; his economic Bible the Grain Growers' Guide.

Since 1914 or thereabouts this man has kept his balance at the head of a movement that split again and again into local factions only to come together again in the head offices of the Grain Growers' Grain Co. and the Canadian Council of Agriculture. He represented multi-millions of investment in land, agriculture, co-operative commercial enterprises and speculation. On the ground floor of the Grain Exchange he was at the head of the greatest organization in the world speculating in visible supply wheat. The grain that Crerar's cohorts bought and sold was either just sown, or heading out, or being threshed, or it was crawling to Winnipeg in miles of box cars on its way to Fort William. In wheat he put his trust ; in railways and steamships never ; in centralized banks and eastern manufacturers not at all ; in old parties at Ottawa still less— if possible.

Crerarism was becoming power to act. Behind Crerar was a sullen but optimistic reformation of such varied emotional character that none but a quiet, steady man could have controlled it in Winnipeg. The novelist's prairie farm was now a power in the land. It was Agrarianism ; that had bolted like an ostrich both old parties in the West, and now offered a new one supposed to contain as a new National Policy a general and itemized contradiction of the old N.P. of 1878—The National Progressive Party.

No economic crusade had ever been so rapid, gigantic

and revolutionary. Trades unionism had taken decades to make head where the Agrarian movement took years. The One Big Union of the Reds, anarching against all Government as it is, merely applied the principle of direct action which the farmers had taught them by suggestion in the unofficial parliaments of the prairie. The Agrarian is himself a One-Big-Unionist. His concern is not with wages and hours, but with exports, imports and elections. The Agrarian will not strike. Crerar knows that. He must not tie up communities and stop trade. He must work through Parliament. His aim is to establish farmerism as the basis of the nation. His creed is, that no matter what use we make of raw material, cheap power, manufacturing experience and capital, Canada's greatest revenue and export production must be in the farm ; and that therefore national legislation must gravitate about the farmer's garage.

This thing came to a head in a part of the country which contains less than one-sixth of Canada's total population, and more than half of them Canadians only by immigration. The one biggest man in the whole movement, besides Mr. Crerar, the man who practically elected the new farmer Premier of Alberta by appointment, is an American born. H. W. Wood, the Czar of Alberta, came as a farmer in search of cheaper land from the Western States. He is a good citizen, and as much entitled to play strong-arm in our politics as any native Canadian is to enter the Cabinet of the United States. But as a rule a free people resent men from other countries agitating for revolution on behalf of an original small minority in a part of the country where industrialism can never become more than a sideshow in the business of production. A people of national consciousness do not relish the idea of a minority group organized to the last man and the last acre, trying to organize a nation-wide group in provinces where the factory and the mine and the fishery are at least as important as the farm.

The whole plan smacks too much of engineering. It is a case of complete, almost Teutonic, organization masquerading as a sort of democracy, but in reality a controlled tyranny whose aim so far as at present defined, is to establish group government under a camouflage of the National Progressive Party, and by means of the power so obtained or by alliances with some other group, to upset the whole economic structure which it has taken fifty years to build up. No true citizen will object to farmers in Parliament and many of them. None but a slave will consent to a Parliament dominated by any group, whether farmers, manufacturers, lawyers or labourites. Democracy means free government on behalf of the people ; not on behalf of a great group which arrogates by organized majorities the right to represent the people. Agrarianism is not a nationwide interest. Quebec has more to hope from the Government now in power than from the farmers. Ontario cannot elect a clear working majority of farmers. It is the West and the West only, which has become Agrarianism rampant. And according to the new officialdom of the West the farmer must save us all. Elect him to Administration and he will open the golden gates of real prosperity by establishing a maximum of free trade, on the assumption that our present protective investment in great railways (two of them bankrupt), in banks, industries and speculative land is all wrong.

The prospect glitters. Mr. Crerar is not dazzled. He sees with a calm and collective gaze into the future. He contemplates with profound elation the scrapping of our present system built by experience, and the setting up of another which makes theories a substitute. Nothing is difficult to a revolutionist. Crerar's success in building Agrarian grand opera is a mere augury in his mind to still greater success in rebuilding a nation, which he thinks is the same thing because the farmer is the nation ; and a nation is the easiest thing in the world to revolutionize so

long as you do not obliterate its institutions. We are not
expected to abolish Commons, or Cabinets, or even the
poor old Senate—until further notice. Mr. Crerar may
need them all in his business. "For this relief much
thanks !" Mr. Crerar is not to be nicknamed Cromwell.

The repeal of the Underwood Tariff and the Agrarian
majority in Medicine Hat gave him great joy. The prospect for a farmer victory in the general election is to him
almost certain by some form of coalition—perhaps with the
Liberals ; possibly with Labourites. In 1920 a man very
close to Crerar estimated a return of 75 National Progressives in a total of 235 had the election been held at
that time. Since then farmer prospects have bulled on the
market. Alberta has gone Agrarian, following Medicine
Hat. Organization has been extended. The old Liberalism on the prairies has been absorbed. Dafoe, of the *Free
Press*, has swung into line with Crerar. There is prospect
of the Government winning some seats in the West, as
there is of the Liberals fielding candidates who will not be
elected. Ontario is already a loose-jointed but effective
part of the movement. Business is not good. A time of
trade depression has always been a good time for a change
of government, even along orthodox lines. The present
economic aftermath of destructive war and a large element
of I-Won't-Work labour along with high wages no matter
what else falls, must look to Crerar like a good time to
make us all believe that we shall all get through to Canaan
if we follow his Ark of the Covenant. He is able to assure
us of cheap clothes and furniture and machinery, because
the farmer needs these things in the production of food,
which must not become too cheap or the advantage will be
lost. What is to become of our industries is not clearly
stated ; but if living is to be so cheap we shall probably not
need employment except on the farms ; though under free
trade we are told that industry, free to flow, is sure to
locate itself at the point of advantage in material, power,

transportation, and getting to market. In fact some free traders blithely tell us that once you get rid of tariffs, living becomes so cheap that people naturally flock to the free trade country, and industry is bound to follow the people ; therefore free trade will give us factories as we need them.

There is no end of the mirage for your head and morass for your feet once you begin to consider the possibilities of a revolution. We had somewhat the same experience forty odd years ago in the forests of smokestacks supposed to spring up in the wake of the National Policy. It took a long while and much hard patient work to get those smokestacks. Now we have got them as part of our national equipment, along with great water powers and long-haul railways and centralized banks and a number of trusts and an undeniable number of dear manufactures under a tariff—and Mr. Crerar purposes to abolish the whole thing, to begin all over again as it was in the beginning, except that even then if the farmer had lost his market town on Saturday he would have been in a very bad way for his Sunday clothes.

In short, Crerar proposes one more revolution, whether by one fell swoop or by a slow process of getting us used to here a little and there a little more—we do not know yet. What we do know is that he proposes to govern this country by a huge economic group that used to go to Ottawa as delegations ; that in his opinion the real Capital of Canada is not economically Ottawa, but the ground floor of the Grain Exchange Building in Winnipeg.

We may not all have been reared on the farm, but be it known to all of us, our natural gravitation is back to the land.

Not many years ago also it was said that one large nation would Boss the world ; later that Soviets would do it. Both the Boss nation and the Soviets seem to be reconsidering the contract. The world is a perversely complicated technicality.

Meanwhile Crerar smiles when the Premier (by appointment) calls the Agrarians "a dilapidated annex" to the Liberals. He thinks he knows better. He smiles even more sarcastically when he sees Mackenzie King chortle over that amusing fiction. He may have some use for King. If the Liberal leader will be reasonable he may permit him to merge his party with the Agrarians. If not he may threaten to rob him of Mr. Lapointe and Quebec, and let him see how he will like that.

Last winter I met Crerar in a Toronto hotel. He had just been down east proclaiming for United Farmers in the Maritimes. An ardent Crerarite who spends his life watching Ottawa closely said as the leader came up :

"Tom, your one best bet is to make an alliance with Lapointe. That combination could upset any other confederacy in Parliament."

Crerar smiled—warmly. He said nothing. At lunch no doubt he discussed this with his supporter. The old ace of Quebec ! When will that home of race Nationalism ever get into the hand of cards held by Crerar who would inundate Quebec with reciprocity ? Perhaps one E. C. Drury can tell. He is talked about as the man whom Crerar may call to the Premiership in a Cabinet of fourteen Ministers of Agriculture and one Minister of Justice.

THE PREMIER WHO MOWED FENCE-CORNERS

HON. E. C. DRURY

MOWING FENCE-CORNERS.

A zig-zag old rack with its ivies and moss,
    Just fifty-odd panels or so ;
A wheat-field, a scythe and a boy his own boss ;
    He had the fence-corners to mow.

He slivered the whetstone clear out to the tip
    Of his snake-handled, snubnosed old blade ;
And he swung his straw hat with a sweep and a rip
    With the sun ninety-four in the shade.

He thought of the water-jug cool as a stone
    Right under a burdock's green palm,
By the leg of a fence-corner hickory half-grown,
    Where the breeze always blew in a calm.

But the boss saw him loafing clear over the corn,
    The next the boy heard was a shout ;
And he wished for a moment he never was born
    To mow all those fence-corners out.

Past the elder-bush blow it's five corners to mow,
    To get to that burdock's green lug—
So he put on a spurt till the sweat blacked his shirt,
    And he mowed his way in to the jug.

What cared the boy then for the boss in the corn
    With a beaded brown jug at his feet,
While he pulled out the corn-cob as glad he was born
    As the bobolink there in the wheat ?

He unbuttoned his shirt and got on the top rail,
    He hung his straw hat on the stake,
And he smiled to the hickory leaves' rustling tale,
    As he gazed at that berry-bush brake.

Till chuck ! went the scythe on a piece of old rail
   That lifted clear out of its bunk ;
And he said what he never had read in a tale,
   To that innocent, rotten old chunk.

And then he heard something that never was sung,
   That no bobolink could have said,
That never was rendered by pen or by tongue ;
   But it made his heart thump in his head,

As he let the scythe drop and he picked up the chunk,
   And sneaked up as soft as a breeze,
And poked at the noise in that rotten rail's bunk
   Till out came a bumble of bees.

Oh ! the jug it was cool and the berries were red,
   And sweet was the bobolink's strain ;
But bumble-bee cups in a rotten rail's bed
   Make a jug and a bobolink vain.

By noon at the nest there was only one bee,
   And only one berry to pick,
And only one drink in the jug at the tree :
   But that boy was as full as a tick.

They have torn the old zig-zag clear out of its snake,
   And the bushes have gone up in fire;
The hickory stands but it's only a stake
   To hold up a fiddle of wire.

The wires are strung tight for the fiddle is new,
   And straight as a beam of the sun :
The plough slides along it, the wind whistles through,
   And the fence-corner blue-grass is done.

The old mossy rails and green ivies are gone
   With fifty grass crooks in a row—
But the bobolink sits on the wire and sings on—
   The music he sang long ago.

And now 'mid the jostle and rush of the street,
   That boy has his dreams in the day,
When he sits on the rail 'twixt the clover and wheat,
   And mows out the fence-corner hay.

WHENEVER E. C. Drury whetted a scythe mowing fence corners he was, so far as can be reasonably surmised, thinking about the tariff and the waters of the Red Sea that swallowed up Pharaoh. It may be a coincidence, but it seems like fate, that he was born in the same year as the National Policy ; the indignity of which was so great that he vowed to spend his life living it down. He went to sleep with blue books and the Bible under his pillow. He gave way to both. He has never gone back on either. The iniquity of a tariff to him was part of the moral law. The more he exhorted at revival meetings and local-preached and led class-meetings, the more deeply he was convinced that tariff-Tories are in constant need of economic salvation. At threshing bees I can fancy this broad-faced, dreamy-eyed, large-mouthed young "Reformer" who never was born to take life mentally easy, saying to himself as he shoved the stack straw past his boots, that the old boys talking so hard about elections knew nothing about economics ; and he wished to heaven that barn was all threshed out, so that he could get back home to read some more tariff statistics.

The Drury farm, hewn from the bush by his grand-father, cost the young man nothing but taxes and upkeep. It gave him leisure in which to study the ills of farming. What a blessing all farmers have not leisure ! Travelling up and down that peninsula between Huron and Erie, constantly at some sort of "Meeting," Drury could see "Hard Times " on almost every telegraph pole. The average farmer had a small lot, a heavy mortgage and a large family ; scrub cattle, thin horses and poor hogs. No doubt Drury read, when it came out, that amazing pamphlet of Goldwin Smith—Canada and the Canadian Question, in which the writer alleged that the Canadian farmer sold the best he produced and ate the culls. Well, with hogs at $3 per cwt., oats 20 cents a bushel, hay $7 a ton, and wheat under a dollar, from stumpy little fields—the farmer in Drury's youth did well to escape cannibalism.

To know Drury, one must understand the oddly interesting epoch and region in which he came up.   The
men with whose sons he went to the village school were
manufacturers first, farmers second.   Their raw material
was the hardwood bush ; their factory the saw mill ; their
common carrier the Yankee schooner.   In my own bush
days a few counties further down in that same peninsula,
I recall heaps of white oak slabs in the forest which I was
told were the remains of the timber-men who had gone
through buying and cutting out the oaks for square timber
that floated away in rafts, probably to build tramp steamers
in England.   The bush farmer hired to wield the broad-
axe on that oak was as much an industrialist as any moulder
in a foundry.   He would have fought with his naked fists
any agitator who proposed to interfere with that wages
revenue.

After the oak was gone came the elm buyers, shrewd
Americans who paid as much for a thousand feet of prime
swamp elm as the pork buyer twenty miles away paid for
a cwt. of dead hog.   Mr. Drury must have known something about those friendly but niggardly Yankee dollars
that saved many a bush farmer from being sold for taxes.
He may have seen bolt mills go up and young men betwixt
haying and harvest swagger down to the docks to get 25
cents an hour loading elm bolts into the three-mast schoo-
ners.   He probably saw stave mills arise in which hundreds
of youths got employment while their fathers at home
fought stumps, wire worms, drought and the devil to get
puny crops at small prices.   He saw the wagon-works and
the fanning mill factory and the reaper industry come up
out of these timber products.   While he was a youth the
farmers were the first promoters of bigger towns, because
the big town meant more jobs for the young men whose
father's acres were too few for the families, and bigger
markets close at hand for perishable products.   The farmers
of that day would have tarred and feathered any revolu-

tionist who came preaching that a good market town was a wicked conspiracy of *bourgeoisie* and should become a deserted village.

Yankee money and Canadian industries were the economics of Drury's boyhood. If he was as good a Canadian then as he is now he must have had more faith in the Canadian factory than he had in the American paymaster, or sometimes even in the Ontario farm. There never was a bush farmer who would not have voted for a tariff that increased the price of timber for the saw-mill.

By the time Drury was old enough to consider being a candidate for Parliament, heaps of sawdust marked the grave of many a vanished saw mill. Young men who could not get work in the near-by town drifted to High School, to college, to law and medicine and the pulpit ; they went to the big cities across the border and got high wages ; to the Canadian West and got cheap land. The counties of Western Ontario began to decrease in man wealth as they increased in the wealth of agricultural industry. The schools that used to have boys sitting on the woodpile by the box stove shrank to about four scholars in a class. Congregations dwindled. Little towns lost their mills and began to feel like Goldsmith's Deserted Village. Then came the age of farm machinery, when the big towns had more overalls than the farms, and every good farm began to be a sort of factory.

All this was meat and drink to E. C. Drury, who came to voting age with the solemn conviction that though the fathers had worked hard, the sons were not prosperous. They paid too much for what they had to buy and got too little for what they had to sell ; a fate which seems to overtake most of us in varying degree. With stagnant local towns the markets for perishable products declined. In the open markets of the world, reached by long railway and steamship hauls, the Canadian farmer's staple products were in competition with nations of cheap labour. Across the lake a nation of twelve times our population was retaliating against our protective tariffs by duties on Canadian grain, cattle and hogs. The Tory party and the Canadian Pacific and the Bank of Montreal and the Canadian Manufacturers' Association were becoming British at the expense of the Canadian farmer. At the back of all the gods of things as they are and ought not to be, stood the damnable, desolating tariff that fattened the town and starved the farmer in order to bloat the banks and the manufacturer and the railways—under the cloak of patriotism! Heaven deliver us! Was it not a Tory manufacturer of stoves who said in Toronto that he would build a tariff "as high as Haman's gallows?" Was it not a Tory President of the C.P.R. who said he would have a tariff as high as a Chinese wall to keep out the Yankees? Was it not the President of a great Canadian bank who deserted the Liberal party when it sought to enact a measure of reciprocity?

On all hands Mr. Drury could see the evidence of a master conspiracy against the farmer, who was to become the helot of civilization. He could see it in his own barn as he reckoned the cost of his machinery, and over against that the price of what he had in the bins of his granary and on the hoof outside. That thousands of farmers voted and talked Conservative proved the astonishing power of heredity. That all farmers did not become Liberals and make the Liberal party a solid rural party proved that even a man's depleted pocket cannot compete with the traditions of his family. Drury looked to Laurier to emancipate the farmer. In vain. Laurier created more farmers, thousands of them in the West; but he only enslaved them with the voters' lists; the very party over which Drury had almost wept with joy when at the age of eighteen he had felt them like the armies of Israel sweeping out the scoundrels of the National Policy.

Thus his hope was no longer in Laurier, who knew nothing about the farmer, nor dreamed that in the very West which he had put on the political map with his prosperity of imported people and borrowed money, there was arising a race that would repudiate him and his. Drury had a weather eye on the West. There were farms in Simcoe county now worked by old men whose sons had gone to that Promised Land. In the constant drift of the hired man and the farmer's son to the town and the city for shorter hours, higher wages and more amusement, he saw the fluidity of labour, the first evidence that there was some common ground between the farmer and the labour class. Working in his own fields, driving his own teams, operating his own machinery, this capitalistic labour-unionist of the soil said to himself that the farmers of Canada were entitled not merely to representation in Parliament, but to the organization of a class interest that should take hold of the country's economic horns and turn it on to the right road.

In the lonely furrow of the farm a man often thinks out conclusions that are gloriously right in themselves, but in the chequered and cynical experiences of men in office tragically impossible. Mr. Drury was no stranger to Ottawa. He had been there on deputations ; and on tariff commissions ; and each time he came back he had a stronger determination to go there some day as the voice of the more or less united farmer against the tariff that had sterilized the Liberals.

Drury was a rural Liberal. He saw in the reciprocity campaign of 1911 some glimmer of hope that Liberalism might succeed without a revolution. The election settled that. From then on to the war the philosopher of Crown Hill bent himself to the deeper study of the one force that now seemed to him to be left capable of breaking the nation's bondage. He no longer had the fervent desire to see a new town grow among the farms that he had when he was a youth. Every bigger town, unless it had industries that could widen the farmer's low-cost market, was a mitigated menace. Every foundry and implement works and furniture factory and boot industry making goods more or less from imported material, considerably with imported labour, and selling to the consumer at a normal price plus the duty, roused in Mr. Drury as much hostility as a natively kind and Christian character would permit.

And at last he saw the predicted slump begin to come in the year 1913, when the boomster dodged the boomerang of inflated and speculative values ; when east and west the farmers, crimped by high railway rates and cost of materials, machinery and labour, ceased to be the backbone of Canadian buying.

And then the War.

Whatever may be traced to the normal development of this Ontario Cincinnatus, it was the War which made Drury. But for the war he would have bided his time to be elected to Ottawa on a straight tariff issue. The war, backed by the man's religion and his tariff theology, drove him to the Premiership of Ontario.

There were times during the war when, if Mr. Drury was as honest with himself as he is about government, he must have reflected that the Canadian farmer was getting pretty well paid back in part of one generation for the wrongs and adversities suffered by generations ago. Pork at $20 per cwt., oats at $1.50 a bushel, wheat fixed by the Government at $2.40 to keep it from bulling to more than $3— none of these could have been economically justified by Mr. Drury except as an act of compensating Providence. The farmer of all people as a class benefited most, when he was driven to the worst labour hardship he ever had by the terrific prices paid for war work, which robbed him of hired help almost at any price. The higher the price and the scarcer the help, the more the Government clamoured for production. The Ontario farmer responded to the call

He was no more a patriot to do it than a man was to buy Victory Bonds. He was simply a profitee (we leave off the r).

And this was the first call of the war to which the farmers as a class made a hearty response. No doubt most farmers were better servants of the nation in the furrow than in the trench. But the time came when they had to leave the furrows. On top of the Government's most frantic call for more production by the farmer came the Military Service Act, which refused to exempt him. The call to the plough-handle came before the election of 1917. The call to the bayonet came afterwards in a crisis unforeseen at the time of the election. Drury himself had been defeated as a conscriptionist Liberal candidate in 1917. No farmer could be in khaki and overalls at the same time. There was no reason given for the drastic change of face except the message from the front that more men were urgently needed or the West front was doomed. It was not even reckoned that a farmer conscripted after seed-time in 1918 could not possibly be of use in the trenches till long after the time when the fate of the West front would have been settled anyway.

Hence the ire of the agriculturist, driven now to become an agrarian. The Ontario farmer made no distinction between the Unionist Government that had conscripted the farmer, and the Ontario Conservative Government which supported Ottawa. The farmer made up his mind wherever possible to defeat both the old line candidates..

Premier Drury was the chief result. He never would have been offered the post but for the cleavage caused by the war. The U.F.O. were not unanimous, and Drury was not anxious. He had his eye on Ottawa. But there was nobody else who could unite the group with labour. Drury had himself been the first president of the U.F.O. and secretary of the Canadian Council of Agriculture ; he was a thinker, something of a scholar, a futurist, and a good deal of a radical ; and he could speak well.

He picked a Cabinet mainly of farmers.   He occupied more time drafting his Cabinet than most farmers take to harvest a crop.   He was in a hurry, but he wanted nobody to suspect it.   He said little ;   wisely.   There was no occasion.   He had no mandate from the people.   He wanted sure-enough colleagues.   The men he chose were all novices.   The old line critics watched him with affected contempt.   They said Agriculture and Labour never could mix.   Drury went along.   No Cabinet had ever been so prayerfully hand-picked.   Labour must not get the idea that it was merely being sopped for the support of twelve men in a House majority of one.   There must be concession ;   common aims understood, even ahead of experience, when there was as yet no common policy.

Mr. Drury had been only a few hours sworn Premier of Ontario when he was summarily turned out—not, however, from Office.   In company with a farmer author friend who had been given the freedom of a certain small but desirable Club and who wanted to show Mr. Drury one place where he could have a quiet time of an evening,he went to have dinner.   As neither of the gentlemen was known to the housekeeping department a member of the Club—a well-known newspaperman—was asked to inquire their identity.   The result was that the Premier of Ontario and his friend left the Club, without dinner.

The next day the newspaperman looked over the shoulder of his editor-chief in office and said,

"Who is the important-looking man in the photograph ?"

The answer came, "Hon. E. C. Drury, Premier of Ontario."

"Great Scott !"   he said huskily, "that's the man I turned out of the Club last night."

Drury had the sense of humour to regard the matter as a joke on both the newspaperman and himself.

The opening of the new Legislature was a spectacle. Dignitaries and judges, professors and generals stood about the farmers—led by the farmer-in-chief, morning-coated, carefully groomed, plainly nervous but sustained by the dignity of it all, His voice was firm; his manner that of a very circumspect bridegroom. The old smug strut and case-hardened pomp of legislature inaugurals was lacking. An undercurrent of deep sincerity stayed many a tremorous hand. Drury was the least nervous of all. I imagine that in the morning he had sung to himself some good old fortifying hymn, like "Rock of Ages."

Since that day the Premier has learned that practical politics is a game that taxes all a man's technique in Christianity. Autocratic Hydro and Mackenzie the loosening octopus ; New Ontario preaching up the old plaint of secession ; better roads and prodigal Mr. Biggs ; what to do with Education that Cody had not started to do ; how to stave off commissions on reform of the school system ; the constant queues of moral reformers ; the new menace of the movies and the censorship farce ; the timber stealers; disconcerting Dewart and redundant Ferguson ; returned soldiers and khaki members ; the Reds and the plain clothes men ; blustering Morrison, and the tyrannical U.F.O.——

Until the Premier, plain, homespun gentleman that he is, longed for Friday evening and the Crown Hill farm and the quiet little church in the village, because one week at his desk took more out of him than a month in overalls, And then to relieve his surcharged soul he made that speech at Milverton in which he boldly proclaimed that he was going to head, not a mere group called the U.F.O., but a People's Party. For this "broadening out" speech he got clods thrown at him by Morrison, and Burnaby put rails on the road to upset the Premier's buggy, and the *Farmers' Sun* tried to change the wheels on his rig so that he would not be able to get home. Worse than any the *Onlooker*, that virile organ of no advertising and of the Meighen Government, said :

"The U.F.O. chose this man and dragged him out of his rural obscurity. In common gratitude he should have stuck to their colours. He should have given fair warning of a change of heart, and indeed we think he ought to have resigned. When a man joins a political party he agrees to subordinate his ambitions and activities to the common good of that party, and failing to do so honour demands that he should leave it."

In spite of the fact that the Premier of Ontario twice made an appointment by request from the writer of this for the purpose of getting a statement for the press as to what he meant to do about this whole business of "broadening out," twice failed to keep the appointment and later came out with the Milverton pronunciamento, we have no hesitation in pointing out that :

Mr. Drury was not in rural obscurity. The U.F.O. had no colours which Mr. Drury had not helped to paint, for he was the first President the U.F.O. ever had. He had no change of heart, because when he made an unstable coalition of the U.F.O. and the Labour party he entered into a pact and covenant which the U.F.O. had never considered ; he had already "broadened out" to drive Labour and Agriculture as a team and had pretty well succeeded in doing it. Mr. Drury did not join a political party. The U.F.O. was not a real party because it went into the election of 1919 without a leader, and in order to get its platform translated into party it had to have Mr. Drury or somebody like him. And if Mr. Drury should resign from the head of the two groups which he alone has made into the semblance of a party, he would be recommended by Mr. Crerar to let his guardian take him to a lunatic asylum.

Drury has done much better than his critics expected he would do. He has been bold enough to keep Adam Beck from being the unelected Premier of Ontario, which is more than Sir William Hearst ever could do. He has made Government cost more than it ever did, though it is only reasonable bookkeeping to believe that part of the cost was incurred by a Government over which he had no control. He has begun to build public highways which being originally a farmer's job should have been done well, but up to the present has been on a smaller scale as bad a case of wasting the public money as the railways of Canada ever perpetrated. The cost of administration being a matter of either experience or graft, it is probable that the Coalition will cut down the cost when they get more experience. The Chippewa Canal is one glaring instance of high labour cost which a Farmer Premier with Labour colleagues did not presume to regulate. If anybody knows what a day's work is it should be the farmer ; but the farmer in this case was not absolutely free to express his opinions, because he depends upon Labour for his voting majority in the House.

In the matter of referendum Mr. Drury has been an advocate instead of a judge. He and his—notably the church-ridden Mr. Raney, who does not even smoke—are a dry lot. They wanted Ontario to be bone dry and therefore preferred to have the people vote either foolishly for the iniquitous O.T.A. or fanatically for absolute prohibition. Mr. Drury should have taken the spark plug out of his Methodist car long enough to reflect that what keeps a man contented is going to keep him from stirring up trouble. If the Government of . enlightened and moral Ontario had brought in a measure to create a referendum on the alternative of prohibition *vs.* effective government control of reasonable liquors, it might have less cause to be panicky over Bolshevism.

The legislation to exempt from taxation houses costing less than a certain amount looks like a pretty straight play for the Labour vote, and the propagation of a semi-Bolshevistic principle that unless checked somewhere will exempt the many at the expense of the few.

But before Mr. Drury has the chance to be truly elected by the people of Ontario to carry on his People's Party, he hopes perhaps that he may have a chance to be called to

Ottawa. It is freely rumoured that Mr. Crerar has no intention of taking the Premiership which the liberated people of Canada are going to bestow upon him by virtue of one more group-coalition. In which case he may invite Mr. Drury, who has given a sparring exhibition of being a Premier, to succeed him. Then we shall have the undemocratic farce of an appointive Premier all over again— for the third time in three years. And then—well, we shudder to think what is going to become of Mr. Drury's hitherto unimpeachable Christianity and of the economic welfare of a country which has as much right to modern factories as the bush farmer ever had to saw-mills.

EZEKIEL AT A LEDGER

RT. HON. SIR GEORGE FOSTER

SIR George Foster is a genius. The world forgives much to geniuses, because it lives by them. Canada has tolerated a great deal in Foster for the very good reason that no man except Laurier has for so long a period without interruption seemed so picturesquely necessary to our public affairs.

In his own temperamental way Sir George somewhat compensates Canada for never having produced a Milton or a Bach. One of his best speeches might be made into blank verse or set to a fugue. He illuminates life. Decade by decade he comes prancing down the vistas of our politics with a vitality that is perfectly amazing. And when some obituarist writes his epitaph, "Foster Mortuus Est," he promptly rubs it out and writes, "Resurgam!"

The first allusion I ever heard made to Sir George Foster was in 1889, on a Sunday School excursion when a Grit lawyer superintendent spoke with admiring deprecation of the then famous divorce case ; adding, as might be expected of a righteous Grit, that it was a pity so eminent an advocate of prohibition should have so compromised, perhaps ruined, his political career.

Well, the compromise has lasted a long time and the ruin seems to be long overdue. Public sentiment over both temperance and divorce has somewhat shifted. In 1889, when virtue shuddered over marrying divorced women, drunkards were being made by hundreds in any town under the very nose of the church. In 1921 when Parliament moves to popularize divorce, public sentiment not only abolishes the bar, but votes bone dry on the eve of an artificial millennium.

A man who for some years has wanted the Ministry of Trade made the remark in a magazine article that if he had Sir George Foster in his employ as a salesman he would have him discharged for incompetence. That man forgets that a genius is not born to sell goods. There were times in the war when less genius and more business in Trade and Commerce would have been better for Canada. Foster was almost seventy when the war began ; a pretty old man to act as the chief business manager for a nation at war. His department was the economic backbone of the Administration. The nearer Canada got to total conscription of resources, the more Foster's work should have towered into the blue. Trade and troops were the life of the nation. Hughes, White, Borden, Rowell, Meighen, were all shoved into greater eminence by the work they did in the war ; Foster was no bigger or more potent a figure in war work or any other kind of work when peace was signed than he was in 1914.

He never was a great executive even at his portfolio under Macdonald in the early '80's. He has always been a prophet. Public speech is his besetting passion. He could rise anywhere and translate logic and economics into ethical emotion. No man in Canada felt the war more intensely. But Trade was not a matter of emotion ; or of oratorical periods ; or the right hand descending upon the left. It was a matter of urgent and colossal business.

In 1916, talking to the war budget, he declaimed against patronage. He had done the same thing in 1910 just as ably when he was the pot calling the kettle black.

"I hope," he said, "that in the white light of the present struggle the two parties will agree to do away with the evil."

But the "white light" was more intent on doing away with the parties themselves.

In the same speech :

"When the trenches call for munitions and supplies, when the blood of the country is oozing from its veins in the struggle to preserve its ideals and its liberties, when those who are at home are contributing with generous self-sacrifice and without murmur or repining, I say that to me as a member of the Government, to you as supporters of the Government, and to you, gentlemen opposite, as a part of the great body which represents the people of this Dominion, the call comes to cut off every unnecessary expenditure, to refuse every improper demand. It is our business to administer the funds of the people with perfect economy, and to devote ourselves to the one sole purpose of prosecuting this war to a successful and final conclusion."

Again, he spoke like a prophet when he riddled the blind optimism of the prosperity pack. At that time Canada had a favouring balance of $200,000,000 just two years after a heavy ledger against us.

"The Optimist speaks of the unexampled prosperity that is to follow the war. I would like to think so, but I can't. The prediction of a Montreal newspaper that Canada will have from twelve to fifteen million inhabitants within three years after the war is a mischievous exaggeration. The first trying period of readjustment will come immediately after the actual fighting ceases and an armistice is declared."

Ezekiel was profoundly right up till the last prophecy. The Minister of Trade, with all his great ability to analyze trade, had not mastered economics. Neither had the President of a great Canadian bank when he said before the armistice, that merchants with empty shelves and able to buy cheap goods would be in luck. It was a bad time for prophets.

However, for a man who aimed at so many nails ,Sir George had a good average of hitting. But while he was talking so much, and in Europe so long, the biggest-business administration of which he was the chief went along on its own more or less mechanical momentum. By 1917 Canada had a total export trade of more than half a billion ; with a possible yearly munition order of 500 millions—no thanks to the Minister of Trade. No nation in the world exported so much from so few people. No Ministry of Trade had such a record. Sir George knew exactly what it all meant. He was used to analytical surveys. But one fails to remember that at any period he issued from his office, the trade centre of the Dominion, any statements that shewed him to be more than a puzzled commentator on the riddle of trade, usually between speeches and journeys. Sir George never did have executive patience for the mastery of detail. In this case he did not even convince the people that he had sized up the great general outlines, so fascinating because so profoundly unusual.

In June, 1916, Sir George issued in his weekly Trade Bulletin a resounding Call To Action for a business conference at Ottawa of all parties interested for the purpose of pulling the country's industries and organizations into one big *ensemble* for getting back to peace. That "Call" was published in one paper illustrated by a picture of Sir George—in the climax of a speech. A few months later a political writer was in Ottawa, and when he came back he wrote an article about the Foster Conference. The following extract shows what he thought of it :

In Ottawa, last week, I met a big bear of a Canadian westerner. He had just arrived from Toronto. He was all smiles, all energy and enthusiasm, and he was looking for the Minister of Trade and Commerce, Sir George E. Foster.

"Tell you what I want him for," he said. "I want to go up and shake hands with a real live man. That's what I want. I read his message 'bout getting together, and it sure set me thinking. I'm strong for this Conference scheme. I'm going to back it for all I'm worth and do my darndest to help a real, live statesman to pull off a big deal. Damn if I care whether he is a Tory. My middle name is—Boost ! I want to help."

We walked up to the Department of Trade and Commerce together.

"Just what line of industry are you interested in ?" I asked.

"Boilers—steam boilers. Vancouver. Little Van-cou-ver. That's my town."

"And if I may ask, what is your idea about this Business Man's Conference ? What do you think ought to be done ?"

"Eh ? Why, I don't know yet. That's what I'm coming to see Foster about."

An hour later I met the boiler-maker coming away from the Department of Trade and Commerce.

"Well," I said, "everything clear ?"

"Clear ?" he roared. "Clear ? Why, man alive ! that fellow

Foster's away in the West with some Dominion Royal Commission, making speeches or something, and back there"—nodding toward the Department of Trade and Commerce—"nobody home !"

"Couldn't they explain it ?"

"Sure. They explain that Sir George is away and nothing definite can be done. I asked 'em when the conference would be called and they said that was indefinite. Then I said where ? And they thought somewhere in Ottawa. Why, all that fellow Foster made was a speech. That's all. A speech ! Now what the h—— good will a speech do to help me and help the rest of us manufacturers to keep from getting swamped after this war ?"

Trade in Canada during the war was of vastly more practical significance than the old fiscal idea of Empire of which Sir George had been such a protagonist when he stumped England for Chamberlain in 1903. But he never seemed able to grasp it as clearly even in a speech. I don't know which seems to me now the greater speech ; that on the Chamberlain mirage to the Toronto Empire Club when he elevated fiscal statistics into a pageant of economic emotion ; or his speech on the war, I think in 1916, when he lifted his thin spectral figure into a sublime paroxysm of ethical appeal, corralled all opposing arguments into a corner and flogged the life out of them in a great message to awakened humanity. The comparison scarcely matters except to show that in fifteen years of great Foster speeches alas for the prophets !—it was not the fiscal Empire of Chamberlain that had leaped to the war.

Still more startling to Sir George, the economics of war riddled to bits the old economics of Empire. In 1917 he was compelled to forget that a tariff was implied in the Ten Commandments and to consent for all necessary purposes to remove trade restrictions across the border. That was after the United States had declared war. The high priest of protection himself invented a phrase "economic unit" to express North America. He wanted markets to find their own levels by their own routes. He no longer had any fear of Canada being Americanized. Canada's nationhood was already defined in the trenches more than ever it had been in tariffs. In Sir George's phrase the food producers of North America were to become one vast international group. When Foster was "Yea" to Macdonald in 1887 and 1891, before he became "Amen" to Chamberlain in 1903, this economic unity was called continentalism, which to Foster was the mother of annexation, and Free Trade Liberals were traitors to the Empire.

Economic unity, however, meant far more than Sir George intended it to mean. He admitted the principle of free-trade only in production. In spite of tariffs North America became, not only a vast group of producers, but a huge family of consumers. Every Victory Loan raised money that was spent in once more paying wages and buying materials for war production in Canada. Every time that money went round the circle, prices for many of the staple commodities went higher. The Department of Trade registered a tremendous increase in the cash value of exports even when the bulk value changed very little. The more loans "put over the top," the more money there seemed to be. The more hazardous shipping became through submarines, the greater the scarcity, and the demand—and the price paid. Sir George witnessed this phenomenon : the fewer producers left by conscription on the land, in the mines, in the factories, the more Canada was able to export—in cash values.

This must have given a good Tory economist loss of sleep. No man could have analyzed the paradox more ably than Sir George. But so far as we can recollect, he published no illuminating bulletins from his Department to tell us about it. How we should have enjoyed his master mind elucidating the phenomenon of a continent being gradually denuded of goods and flushed with money ; of prices inexorably mounting ; of money hungering for goods ; of fabulous wages for munition-making and any-thing else that could be scaled up to meet the competition unloading themselves into Victory Bonds at a sure profit, and the surplus into commodities most of which were not made in Canada and must therefore come from the United States. What a prophetic commentary it would have made on the "buyers' market" which followed the armistice. What wonderful reading it would have made if Sir George had issued replies to those commercial newspaper editors over the border who rushed jubilating into print to say with fabulous statistics that Canada was now the heaviest customer that nation had. How we should have liked to hear officially from the Minister of Trade how Broadway was infecting the country, luxuries reeling in argosies over the dry land to Canada, and Canada buying herself bankrupt on the exchanges ; and that though there were powerful economic reasons for it all, we had better enlist in an army of economy instead of being conscripted later by the super-tariff on luxuries and the luxury tax.

But the Minister of Trade confined himself to growling that we should all wear patches and old clothes. Which was one good reason why many people did not. It was easy for Sir George to wear patched trousers if he felt like so doing. He would have been merely picturesque, like those ragged prophets of old. Most of us still had to invest in some sort of decoration. Anyhow a large number of people had the money to spend ; and the more they spent the more they approved of self-denial in other people.

This problem of American penetration is big enough at any time here. The Department of Trade is the place where it is most clearly understood. We are constantly warned about the danger, not only to our Canadian dollar, but to our national independence if we persist in importing motor cars, fashionable footwear, party gowns and lingerie and hats, art furniture, home decorations, phonographs, moving pictures, and magazines. But we go on doing it ; because Canada, whether in war or peace, fails to produce

g

a great many things that people like to have and to wear and to go about in ; and for those that she does we are charged the foreign price plus the duty and more ; so that in many and many a case it has been found more economical to buy the article from catalogue, paying the duty and the express charges.

Has Sir George ever enlightened us about this ? Has he ever tried to inform the Canadian manufacturer that if he expects to hold our allegiance even under a more or less protective tariff, he must refrain from charging the consumer all the traffic and more than the consumer will stand ? We fail to remember ; even when we recollect that on thus and such an occasion somewhere in the Empire he made some glorious patriotic speech. On a subject which causes many Canadians to explode, often with ill-considered accusation of "the Yankees," our greatest maker of pure and applied speeches seldom has a word to say. But he knows. Sir George Foster knows our economic subjugation by the 12 to 1 method, even under a tariff. Alas! he hails from the Maritimes, a land of great people, of constructive Canadians who have too often been in absolute economic need of more of that sort of subjugation.

Then there was the never-dead dragon of high prices for everything, which our St. George made no real attempt to spear. That is a long story. It was his department which furnished the Food Controller, the duties which the Trade Department could not discharge. Well remembered are the evangelical injunctions of the Controller to consume perishable and export other products ; to live on garden truck grown in back yards and corner lots so that grain and butter and bacon and eggs and oatmeal might run the submarine blockade on the high seas. There was no fault to find with this, so long as it was economy. But heaven knew what armies of housewives, already desperate from lack of help, were dragooned into making their kitchens amateur canning factories where they wasted good fruit along with tragically expensive sugar in jars that approximated the cost of cut glass. And after all the slavery and the self denial, butter and eggs that were not shipped abroad because there was no room in munition ships to carry them, vanished mysteriously in the lower price season into some limbo known as cold-storage, only to emerge when it suited the storage barons at prices as high as were paid in Europe. No doubt there is an economic philosophy in cold-storage just as there is in hydro-power. But we have always supposed its virtue was in taking care of a perishable surplus, so that when there is a scarcity the surplus can be released at a reasonable profit.

Did the able Minister of Trade ever stoop to enlighten us with the economics of this ? If so, the recollection has faded.

There is at any time, whether in peace or war, a great function for the Department of Trade to perform in the matter of what is the reasonable cost of any commodity in general demand. But no Trade Department in this country has ever done it. There is always plenty of time for the consideration of new markets, the plotting of new trade routes and the planning of mercantile marine for export ; all very well, and if we are to pay our bills by exports, very necessary. But the common consumer has many a time, long before the war and often since, found himself in the jaws of a nutcracker in the shape of some combine or trust or confederacy of middlemen ; and if there was any sphere of government to deal with these things it was the great Department of Trade.

This has nothing to do with party politics. Any party up to date has been capable of neglecting the people in these matters. But it is quite as important as the abolition of patronage.

We have ceased to expect any such function from a Minister so old, so eloquent, so Imperially-inspired as Sir George Foster. There is always something else to do.

The party must be led in the House. Sir George was the House leader. Magnificent ! No man ever rose at a desk in Parliament who could more superbly play upon the bigotries and the high patriotic emotions of even a remnant party. The man is a genius. There must be the valley of dry bones for Ezekiel. And the bones must come together and walk. Sir Robert Borden on such occasions was a mere interested gargoyle. Patriotism demanded that the party's desks be thumped. Sir George saw that they were thumped without stint.

Twice during the Opposition period Sir George was dead and buried by the Grits ; once over the Union Trust land investigation ; again in a libel suit which he lost to the *Globe* when Rowell was against him. None of these things defeated the able author of Resurgam ! who was made Minister of Trade, went for a six-months' journey in the Orient trying to convert the yellow races from rice to Canadian flour, and afterwards got his title. So when the people, in 1917, asked Ezekiel for a prophecy, the Minister of Trade stoically advised them to eat less, save more, waste nothing, wear what their grandmothers wore if possible, and hope for the best. In the matter of fixing prices Sir George had as much wisdom as most, though he made a very awkward attempt to adjust the price of wheat and only then at the instigation of the British Government.

The world by this time was full of upsetting anomalies to Sir George. Even government was perverted. He had no desire for Unionism ; to sit at Council with even win-the-war Liberals—once plain Grits. It needed political philosophy to make colleagues of such men as Calder, the Grit enemy of Toryism in the West, Crerar, the avowed apostle of free-trade, Sifton, the Alberta mystery man, and Rowell, who had won the libel suit against him for the *Globe*. It was not to be expected that so complete and historic a Tory as Sir George could at first easily regard such men as anything but interlopers, even though he admitted their strength in the Coalition. One can imagine Meighen making up to his old trade enemy Carvell, but not Foster making overtures to Rowell.

But the vital element was gone out of the Administration, and Sir George had to admit it. Cold and repellent as he has always seemed in politics, without a crony or even a man who cared to make him a confederate, he has never been a man of implacable resentment. He was yet to regard Rowell as a real man, worthy his confidence.

A newspaperman sent to Osgoode Hall to report the *Globe* libel suit for an Ottawa Liberal paper relates how the night of the conclusion of the trial he met Mr. Foster at the Toronto Station. The reporter had already wired the decision of the Court adverse to Mr. Foster, who had not even taken the trouble to inquire what it was. The two chatted amiably on the train and met the next morning in Ottawa. On his way home Mr. Foster saw the Liberal bulletin at the newspaper office. A few days later he met the scribe.

"Tom," he said, genially, shaking hands, "why didn't you tell me about that decision ?"

."Well, sir, I really thought you knew, and I didn't care to hurt your feelings."

The member for North York laughed.

"Feelings !" he repeated. "You are the first Grit that ever said I had any."

A prominent Liberal described to the writer the exit of Mr. Foster from the House after the Royal Commission investigation into the Union Trust.

"Mr. and Mrs. Foster," he said eloquently, "went together down the terrace in a fog of rain, into the shadow of the night, under one umbrella. And I said to myself as they went, dejected and pitiful, 'Well, that's the final exit of Foster from political life.' "

The author of Resurgam knew better. He could always somehow come back on the stepping stones of a dead self.

Something made him feel that without him the Conservative party would have been like the Liberals without Laurier, or in an earlier day his own party minus the old chief Macdonald.   He was almost right.

One other episode illustrates how spontaneously the emotional aspect of things sometimes sways this cold politician who never could lead a party.   When the Premier by request called a caucus of his Union supporters for the purpose of discovering what could be done with the Coalition to make it a party, it was not the Premier who held the floor, but Sir George, who made a long passionate speech upon the vicissitudes of men who—like the Premier and himself—had carried the burden and the heat of the political day.   When Foster had finished, there were tears on case-hardened faces and the caucus adjourned. Asked later for a copy of his great speech, Sir George said he had not even prepared any notes ; when he went to the caucus he had not intended making any such speech ; he did not now remember what he had said.

Can we call such a man anything but a genius ?   As Minister of Trade he may be a poor salesman.   He is not less a poor salesman of his party, his country, or his big original belief in the Empire, whatever form of government it might become, or of his birthright to spend his tremendous talent in public service rather than in private gain.   And he has been for almost a generation the most interesting personality in the ranks of the Conservative party.

There is but one other politician in America with the political vitality of Sir George Foster. "Uncle Joe" Cannon is the man.   In Washington Cannon is regarded as a miracle because he was once the autocrat of Congress and is still a member of the House and a very old man. Sir George Foster is almost as old a man and has been in public service much longer.   He has held portfolios under all the Conservative Premiers that Canada ever had—Macdonald, Thompson, Abbott, Bowell, Borden, Meighen.   There have been times in the shuffles of these men when for ability he, rather than Abbott or Bowell or Borden, should have been Premier. But there was always a fatal obstacle in the personality of the man whose leadership always depended upon making a great speech. When he was first Minister under Macdonald, a lad named Arthur Meighen was getting ready to attend a High School. Could that Minister and that lad have been introduced, would Ezekiel have prophesied that in 1920 he would be holding office under the lad, Premier of Canada ?

Anomalies like these are the rule in a life of a man so unusual as Sir George, who is now a Senator. Even in the Senate he is not dead; for in Ezekiel, 37th chapter, it is written, "Son of man, can these bones live? And I answered, O Lord God, thou knowest."

A HALO OF BILLIONS

Hon. Sir Thomas White

Sir Thomas White was the world's only continuous Finance Minister for the whole period of the war—and after ; when nobody 'else cared to have his job, and Sir Thomas did. He seduced billions of patriotic dollars out of the pockets of this country and smiled as he did it. No man in Canada was so exquisitely fitted to the task of making an average dollar burn a hole in a man's pocket in order to do its bit. It gave him "the pleasure that's almost pain" to feel that no man except Henri Bourassa or an Eskimo could escape the snare of a Victory Loan advertisement prepared by Sir Thomas and his committees of ad-men and brokers. Never before on this continent had a nation been so advertised into patriotism. In England some expert had done it for Kitchener's Army. But it was easier to recruit England, with 30 millions of people within the area of our maritime provinces, than to mobilize billions from a vast emptiness like Canada.

It must be admitted that the divinity which keeps governments from wrecking nations had somehow picked the right man for this stupendous task. Sir Thomas had a quality of mind and a political experience which made it possible for him to pull the last dollar for victory. In the war annals of Canada he will have a halo of billions, while Sam Hughes has one of bayonets. He mobilized our financial resources by a system that stopped only short of conscription.

I seldom see Sir Thomas standing at a street corner when I do not feel like urging him to run along and attend to his office and not to be losing time. He seems to belong to that cold group of men whose time is naturally money.

In 1912 I asked Mr. White in Ottawa for an interview. He appointed an hour when I might see him. As soon as I entered the office he began to talk. The ease and fluency of his conversation amazed me. No other Minister of that Cabinet could have been so suave and entertaining.

"Er—with regard to the question of railway fin——?"

He saw the question coming in a sort of parabolic curve and he dodged it. By a neat evasion he got the topic switched to sociology, from that to philosophy, to heredity, literature, journalism, art, and finally prenatalism. Every effort I made to probe him on public finance was met by some calm and smiling barrage of eclectic interest. For an hour we played conversational pingpong in the most amiable style. And when Mr. White urbanely confessed that he liked everybody in the House of Commons, even "Bob" Rogers and Dr. Pugsley, it was time for the interviewer to go, before so charmed a Utopia should vanish like a film on a screen, and to conclude that the Finance Minister of Canada was no novice in a certain species of diplomacy.

Time made some heavy changes in him. A press gallery observer, asked by a certain Canadian periodical to name a possible successor to Sir Robert Borden four years before the Premier's resignation, picked Sir Thomas whom he said he had watched turn grey and careworn in office, sedulous at his desk, always busy, never at ease. Yet in 1912 he could lecture hon. gentlemen opposite seasoned in political intrigues as though he, himself, had discovered some new coefficient in politics.

Sir Thomas White has always been a political emergency, a sort of administrative occasion. For real politics he was never meant. For government by business he had great aptitude. To him government is big business, and the human side of democracy a sealed book. He has an almost

exquisite sense of prerogative. His equilibrium is adjusted
to the niceties of a seismographic instrument. Yet he has
never held himself aloof, and is not commonly proud.

There is an idle story that near the end of his term in
office he went to a bank teller's wicket—being in urgent
temporary need of a little common money—and presented
a cheque. On being courteously reminded by the teller
that he had not brought the customary identification, he
blandly announced, "I am the Finance Minister of Canada."
The manner in which the Minister spoke is said to have left
no doubt in the teller's mind that he was indeed the very
man whose photograph had appeared in the newspapers.

There is also a little story that during one of the Victory
Loan conferences in Ottawa, one of his older associates in
newspaper work politely called him Sir Thomas, and that
the Minister replied, "Oh, forget it ! Call me Tom."

The first may be fiction. The second is a fact. But
the number of men who without invitation would call him
Tom, is not very extensive.

From his youth up Tom White had a powerful capacity
for ordered work. There was "a time to work and a time
to play, a time to laugh and a time to weep." Nor did he
acquire this from Sir Joseph Flavelle, with whom he was
so long and intimately associated. He had it from the
cradle, which he must have left at the appointed time with
some impatience at too much rocking. As a student at
the University, as a law student at Osgoode, as a barrister,
as reporter on the *Telegram*, as an employee in the Toronto
Assessment Department, he had always a sort of mathe-
matical regard for the diligence that makes a man fit to
stand before kings, and the sensation of a superbly pigeon-
holed mind.

By heredity Sir Thomas was labelled a Liberal, and at
the time of the Taft-Fielding reciprocity junta he sat on
the edge of his political bed pulling the court-plaster off.
Next morning, without a single new grey hair in his head,

he found himself a Conservative. The Liberal regime of
shipping in people and booming up speculative towns on the
prairies was a good thing for any Trust. But when the
Government began to barter its preserve for another lease
of life, Mr. White decided that it was time for a change.
When he quit the National Trust to take on a trust for a
nation he was a new-born Conservative, and in the eyes
of the new Premier a lovely child. And as Finance Minister
in a Tory Government he became the real author of
Coalition.

Mr. White took into the Finance Department the
atmosphere and the technique of the fiduciary corporation.
Hence he was never able to read himself into the life of the
country, never became more than a superficial master of
its political forces, never rallied men about him in a great
effort to save anything but a financial situation, and never
lost a superb sense of himself. The fact that without ever
having been elected to Parliament or Legislature, or even
a County Council, he could walk into what is usually
regarded as the most important department of administration in any country, is a proof that government as big
business was more important to him than politics as experience.

The average portfolio is handed to a politician, not
because he knows anything about the matter in hand, but
because he is a good politician, a big enough man to represent some electoral area, and may be left to learn his public
job after he gets it. Such is democracy. White was a
tyro in politics and public administration. But he did
know finance. When Laurier picked editor Fielding from
Nova Scotia to look after the Budget he chose a good
deal of a genius. Mr. Fielding was a master of tariffs and
of inspiring fiscal speeches outside the House. He had
almost a Gladstonian faculty for making statistics scintil-
late with human interest. He had made a survey of the
country on tariff for revenue ; and he usually had a book-

keeping surplus at a time when he practically boasted on the platform of what it cost to run the country. Much thanks to him the Liberals had given Free Trade a profoundly respectable burial, with Michael Clark, headmaster of the Manchester School in Canada, as chief mourner.

But the ledgers of Canada looked to be in a bad way to Mr. White. "The cost of high living" had been demonstrated by the Liberal Government some time before James J. Hill coined the phrase. Laurier monuments to high living were dotted all over the country in the shape of armouries, post offices, customs houses, docks, courthouses, the Quebec Bridge, and vast systems of unpopulated railways.

When Mr. White's sensitive finger came to that prodigal item in the public ledger he had almost excuse, in spite of his pre-knowledge of the business, for curling up like a cutworm. His knowledge of banks and their customers was very extensive. He had dealt with those banks. The ex-manager of the National Trust had long known that Canada was overbuilt with railways and going-to-be-bankrupt towns. The orgy of expansion whose familiar figure was the prodigal with the scoop shovel in the gold bin by the open window with a huge hole in the ground beneath, was just about at the crest of its master carousal; and the transcontinental railways with their entails of cash and land grants and guaranteed bonds was the thing that gave the new Minister the greatest concern of the lot, though he never said so. An ex-Cabinetarian who used to agree with Sir Thomas in politics still stoutly alleges that the 1911 "bolt" of the famous 18 Liberals, of whom Sir Thomas was one of the leaders, was a tactical manœuvre to save the Canadian Northern from bankruptcy by reciprocity.

Sir Thomas should have made the railways his first drastic item of reorganization. Here was a Verdun for the Finance Minister to take But for two years while the railway cataclysm was coming he went along with business as usual. It would have been less of a burden to unload that railway bankruptcy in 1913 than it was during the stress of after the war.

But of course the Finance Minister was only the chief subordinate in the Administration. Time would force the railways to terms. The war and war business came faster than the time. Sir Thomas probably dreaded the public ownership in which he has never profoundly believed. In conversation with the President of the Canadian Pacific he practically admitted that a Government cannot compete with a great corporation in operating a railway. But in 1912, on the principle that an egg hatches into a chicken, he must have foreseen that national ownership of half Canada's railways would be thrust upon him.

It is not explicitly known what are Sir Thomas White's opinions about the Government ownership of railways ; but one can easily imagine what he would have said prior to 1911 to any proposal of any Government to begin owning and operating banks and trust companies. And as Government is the owner of the Royal Mint in Canada and does its own coining of the metals used in our currency, it would seem to be vastly easier for a Government to own banks and loan companies than to own and operate transportation systems. Sir Thomas would scarcely deny that. He is too shrewd in experience. It is one thing for a municipality to own street railways, because all the streets are automatically part of a city's property. It is quite another matter for Government to own and operate railways, because the routes of these highways and the machinery necessary to conduct traffic are not naturally the property of a Government, which exercises its power chiefly through the regulation of rates and the functions of the Railway Commission.

One imagines that Sir Thomas sincerely hoped that the railways built from cash borrowed on Government guaranteed bonds, and by direct loans from the national exchequer would some time develop business enough to pay their own way. But it is not remembered that he held any conferences with the Minister of Railways to prepare a public statement on this question. Both these Ministers had troubles enough without creating more. The country was on the crest of a wave whose trough was not far ahead.

Sir Thomas had made but one really constructive budget speech when the inevitable slump began to come. But as yet he seemed to be rather charmed with the novelties of Parliament and the ironies of preparing to win elections. The war plunged him into a system that cared no more for his budget than a cyclone for a baby carriage. Tariffs, bankrupt railways, the banking system, exchanges, and the common cost of living were all but obliterated in the campaign of war loans, not the least marvellous feature of which was that selling Victory Bonds almost made the Finance Minister a friend of the common people. The "vicious circle" of higher wages and higher cost of living was offset by Sir Thomas White's virtuous circle of money raised in Canada, spent in Canada, for goods needed by Canada and the Allies at the front. The formula was $5\frac{1}{2}$ per cent with no taxes, and the best security in the world—if the war was won, which of course it would be if people bought Victory Bonds.

In this era of the patriotism of the pocket, common reason almost tottered from her throne. Ordinary financial logic was forgotten. Economic delirium took hold of the nation. A broker in those days could talk in language more mysterious than the polite attentions of a juggler who pulls an egg from your pocket. Newspapers were full of jargon that sometimes seemed more fantastic than the theories of the Holy Rollers. The citizen who could not cash a Victory Bond to pay a debt was considered behind the times, and the banker who told you that it was better to sell bonds than to borrow on them at the bank was regarded as an oracle, even though you could not begin to comprehend his logic.

But the Finance Minister was as calm as Gibraltar. He was the man behind the curtain and the show. He was seldom absent from the Orders-in-Council convention, commonly known as Parliament. He was again and again acting Premier. He cared little for Imperial Conferences. His war was at home. His firing line was all over Canada. He was the most stay-at-home and sedulous of our ministers. He worked while others slept or sailed the seas. No Victory Loan advertisement proof escaped the eagle eye of this ex-newspaperman before it went to press. He scanned and corrected every syllable. Every advertisement was a sermonette from the Finance Minister.

An independent writer visiting Ottawa in the fall of 1916, wrote concerning the Finance Minister :

"One of the best evidences of Ottawa's frame of mind is the way it talks about Sir Thomas White—and the way Sir Thomas talks about himself. Sir Thomas White has probably rendered more real brain service to this country in his few years of office than any one man who has held office as a Minister—I am not now speaking of Prime Ministers, whose functions are particular and peculiar—since Confederation. To Ottawa, Sir Thomas is little short of a miracle. The frame of mind on both sides of politics regarding Sir Thomas is not unlike that of the farmer who saw a two-humped camel for the first time. "Hell," said Ottawa, "they ain't no such animal !" Now it calls Sir Thomas White 'great'—and even Sir Thomas admits it !"

Vol. I., No. 1 of The Onlooker, had this to say on the other side of the ledger :

"One would gather from the way some of his admirers talk that he, and he alone, was responsible for the success of the various loans issued during the war. He had it easy. The country was literally bursting with money seeking investment. One could almost have raised it with his eyes shut. The whole community was humming with activity like a top asleep ; and still the orders from abroad came pouring in. Every fresh loan stimulated activity anew. All that was required was to issue the prospectus, pass the solicitation of funds to interested canvassers, newspapers, publications, loan companies, banks, brokers, and hurrah at the end."

Some things do look easy to the man who is not doing them. Common sense admits that the man who patriotically juggled the billions from pocket to exchequer and back to pocket again would have had a much harder task to undertake what somebody called "the Gethsemane" of paying the nation's bills when the "hurrah" was over. The method of financing Canada in the war may be vastly different from the method necessary in peace. But when money must be had quickly in vast quantities there is no time to debate on just how you are going to get it. Sir Thomas White's raid upon the pockets of Canada was a financial spectacle not to be judged by standards of thrift, for the very good reason that the people were nauseated with thrift talk, were looking for something easy, and White had the instinct to know that the easier and the more spectacular he could make a Victory Loan the better for the war. He rowed with the current and knew he was doing it. In his own financial brain, which is not un-thrifty, he knew that the "hurrah" was not healthy in the long run and that it could not last forever. But once it was started there was no other way bu to keep it up.

Thanks to Sir Thomas, every citizen had an oppor-tunity to get himself rubber-stamped on behalf of the nation ; which on general principles was a good thing, because a large number of people at that time indulged the fiction that as the Government was paying its debts, a good way to do it would be to print more paper money. It was the Finance Minister's opportunity to instruct us, that the Government was not paying debts—but making it possible to pay wages. Unless the surplus of every man's earnings was invested in Victory Bonds there would shortly be no big industries left to pay the earnings at all, Canada would cease to export munitions—which might be the one thing to lose the war, in which case nothing would be left for any of us but to pay war indemnities to he enemy. Critics declared that non-taxable bonds were an iniquity in favour of the big investor who could heap up bonanza investments without taxes ; another way of

accusing the Finance Minister of being in league with the
"big interests." But we must do Sir Thomas the credit
of taking a sure way to encourage the small investor by
refusing to tax his patriotism. A 100th per cent tax on
some people's patriotism might have squelched it altogether. It would have been a public service if Sir Thomas
White had plainly told the people, not less about why they
should buy Victory Bonds during a period of inflation, but
more about what would happen to them when deflation
began to set in ; when, ceasing to buy Victory Bonds at a
low price, we should have to buy bread and butter and
clothes at higher prices than ever at a time when money
began to sneak away, we knew not whither.

Perhaps it was too much to expect one man to organize
the "hurrah" and afterwards to conduct the "Gethsemane." At any rate, before we had an opportunity to
test the real size of Sir Thomas as a public servant he
resigned office.

Whether the Finance Minister at the climax of his big
opus was shrewd enough to imagine that the kudos of the
loans might get him the Premiership, we do not profess to
know. He is not considered famous as a political strategist.
He has far too much serenity.

In 1917 Sir Thomas was chairman of a monster meeting
in Toronto when ten thousand people who tried to hear
Theodore Roosevelt speak on behalf of that year's Victory
Loan of Canada were turned away. For some hours he
had been in company with a man whose mastery of the
unusual was almost the equal of Mark Twain's. If ever
he had a chance to be startled out of his headmaster poise,
here it was. But he made a long, tedious preamble of a
speech the only sentence of which that sticks in my memory
is that sincerely girlish utterance of Portia to Antonio after
the trial, "Sir, you are very welcome to our house." It
was like pinning a pink bow knot on the head of a lion.

Sir Thomas showed strategic ability when he refused

H

the Premiership. After declining the Premiership he was not likely to need a portfolio.

Public life is considerably like war. Every time you move there must be a motive.

A former political crony of Sir Thomas said to the writer that the excess profits tax imposed by the Minister was one of the cleverest political manœuvres ever perpetrated in Ottawa, because it drove manufacturers and merchants to advertise in the newspapers in order to reduce their profits, thus paying part of the excess to the newspapers rather than to the Government ; which was supposed to have made the Government popular with newspapers on both sides of the political fence. This is a genially cynical way of saying that every publisher has his price, and that the Finance Minister had made some startling progress in his mentality since the day when he was charmed with everybody in Parliament. But it is a Machiavellian touch quite uncharacteristic of a man whose friends had designated him for the Premiership.

The friends of Sir Thomas may have had good reason for considering him as the next Premier. On the evidence of the mere handling of executive big business demanding cool judgment, practical vision and powerful action he was the equal of any other candidate for the office. His defects were less obvious, but perhaps more vital in the case. Sir Thomas was not designed to lead, which in these days means to be constantly recreating a party, not to operate a well-built governmental machine. In his nine years of public life he did a big national work and justly earned all the real distinction he ever got. He did so much in a big, unusual way for the nation that his passing out becomes another example of how easy it is to cripple administration by sacrificing public service brains to private business.

CALLED TO THE POLITICAL PULPIT

Hon. Newton Wesley Rowell

N. W. ROWELL has the bearing of a man who long ago felt that he was called to do something for a cause or a country and has never got over it. Meanwhile he has done much for both a cause and a country, and seems to have quit before the country had begun to enjoy more than the least agreeable elements in his character. To have suffered the insistent righteousness of Mr. Rowell so long, and at the close of the first period of his life when he seemed to be getting his own measure as a public man on a big stage, to see him withdraw like a chambered nautilus into his shell, not only from the Cabinet but from his seat in Durham, is a little hard on public patience. But of course the chambered nautilus may emerge again.

Years ago Mr. Rowell had moral energy enough to reconstruct a large part of the world in Liberalism and in the Methodist Church. Today he finds evangelic Liberalism rampant out on the skyline under such men as Crerar and Drury, and the church discussing social reformation in phraseology associated with dynamic ideas to which he never could be assimilated.

Mr. Rowell's career reminds us that there are four brands of Liberals in Canada : Evolutionary ; Manchester School ; Laurierite ; Agrarian. Tories never evolve. There are only good Tories and bad ones.

He belongs to the first group, and there is nothing in his temperament to make him anything else. Free Trade never did convince him ; he broke away from the enchanting tyranny of Laurier ; and, though born on a farm, he never could revert to the plough-handles for a vision of the world.

Judging from some fairly recent preachments by able reverends such as Wm. Woodsworth and Salem Bland, there may be as many brands of Methodism. If so we unhesitatingly place Mr. Rowell in the evolutionary group.

Therefore by personal development he is next thing to a Conservative ; and the latest phase of his career proves that in working it out he has practised the fine old platitude of Polonius to Laertes :

> "To thine own self be true,
> And it must follow, as the night the day,
> Thou canst not then be false to any man."

Mr. Rowell is one of our most encouraging types of what is called the self-made man. Any Oxford professor hearing him make a typically good speech in London on "The Commonwealth of Nations under the Union Jack," would infer that he had taken a post-graduate course in political history after graduating as a B.A. But Mr. Rowell never even attended a High School He went from the farm as a lad to be a parcel boy in a London, Ont., dry-good store. The class-meeting and the sermon and the Mechanics' Institute gave him a taste for serious literature. He came up in the oratorical county that produced G. W. Ross and J. A. Macdonald. He must have regularly read Talmage's sermons. He was a youth when the Y.M.C.A. movement invaded Canada along with baseball. He made the choice. He passed into the Law School, somehow dodging all the good brethren who advised him to go into the ministry. And through the opportunity afforded him by the successful practice of law and Liberalism on a large scale he has been able to preach his sermons to much bigger audiences than he ever could have found in the Methodist Church.

If some of the advanced radicals of these days would con over the outlines of a career like this, they might get rid of some of their fantastic notions about State-devised equality and emancipation. Mr. Rowell instinctively reached out by industry and enthusiasm for the forces that would better his condition. In so doing he spent a large part of himself upon the betterment of society. The result is an intellectual, moral and financially successful character of which any community might be proud—so long as the community contained but one of the kind.

Rowellism is a good salt. It is not good porridge. The average unprofessional Christian man cannot live on the levels where Mr. Rowell breathes so easily.

Time and again have we heard the equivocal remark about this man ; if such, and however so. Why not take the man as he is and make the best of him ? Surely by now he has proved that he has a definite and uplifting leverage on public life. It is of no use to complain that he never was cut out to be a leader in anything but ethical ideas of statesmanship. It was political makeshiftery to make such a man the leader of Ontario Liberalism, which did not ask to be led but to be cajoled and tricked up for the carnival. It was fatuous to imagine that he could ever become a chief of the National Liberal and Conservative party to which he now inextricably belongs. If secret ambition ever spurred him to indulge that dream—which seems incredible—sober reflection at the looking glass should have corrected the strabismus. Mr. Rowell is not a leader of men, in action ; never was and never could be— without some drastic transformation in his outward character such as he has never shown.

The last time I observed Mr. Rowell he was in the lounge of a club where he had just finished lunch. All about him were scores of men in groups, each group animatedly intent upon some topic from baseball to high finance. A few weeks earlier that same club had given a public dinner to Mr. Rowell and Sir George Foster, when each seemed to overdo the other in gripping those present

by the presentation of a world theme backed by a striking
personality. In the lounge Mr. Rowell, our best authority
on the ethics of the Empire and the League of Nations,
went about alone, unobtrusive, drab-coloured, almost
insignificant. He spoke to nobody and few men as much
as noticed him. He nodded gravely now and again, but
never smiled. Both hands in his trouser pockets, he seemed
to be gazing at some vagabond blind spot in the room.
He almost seemed to be whistling to himself like a lad in
a forest. Presently he wandered out.

By no exercise of imagination could one conceive such
a man as a Canadian political leader. If there is anything
in an aura he has it not. A halo would have suited him
better.

Three elements conspire to make Rowell :

Conscience ; oratory ; opportunity.

Most men have trouble enough with any two of the
three. Mr. Rowell continues to hold our respect in spite
of the whole trinity. Too much conscience always on
duty at a peak load is no way to attract a vast variety of
people who relish a degree of sinfulness now and again.
We do not repudiate the value of conscience in public
affairs. The public man without it provides almost the
only sane argument for the preservation of the gallows.
But when one man carries so much of it, a number of others
may be excused for carrying less. This is an age of special-
ties.

It is required of a truly efficient conscience, however,
that it be instant in season and out of season, and that it
do not wait upon opportunity. When the Ross Government was so old in sin that even the new *Globe* editor
accused the ship of having barnacles, we fail to remember
that Mr. Rowell lifted his voice against it. He was a candidate for the Commons five years before James Whitney
began his regime of government by indignation ; at a
time when if Ontario went on a political spree Ottawa got

a headache. Big-party government was pretty strong in those days to keep a man like Rowell from talking out in meeting. The value of a conscience to a community, whatever it may be to an individual or a party, is in giving it a chance to speak out when something is wrong with your own group, not when it is politically convenient to take off the muffler. Mr. Rowell's method of opening Durham as a safe seat for himself by making a Senator of the Conservative member for Durham, was one way of reforming the Civil Service, which was one of his Government hobbies. But in practical politics it is sometimes necessary to do evil that good may come. Mr. Rowell needed a safe seat—in order to do his work for the country. It seems a pity that a constituency so shrewdly obtained could not have been steadfastly held.

As an orator Mr. Rowell is remarkable in spite of two defects ; no classical or humanities education except what he diligently dug out of books, and a very thin voice. Few public speakers of our time use such admirable diction, and it is a rare one who can make so lean a voice thrill so completely with passion in the presentation of powerfully synthetic ideas. This is a great gift ; but like personal beauty it has its fatal fascination. Mr. Rowell has not ceased to suffer from a sort of bondage to his oratory as he has from the tyranny of his conscience. In conversation he seldom just talks. He seems to deliver dicta. He rarely glows with the fire of the moment ; he seems to be preparing for the grand occasion. The stage must be set. When did he ever make a poor speech that he had time to prepare ? Or a good one impromptu ? One cannot soon forget his remarkable speech in the Toronto Arena at the citizens' reception to Premier Borden in 1915. Here this lifelong Liberal made what up to that moment was the greatest speech of his career ; and he was speaking as a British citizen, not as a Canadian Liberal.

With equal power, to a small group, but with even more

passion as a broad-minded Canadian, he spoke to the
Bonne Entente in Toronto in 1917 on a subject which may
have had something to do with his future as a Dominion
instead of a Provincial statesman.   In this connection I
quote from a report of that meeting made by the writer :

"He took his preconsidered skeleton of argument
with all its careful alignment of crescendos and climaxes
and clothed it with the passion of a rousing, emotionaliz-
ing speech. The points somewhat roughly made by
other men he remade by a new grouping of the ideas.
With eminent juridical clarity he worked himself up
the ropes of oratory, and when he got to the tiptop of
the trapeze he flung out his big compliment to the
French-Canadians now at the front. Of course he
said other things. He made fine use of the historic as
he always manages to do But when he got away
from that into the great little story of Courcellette and
the gallant 22nd with its sole surviving eighty men and
two officers besides the C.O. "fighting the Germans
like devils," he had voltage enough for an audience
of ten thousand."

It is doubtful if Canada ever had a public speaker who
with so little personal makeup for the part could so wonder-
fully deliver himself in orational speeches on any topic of
nations, commonwealths and empires. If Rowell were
less of an orator he would be more of a power as a public
man.   Carrying around loaded blank pistols is not nearly
so congenial to most men as a cigar in the left hand vest
pocket. There is in most of us a strain of buncombe
which we exhibit often when others are not looking. I
think Rowell exhibits most of his in solemn form in public.
If one has not what is called *savoir faire* he must make his
abstractions and silences confoundedly interesting. Rowell
packs all his power into a speech. Therefore even his
greatest speeches are sometimes to some people a bore.

I think he must have risen to about his height of unceremonious informality at a Peace dinner in London when he sat next to the plenipotentiary from Serbia, to whom he remarked :

"I should think so many dinners and public functions would be hard on your constitution."

"Yes," rejoined the Serbian with a gravely astute look at his companion ; "but we have an upper and a lower chamber."

Rowell told this on himself. Even that he could not have done five years ago. Mingling with men more solemn than himself he observed the inconvenience of solemnity. He really wants to be a conductor of the little currents of energy that make men think and act in small groups. Some good parson years ago should have encouraged him to smoke between speeches.

Opportunity. This focuses the other two. Rowell has seldom neglected this mistress. It is comparatively easy for many men to make themselves at the Sign of the Dollar ; as a rule more difficult at the Sign of Culture. Mr. Rowell is a man of fine intellectual attainments, which he has seldom failed to use in furthering his public success. Yet he was a good while becoming incorporated into the body politic of Liberalism. The world was his parish. Wesley was his idol ; then Laurier. Between these two it is a marvel that even at the rather late age of forty-four he came to the leadership of Liberalism in Ontario. Here he became the prophet who would abolish the bar even before its time, not without provocation. There had been stories of wild drinking escapades among some of the Liberal leaders in Queen's Park. Mr. Rowell can therefore be amply forgiven for having been the instigator of that poster, "Is That You, Daddy ?"

This can be remembered from his five years of misfit rule in Queen's Park when many of his good offices there are mainly forgotten. It was rather pitiful to observe how incapable Mr. Rowell was of giving vent to his great talents in that Legislature. He did not understand the lingo. Most of it was too piffling and small. He knew Ontario better from the angle of corporation law. He made a poor showing as leader, for there were no great issues in which he could lead ; though he did initiate a great deal of useful welfare legislation. He made one heroic effort to understand New Ontario in the rough when he donned overalls and went down in some of the mines. But it was all too much in the rough. One imagines there must have been many a moment when he wished he had never taken that leadership with so precious little to lead, and yearned for some larger way. But it was a long, long trail. And Laurier was now a strange old man. Whichever way he looked he was in a blind alley.

The Coalition gave him a way out. The old chief's attitude towards the war made Laurier Liberalism still more unpalatable. Rowell was deeply stirred by the war. He could see in the upheaval of old and new world ideas the sort of grand realignment which he could understand ; the assertion of true Liberalism in true democracy. Any average speech of his during the war demonstrates that he was among those few leaders of thought whom the struggle lifted into a larger conception of manhood in the State.

Again, honesty to himself suggests that Mr. Rowell did not suffer such pangs at his severance from Laurier as did men like Carvell, Guthrie and Clark, who had fought under the old man in Commons. At the Liberal Win-the-War meeting in 1917, he threw off all disguises and fervently proclaimed that he had chosen to take office under "the greatest Premier in the world." The statement smacked not so much of insincerity as of a sense of emancipation. Mr. Rowell was no longer labelled a Laurier Liberal. He was a free agent in a new great conflict of force. He was stirred as never he had been. Of all the Liberals who took oath under the new administration he was the strongest, and the most difficult to assign a com-

petent task. He was made President of the Council and
Minister of Information. The peculiar advantage of the
latter was that as real information was the last thing that
seemed to be wanted by anything resembling a Government,
there was very little for Mr. Rowell to do at his desk and
very much time for him to be absent where he felt much
more at home, in Europe. As President of the Council
he had great ability.

This one year of Ministry before the end of the war
gave Mr. Rowell an opportunity to survey forces of whose
operation he had no knowledge while he remained a mere
Liberal. He became officially familiar to London and as
the constant companion of the Premier came very near
to the elbows of the great, when he did not suffer by comparison.

But it was the Peace Conference that gave him his real
work. During the war any nation got the prestige that
it could win, either by its own efforts or in league with
others. All nations on each side were more or less animated
by the one great purpose. Suddenly the golden grip of
union was off. The second war began around the Peace
table. In this new and more precarious conflict of pour-
parlers and old secret diplomacies under the dangerous
flare of the self-determination torch, national selfishness
rushed to the front of the stage. Every pocket of people
in Europe hemmed between a river, a mountain and a
dialect claimed the rights of a nation, when more than half
of them should have been conveniently merged into work-
able groups having some form of government with which
nations of experience could deal.

In this clamour of the *voces populi* the voice of Canada
was not to be disregarded. We had reason that it should
be heard. We were in sudden danger of being overshadowed at the Conference by the vast figure of the other
half of North America. Mr. Rowell has never been an
anti-Yankee. He has too much fine sense ever to pull

feathers out of the eagle in retaliation for twisting the
lion's tail. He knows as well as any man the strategic and
moral necessity of Canada being the real House of Interpreter to the two leading Anglo-nations. He knew it at
the Conference. But he knew also that in proportion to
service and sacrifice in the war, Canada in the Council of
Peace had a right to be heard and considered as the voice
of a nation occupying the northern half of North America.

There was great sense in the estimate of a leading
London correspondent that among the four most impres-
sive and masterful personalities at the Geneva Assembly
of the League, Rowell the Canadian was at least the fourth.
This was not merely a personal or natural compliment.
It was the sincere recognition of a fact.

Mr. Rowell had the gift and the energy of will to translate the Peace into Canadian language. He gave Canada
a voice in Europe. He did try so far as one man might to
play up to the voice given to Canada by the dead in Flanders. In the big occasion when great tumult of forces
were rushing to a climax Rowell rose to the opportunity—
as he always has done—and he earned the lasting gratitude
of his country. We needed just that intellectual power
and that moral audacity, not only in Europe but in Washington.

Yes, N. W. Rowell has made a big use of opportunity.
He has even created it. But it was seldom the little simple
thing at his door that roused his great qualities. It was
the bigger issue that lay out among the mountain tops.
He was overwhelmingly eloquent for the universal eight-
hour day when he attended the International Labour Conference in Washington. The League of Nations had recommended it. But what of the cheap-labour competition in
the Orient ? And what did Mr. Rowell know about
Industry and Democracy at all ?

Mr. Rowell made a bold bid for recognition as a statesman of international repute. And he got it. His speeches

on the Empire were consistently a greater voice than Borden ever could have had. The colleague of the Premier became his Imperial master because he had the power which Borden lacked, of making the British world-Commonwealth live in great public utterances.

What a journey had this man travelled now from "Is That You Daddy?" in Queen's Park!

And it may be sensibly asked—What was his great intention? Canada is interested to know what is "the big idea" in this man's mind. Corporation law cannot contain him now. He has tried his strength and knows it. He knows that other men know it.

Once during the derelict days of the Coalition it was rumoured that Rowell on a Western trip would sketch out a new leadership—for himself. But he was not a man to throw Borden overboard. He had a profound respect for the Premier, who had made great use of him.

Perhaps, if only Rowell had been born Conservative instead of a Win-the-War Liberal converted into a Coalitionist, the Premier might have called him to succeed. We know not. There was a predicament. White, Meighen, Rowell—all must be considered. There was the Washington post, if ever it should come to be. Did Mr. Rowell ever intimate that he wanted either of these? Nobody has said. But Sir Robert was wise at least not to have offered him the Premiership. Too long had that been the office of a man who could not lead. It was time for a leader. It is not surprising that Mr. Rowell should have stepped out of the Administration when Meighen went to the head of it. He could not comfortably serve under Meighen. Ambition is a tyrant. Self-sacrifice is usually easiest when great moral issues are uppermost. For more than one session he would not even retain his seat in the House. His retirement opens Durham, a safe constituency under Rowell, and may weaken the Government.

But what if it does? Mr. Rowell took office as a

Coalitionist to win the war. The war is won. But his work—is only nicely beginning. How is he going to finish his work for this nation ? He has not said. Not by making sundry speeches about the League of Nations.

If this country is to go ahead on its own native steam, it must be wise enough to find a big public place for the great talents of N. W. Rowell. And if Mr. Rowell, or any other disciple of opportunity in public affairs, wants to give Canada what she has a right to expect from him, he will do well to make his needed money now at corporation law, and when he comes back to public life have a constant eye single to the glory of his country.

To evolve men of that stamp is not easy. Rowell, like Meighen, is a product of the older studious days when youths buried themselves in books for the sake of getting on in the world without reference to mere money. He is now at an age when the best he has made of himself might be of incalculable good to the country if he could help the Government to go back to power and go with the National Liberal-Conservative Party as conscientiously as he entered the Unionist Government.

Conscience ;   Oratory ;   Opportunity. The greatest of these is Conscience; the least, Opportunity.

AN AUTOCRAT FOR DIVIDENDS

BARON SHAUGHNESSY

CANADA has a national habit of veneration for the C.P.R.
just as England used to have for Kitchener in Egypt. The
travels of H. M. Stanley in Africa were not more wonderful
than the everyday lives of Sandford Fleming's engineers
routeing that great new line through the Rockies ; and
the legend of Monte Cristo scarcely more fabulous than the
exploits of Van Horne in getting the money or the work
done without it. The man who bought supplies for Van
Horne (when there was money) and wrote letters or sent
telegrams when there was none, got a finer preparation for
being a great railwayman than most Premiers ever got for
the duties of public life.

The sensations of the cured scriptural blind man who
saw "men as trees walking" were repeated to Canadians
of thirty-five years ago who read about those legendary
Scots, Yankees and Canadians who flung that *chemin de fer*
over Canada to start a Confederacy into a nation. And
there was no *Boys' Own Annual* in Canada to tell the tale,
as it should have been done, along with the tales of the
Northwest Mounted Police and the adventures of the
Hudson's Bay Company. George Stephen, Donald A.
Smith, Robert Angus, Sandford Fleming, John A. Macdonald, Van Horne, the young Shaughnessy—all seemed
then to be not merely doers of the undoable, but men of
mighty imagination and a sort of Old Testament morality.
Even the Pacific Scandal seemed as necessary a part of
the narrative as the story of Joseph's coat and of Jacob
and Esau were of the epic of Israel.

127

Well, admittedly, most of that has faded from the Canadian Pacific. We read the annual address of the C.P.R. President with yawns. It all seems considerably like what is said and done at any directors' meeting of a rubber factory or a street railway. You read the names of the directors and few of them strike you with any sense of novelty or of awe. The room in which these magnates meet is—just a room ; it used to be thought of as a sort of Doges' Palace of finance. You may even note that one of the directors is baggy at the knees, and any two of them may be talking along the corridor about that very ordinary thing—the cost of living.

Of all the men at any C.P.R. directors' meeting, Lord Shaughnessy knows most about the steep side of finance. He was the spender when there was nothing to spend. The romantic adversities of those days never left him. He came down to the presidency with the fear of no-funds in his soul. From the beginning until then he had felt all the ragged edges of C.P.R. life. He had grimly chuckled to Van Horne, the occasionally helpless wizard, over the hard times. And hard times never really left the road until Van Horne handed the C.P. over to Shaughnessy just at the edge of the era when the system was getting ready to handle phenomenal traffic arising out of stupendous immigration.

From then on till the day that he also went out was the epoch when traffic and travel became vaster than the road, and greater than the men. It was his to operate, and to build as well. But the operations were all of a system which had creaked into through traffic from Yokohama to Montreal as far aback as 1889 ; and the new lines built under Shaughnessy were just branches of the old trunk. Shaughnessy took over bulging receipts after he had spent years at painful expenditures. He took over a despotism and made it an autocracy.

It was not in his practical, unromantic temperament

to play the Gargantuan role. He had not the mentality. Van Horne left the road when the road threatened to become bigger than its creator. Shaughnessy began to work on it when he knew that the bigger he made the system the greater would be his own executive authority, and the bigger the dividends to the holders of stock.

There was a radical contrast between these two men ; and as much between the road built by Van Horne and the system operated and magnified by Shaughnessy. The former would not have his shadow dwarfed by the dimensions of his own creation. The latter had created nothing : he would have the shadow of the thing fling itself so vastly over the nation—and the nations—that whenever men spoke of C.P. they thought of Shaughnessy, and when they said his name they mentally took off their hats to the headship of the greatest system of its kind in the world.

This may or may not have been Shaughnessy's intention. It was certainly the effect. We have all gone through the era of profound respect for the cold autocrat of the twentieth century, as some of us did that of awesome veneration of the railway giants of the nineteenth. We have read newspaper stories—some of them buncombe—about this man's all-seeing eye as he travelled over the system, as we did of the peripatetic omniscience of James J. Hill and the Gargantuan humours of Van Horne. We have consented that the system perfected by Shaughnessy was the most marvellous known of its kind, and therefore the man at its head must be a phenomenal administrator.

Very likely we have been warped by our enthusiasm. Shaughnessy was no miracle man. He was a wonderful *maestro* of details, a clear-headed organizer of systems and a man to provoke high respect in those who had to deal with him at close range. But he had perhaps less sheer ability for detail than Van Horne, who as a rule despised the botheration of it. I have heard Van Horne dictating to his secretary a mass of intimate instructions to a con-

tractor about how to build a rotunda in a hotel in Cuba, at
the same time with his left hand on a drawer full of complicated notes on his philosophy of life, which with the
other lobe of his brain he was traversing in order to engulf
the interviewer as soon as the letter was finished.   Shaughnessy never could have carried on such an interiew, lasting
four hours of a busy life.   His talks to the press must be
curt and comprehensive—or else elliptical.   He had no
exuding vivacity.   When I talked to him—or listened to
him—he was cold and exact.   He left his chair only to
walk erectly to the window.   He deviated not a syllable
from the subject in hand—the system.   He worshipped
that : as much as any Mikado ever did his ancestry.   He
paid passing veneration to Van Horne—when from the
slant of his remark I surmised that he was critical even
in his admiration for that epical character.

Shaughnessy is essentially a system-man.   When he
travelled he had his practical jokes and his Irish stories
and his fondness for the social side ; but he was conventionally as correct as a time-table.   Had there been a
spark of genius in him he would have extinguished it for
the sake of betterments to the most conventional Colossus
in Canada.   The C.P.R. was supposed to lead.   It was
built for dividends, and born in politics.   It had craft at
its cradle.   The new policy under Shaughnessy was bigger.
It had to do less with Asia, with spectacle, with carved
gods ; more with Europe, with immigration posters, with
land settlement.   Shaughnessy had taken over a system
which could be used ostensibly as the agent of the Immigration Department and of the Interior ; effectively as the
base of population-supply on its own account.

As Shaughnessy worked it out the C.P. had a scheme
of national expansion that acted independent of government ; its own ships, trains, roads, docks, land offices,
immigration agents, poster-advertising—until the average
European looking for a way out of economic slavery be-

lieved that the C.P.R. was the owner and operator of Canada. A belief which was not contradicted, except officially, at home.

William Mackenzie set the pace for building ; Shaughnessy for operation. But Shaughnessy built fast. He did it under a handicap of two systems against one. The difference was that an average new line under Shaughnessy paid dividends, or at least did not appreciably lower dividends already declared.

Under Lord Shaughnessy it was unofficially believed that the head of the C.P.R. was somehow overlord to governments. Shaughnessy the impenetrable was not the agent of a democracy, but an emperor. He had his counterpart in Japan. The Orientalism which Van Horne infused into the system even while he laughed it out of court, was solemnly accepted by the man who came after. But it was the Orientalism of efficiency. Shaughnessy was its symbol. Away from it he was of little consequence except as a benevolent citizen with statesmanlike views upon how governments should govern. Within it he was mighty. He felt himself the apex of a thing that knew no provincial boundaries. He consciously made it the instrument of Empire. He was inordinately proud of its morale. To him it was a complicated army. He felt it assimilating men who lived, moved and had their being in C.P.R.—as he had. He was the great human rubber stamp. He had extra power. He lived on fiats and papal bulls. Men learned to tremble at his nod—not at Shaughnessy, but at the man who personalized the infallible system. And as governments came up and capsized in the storms of public sentiment, the great system went on in its sullen but splendid way, a sort of solar system in which parties and governments gravitated.

It would have needed a greater soul than Shaughnessy to be cynical about C.P.R. It often needed his latent Irish humour to appreciate the larger cynicism which it expressed concerning the country. The pap-fed infants of Mackenzie and Hays served but to illustrate by contrast the perfection and the well-oiled technique of the dynamo operated by Shaughnessy. It became an obsession with him, as it did with Flavelle over a commercial company, that "the king can do no wrong." His annual report bristled with pride over the Company's achievements. He insisted upon the inherent morality of the thing and of the men who were its officials. And the older he grew the more Shaughnessy became absorbed in it. In his career the office of President reached its climax. It was shorn of much of its aspect of awe as soon as he left it.

His knighthood was a slight decoration on so august a personage ; as though the king had decorated the Mikado. The baronage more nearly fitted the case. Shaughnessy was not too passionately a Home Ruler to take it. But he was never so good a president of the C.P.R. after he got it. He became particular over forms and etiquette. One almost looked for a change of guard at the gate when entering the President's office.

No pomp, however, could undo such efficiency , and in the main such national sanity. Shaughnessy always liked to have a voice in national affairs. That was partly tradition. It also kept the public from remembering that the railway after all was a creature of government and of politics. It sometimes deflected public attention from the "melon" patch which was the *Toronto World's* sobriquet for the C.P.R. "pork barrel," and from the ever potential lobby maintained by the company at Ottawa. Of course lobbies are always repudiated. No self-respecting railway ever knows it by that name. There is no department of lobbyage in the head offices. The art is never taught. But it is childish to dodge the public necessity of a great corporation being represented at the centre of national legislation. In fact, C.P. has loomed so large in public affairs that a member of Parliament for the Company would sometimes have been scarcely ridiculous. Whenever Lord Shaughnessy went to Ottawa, it was public news. He never went for his health, seldom without some issue too big for a subordinate to handle. Had the Minister of Railways gone to Montreal to see Mr. President, it would have seemed quite as natural.

The war gave Lord Shaughnessy for a time almost equal prominence with Sir Sam Hughes. His quite sensible speech criticizing the haphazard and costly methods of recruiting made Hughes retort that to raise the First Contingent was as great a task as building the C.P.R. Lord Shaughnessy earned that absurd retort because of his announcement to the Government that he meant to make the speech ; as though the nation would be waiting to hear it. There was room for one super-governmentarian at Ottawa ; never for two. It was Hughes vs. Shaughnessy.

Lord Shaughnessy's retirement from the presidency was not sudden. He had reached his zenith. His eyesight was bad. But he had not lost his grip. The war threw such an unusual load on the system and so changed its complexion that it became necessary to have a younger man. There is reason to believe that the war rudely upset much of the Imperial dignity of the great system. The C.P. was no longer a law unto itself. It was part of the national pool. The President was no longer a sublime autocrat ; he was a public agent. The life blood of a globe-girdling system was drained by the war, even while it retained its supremacy as the greatest railway and more than held up its end compared with the railway muddle in the United States. Never again could the C.P. recover its splendid isolation of greatness. Public ownership was being thrust upon the nation by the bankruptcy of the other roads. Shaughnessy had no real fear that it would ever absorb the C.P.R. But he had reason to suspect that a huge Government system would be more or less of a menace to the system which he had spent his life to build up.

There was no better way than to retire, leaving the chief administration to a man of his own choice and retaining the post of Chairman along with the room occupied by the old President.   Even here the old autocrat survives. The proposal made by Baron Shaughnessy to pool all the railways, except the Grand Trunk, and to put them all under C.P. administration with a guarantee of dividends to C.P. shareholders—was a magnificent play to the gallery. The other roads were undeniably bankrupt, when even the splendid showing made by the management could not make their records palatable to the public.   It was a strategic time to advertise once, finally and for all, the unequalled efficiency of the old Transcontinental.

But Canadian railwaydom is dominated by C.P.R. as naturally as tides by the moon.   The Railway Association, once the Railway War Board, are now a junta of dividendists and of paid chiefs of the Government system, to oppose—whenever necessary—the adverse judgments of the Government's Railway Commission. The road which was the tangible nexus of Confederation was built by two Americans, one of whom became a high-tariff Tory and a knight, the other an Imperialistic baron who believed in Dominion Home Rule for Ireland when the average Canadian considered Home Rule as treasonable as annexation.   It is the prerogative of any robust Canadian to oppose either infection from Broadway or domination from Downing Street. But, regarding the strategic position of Canada in the misnamed "British Empire," we might all take a cue from Lord Shaughnessy, who has had all the internationalizing emotions of which any man is normally capable, and can challenge any man to shew where he has ever compromised conscience or country.

THE PUBLIC SERVICE HOBBYIST

SIR HERBERT AMES

WHATEVER may be done by the Washington Conference to the League of Nations, there still live two men to whom it is and shall be the hub of the world. Lord Robert Cecil and Sir Herbert Ames at least will never admit that the League was a mere Wilson-Democrat device for making the world safe for humanity, and that the alternative is a Harding-Republican expedient for making Washington the new hub of the world.

Sir Herbert is much too cordial a cosmopolitan to begrudge Washington any eminence she can get from imitating the League. He is too charitable even to admit that if Dr. Wilson had stood for peace first and covenant second, no Washington Conference would have been needed. He is also Canadian enough to realize that transferring the centre of the Peace progaganda to the leading Capital of the New World is a good way to remind the Old World that Ottawa has more to do with Washington than even London has. Out of the Washington Conference may arise the Canadian envoy. Whatever happens in the Pacific zone of the world-open diplomacy can never hurt Ottawa—nor disturb the complacent optimism of Sir Herbert Ames, Financial Director of the Secretariat to the League of Nations. The time may come when even Ottawa is considered a better place than London or Geneva for the conduct of world-peace agenda.

When Sir Herbert Ames was chosen Financial Director of the League Secretariat he was chosen less to please Canada than to vindicate his own ability. When he

spoke in Canada on how the League works he showed his
remarkable optimism by extolling its operations at a time
when Europe was more anarchic than at any time since
the war.

Every forward nation should have its Ames. This one
justified his existence in Canada long before he became a
knight or even an M.P. for St. Antoine, Montreal. At one
time in his citizenship he was the incarnation of what a
large number of people would be anxious to avoid ; in the
days when he used to pack his grip from Montreal and go
forth on lectural pilgrimages over Ontario and other parts.
On a platform he always seemed like a long, lean school-
master. Sometimes he used a blackboard. One of his
pet subjects was prohibition. He looked entirely like it.
One could scarcely recollect having heard quite so dry a
man on any subject. He looked like the genius of self-
denial—like a man who long ago should have gone into a
monastery, doing penance for the uplift of the world as
mirrored in his own conscience, instead of remaining at
large a common Presbyterian and a very uncommon sort
of Tory.

I was agreeably startled to find Sir Herbert in 1920 one
of the most cordial and amiable men on the roster of Who's
Who. He was no longer dry, bigoted, or pedagogical. In
fact he was almost benignly human, even humourous.
And I concluded that if intimacy with the League of
Nations could work such a change in the average man connected with it, there is surely some function for the League
as a cheerful solvent for the world.

Sir Herbert Ames' previous work as Hon. Chairman of
the National Patriotic Fund of course did a good deal to
reclaim him. Of all war work this was among the most
destructive of personal bigotry and political prejudice. If
Sir Herbert imbibed the real philosophy of the Patriotic
Fund he must be, speaking humanly, one of the wisest men
in Canada. It was a scientific fact that at a time when

men in the army were displaying incredible heroism, certain
people at home were exhibiting unbelievable meanness.
The people who used to attempt graft on the Patriotic
Fund were the kindergarten of the college of national
profiteers who came later. They were happily out-num-
bered by the people who were thankful for all they got and
who in the greatest losses that life can inflict showed almost
sublime fortitude and patience.

Preparation for some form of public service by doing it
as he went along has always been Ames' strongest characteristic. He had eyes for the homely, sometimes mean,
job under his nose. There was an evangelism about him.
Why ? Because he was a citizen. Where did he live ?
In Montreal. No man can be a reforming citizen in Montreal unless he has plenty of time, and some money. Mr.
Ames has always had both. He also has endless patience.

Perhaps the most remarkable proof that he intended to
be a practical philanthropist is the fact that for eight years
he was one of the feeble Anglo-Saxon minority in the Montreal City Council. An artist in search of contrast could
never have found a finer example than a comparative study
of the leader of the English section Ames, and the French
boss, the late L. A. Lapointe. In the bilingual Legislature
of an incorrigible city Mr. Ames spoke two languages. If
he had mastered twenty he never could have equalled
Lapointe, who in my recollection of a long conversation
some years ago could genially and grandly boast that the
fad for reforming the City of Montreal would never make
much headway so long as he remained boss of the French
section in Council. Lapointe was Montreal's Tammany.
He held Montreal under his patronage and executive thumb
before Mederic Martin had begun to achieve any fame
beyond that of a maker of cigars. He knew every cranny
of Montreal as intimately as the late John Ross Robertson
used to know Toronto. Mr. Ames' knowledge of the big
town was fairly complete. But if Mr. Ames and Mr.

Lighthall, the genie of civic information in Montreal, could have been one two-headed man, they never could have matched Lapointe in the expert business of knowing where to plant a man to give him a civic job or how to create a job to suit a man in need of it.

Yet for eight consecutive years Mr. Ames with no other desire than to do his duty, to study Montreal, and perhaps qualify for larger service later, remained a member of the City Council. And he did his work there before the English-speaking element undertook to clean up the city— the most genial, sarcastic failure of modern times. He wrote little books about Montreal. He mastered French by studying it first-hand in France. Those who used to listen to his evangelical speeches in his own tongue some-times wished he had learned a few nuances and inflexions in English. He was for some time Chairman of the Muni-cipal Board of Health, in a city where infant mortality is such a constant epidemic that babies' coffins are displayed in shop windows. In 1907 he wrote a tractate on the housing of the working classes, just on the eve of the period when Montreal began to be the worst city in America for high rents, extortionate charges for moving and intolerable congestion. The publication of his views on the subject, however, showed that he had the courage to point out what was wrong, even though he had no concrete con-structive proposal which any municipal government in Montreal or any Legislature in Quebec would ever accept as a working basis for putting the thing right. As far back as 1901 he indited a treatise on The City Problem, What Is It ? Twenty years later, after all Mr. Ames' burnings on the subject, Montreal has slumped back into sheer mediaevalism in civic government under the wheedling despotism of Mederic Martin, who presided at the public funeral of the only effort the city ever made to establish a real business administration. In that Quixotic eruption of public virtue in 1912, Mr. Ames, after all his publicity on the subject of redeeming Montreal, was not even considered as a candidate for the Board of Control.

On the whole scarcely a public man, or even a reforming editor, in Canada has talked so consistently and so cheerfully for so long a period and to so little apparent purpose, on the need for cleaning up civic government. The difference between Mr. Ames and the average public-service expert in Montreal on this question is that Mr. Ames has never been worldly-wise enough to become an avowed cynic on the question. He probably knows as well as anybody that to clean up Montreal is in the same category as making Europe safe for the League of Nations ; a much harder city to regenerate than even Philadelphia. Muckraking has no effect, when two-thirds of the population read French papers which never use the rake, and when the boss of three-fourths of the rest is himself often a target for the yellows. Mr. Ames should long ago in this connection have propounded a thesis, Hugh Graham, What Is It ? He would then be free to dissect the ethics of Mederic Martin and the late L. A. Lapointe.

Martin rules Montreal in spite of Lord Atholstan, the Archbishop and the International Union, because in his own person he interprets the distinction between Anglo and Franco. In Montreal a dominant minority controls three-fourths of the commercial wealth. A couple of dozen men control big industries, railways, electric and water powers, finance and newspapers. When these men want the City Hall they consult the directory. To them Montreal is a convenient sea-wharfing spot to conduct big business ; otherwise a French Canadian city and so, hopeless. The chief common bond between this group and the city at large is the labour market. The elections are a mere superficial disturbance. The old courteous alternative of a French mayor, an English mayor, and an Irish mayor has been discarded. The mayors are all French now. The population is overwhelmingly French. The

City Hall is as French as the courts. The civic jobs are given to Frenchmen. As a rule there are plenty of jobs. It is a fair compromise—that if the Anglos will monopolize most of the big productive business, the civic administration must go to the Francos who are the elective majority.

Sir Herbert Ames ,who was born in Montreal and is the only man who has ever undertaken to theorize openly as to its redemption, knows exactly why the place is so absorbing to the cynical mind. He understands that a man cannot have the same geometrical and diligent enthusiasm for Montreal as he has for Toronto. To be a thoughtful citizen of Montreal stimulates the imagination and disgusts the economic sense. For the past ten years Sir Herbert has been too much absorbed in Ottawa and the League of Nations to care much about the city where he spent so much of his earlier zeal for reclamation. The member for St. Antoine has a larger orbit—to negotiate which he has resigned his seat in the House.

One is tempted to consider whether there are not enough secretarial minds in Europe from which to take a man as Financial Secretary for the League of Nations, and let Sir Herbert come back to Canada to finish his work. He has had world experiences enough to come back and be of some real use to the country. He is not yet sixty. He has ahead of him twenty years in which he could do a great deal more for the Empire about which he is so earnest by working in Canada than by occupying a conspicuous post somewhere in Europe. It is not the fashion for ex-Canadians who have had political or other experiences abroad to come back here for anything but speeches and banquets. Sir Herbert may be permitted to change the fashion. With his versatility in French, his knowledge of Europe, his acquaintance with large public questions of finance and his general *savoir faire*, he seems to be just the kind of man who could head a movement to nationalize Montreal.

But of course he never will do it.

THE SHADOW AND THE MAN

HON. SIR SAM HUGHES, K.C.B.

THE career of the late Sam Hughes is a tragic reminder that no man in public life can afford to regard himself as bigger than his suitable job. When a nation has to retire a genius for the sake of enthroning what remains of common democracy the nation's loss is nobody's gain. In the jungle book of our aristocracy Sam Hughes should have been Lord Valcartier. Not that a democratic country cares at all to be given any more lords, even if Parliament had not asked the King to abolish the custom. But while peerages and baronetcies were being handed about for honour, Hughes was the kind of man that should have got his— except that he made it impossible.

However, it is more interesting to record the short-comings of Hughes than to report the success of medio-crities. Canada had in Hughes a name with which for a year or so to poster almost any part of the Empire, especi-ally England. We are in danger of forgetting at this distance—five years now since he resigned office—just what were the conditions that made him such a tre-mendous figure.

Sam Hughes, M.P., born in County Durham, Orange-man from the town of Lindsay, editor, soldier, adventurer, school teacher who once taught English and who never could make a speech, though he talked in public—what was there about him up till 1914 to make any nation wonder? The first time I saw Hughes, in 1910, a man whose office he had just left said, as though imparting a State secret :

"There goes the next Minister of Militia."

Up till that moment if anybody had asked me, "Do you know Hughes?" I should have said, "Oh, yes, everybody knows Jim Hughes, the School Inspector."

The story of Canada's Army is immortal. It is yet to be truly told. When it is told by the right man—whether historian or poet—the name Hughes, as we know it at its best and biggest, will shine out like a great fixed star that tried to play being a comet. On April 22nd, from the sick bed that even he probably knew he never would leave of his own will, in memory of St. Julien, he sent the army boys a brief message, that he still believed in them as he always had.

Simple little message, it meant much. It would have meant a million times more if the "boys" could have flashed back a helio to the wan old General who used to be such a noise in the world—"Same to you, General." The boys somehow liked him. The defects of Sam Hughes were of the sort that soldiers love. He was a man's man.

"Tipperary" was just becoming popular to whistle when a camera man authorized by the Government of Canada took one of the most striking pictures in our part of the war outside the zone of the shell areas. Gen. Sam Hughes, jack boots and oilskin cape flung back by the gale to show his belt and the flap of his khaki, wide-legged on a rope ladder, coming down forward from a troopship in the Gulf, almost baring his teeth to the October wind ; bidding farewell to the First Contingent 33,000 strong, that steamed out of the Gulf into the convoy.

You recognize in such a picture a man who perhaps understood the sensations of Alexander. Sam Hughes had finished his first job for the war. Among all the war achievements that thrilled nations when big men suddenly took hold of them in after years, this one holds its own. Hughes never could match it again. Here was the greatest army that had ever put out to sea at one time ; an army

forty per cent bigger in three months than the total force
that Gen. Ian Hamilton estimated Canada could send as
her whole contribution to a great war. This was Hughes'
answer to Hamilton. Not only were the men Canadian
—if not many of them Canadians—but their uniforms,
boots, kits, rifles, horses, tents, artillery, machine gun
batteries, army waggons, cook waggons, engineering out-
fits and munitions, were as far as possible produced in
Canada. Troop trains and transport steamers were
Canadian. The money that paid for the army was Canadian. The pay of officers and men was Canadian. And
we know what Hughes was.

But the moment Hughes let go the rope ladder that
should have made him Lord Valcartier, he began to undo
his own career.

In a misguided speech afterwards Sam reminded Lord
Shaughnessy that to raise, equip and dispatch the First
Contingent from Canada was a heavier contract than
building the C.P.R. The comparison was foolish, but very
human. Shaughnessy had provoked it by announcing to
the Government that he intended to make a speech in con-
demnation of Hughes' methods of recruiting.

The author of Canada in Flanders describes exactly
what the work of organizing that Contingent was. A few
extracts will do :

"In less than a month the Government, which had
asked for 20,000 men, found almost 40,000 at its disposal. . .
General Hughes devised and ordered the establishment of
the largest camp that had ever been seen on Canadian soil.
The site at Valcartier was well chosen. . . ."

"The transformation effected within a fortnight by an
army of engineers and workers was a remarkable triumph
of applied science. Roads were made, drains laid down,
a water supply with miles of pipes installed, electric lighting
furnished from Quebec and incinerators built for the
destruction of dry refuse. A sanitary system second to
none that any camp has seen was instituted. Every company had its own bathing place and shower baths: every

cook-house its own supply of water.   Troughs of water for
horses filled automatically so that there was neither shortage
nor waste.   The standing crops were garnered ;   trees cut
down and the roots torn up.   A line of targets 3½ miles
long—the largest rifle range in the world—was constructed.
. . . . Camp and army leaped to life in the same hour.
Within four days of the opening of the camp nearly 6,000
men had arrived in it.   The cloth mills of Montreal began
to hum with the manufacture of khaki, which the needles
of a great army of tailors converted into uniforms, great-
coats and cloaks.   The Ordnance Department equipped
the host with the Ross Rifle.   Regiments were shuffled
and reshuffled into battalions ;   battalions into brigades.
The whole force was inoculated against typhoid.   There
were stores to accumulate ;   a fleet of transports to
assemble ;   a thousand small cogs in the machine to be
nicely adjusted.

Sir Max Aitken did not mention the message to "My
Soldiers " in every man's knapsack, an imitation of
Kitchener's knapsack message to the "Old Contemptibles";
or that he himself had applied to Sam Hughes for a "job"
in Canada's army.

Hughes was Minister of War, not a Minister of Defence.
In the tramp of battalions down the street he felt Canada
to be a young nation, not an overseas Dominion only.
Yet the First Contingent was the work of one of the most
scientifically unprepared-for-war peoples in the world.
Valcartier was the glorification of Hughes, who was always
personally prepared for war ;   what or where he was not
always sure, except that it would involve the Empire, that
when it came, the sand-bags of Canada's front line would
not be in Canada, and the Canada Militia Act would be as
useful in the case as a page from Pickwick Papers.

Allow for the British-born majority in the First Contingent, the patriotic enthusiasm of Militia officers, the
commandeering of national resources and the great work
of subordinates ;   the fact remains that had he not been
as much his own enemy as he was a soldier born and bred,
Sam Hughes should have been Lord Valcartier.

The sad fact about Hughes is that he did not estimate what Canada did and did not in her first impact upon the war. He could not see Canada except as the shadow of Sam Hughes. In the light of the war as he stood in front of it, that shadow of Hughes seemed to him to cover the country. For two years, it seemed to grow. Then it flickered. In 1916 it went out. And there never was in Canada a going out like it.

Hughes was the embodiment of force without power. He began to mobilize a nation, not merely as battalions on parade, but as an army equipped by Canadian science, industry, transportation, intelligence, and citizenship. So far as he carried that out, the editor of the *Lindsay Warder* and M.P. for Haliburton and Victoria had no superior in organizing force in this country. Up till 1916 he was a patriotic cannon-cracker exploding without any particular objective, except that he wanted a Canadian Army in Canada, not an overseas Contingent, or an Imperial Army. Between 1914 and 1916 he was a great organizing soldier, at his best comparable to any men who were doing wonders at the front. As Nationalist as Quebec, he thought of Canada as a unit in the Empire, most of which he had seen for military reasons. Canada could not declare war ; but in the mind of Hughes the force that held Canada and other overseas dominions within the Empire was not in trade and tariffs, but in ships, armies and victories.

Sam Hughes failed to translate his force into power because he failed to estimate the elements which carried him to success, and therefore could not measure the energies that would defeat him. He never understood what Bismarck called the "imponderables". Nature gave him the energy ; Fate the ambition : Destiny denied him the vision.

The electric energy of this nation in response to the call of war made a flash that blinded Hughes. He seemed to think that he was the man who was running the cataract.

He had a wholesome contempt for Kaiserism in Germany. He tried to express it by an imitation of Kaiserism in Canada. He had a sense of relative omnipotence. He put editors in jail, went over the heads of District commanders, inexcusably humiliated General Lessard in command of the most important military district in Canada, openly browbeat officers in front of their men, played Napoleon on a white charger at the crest of a mound in Valcartier, and trod on the official corns of his colleagues.

Such things are now somewhat blurred by perspective. At the time they were glaringly in the spotlight as the pranks of a Jack the Giant Killer. In December, 1914, Premier Borden made a tactical visit to the headquarters of Military District No. 2, nominally commanded by General Lessard.

A military writer had this to say about the Premier's speech :

".... He thought the accomplishment of this task (Valcartier) was a tribute to the spirit of the people. He claimed no special credit for his Government ; inferentially it was a high compliment to the organizing ability of the Minister of Militia, but Sir Robert deftly left that to the imagination of his audience. . . . . A curious feature was his avoidance of any mention of the 'Minister of Militia.' When he desired to speak of the military programme, he stated that he had decided, after consultation with the 'Chief of Staff'. This was done repeatedly and apparently with definite purpose. Once he mentioned the name of Major Lessard, and a shout went up from the audience."

Further quotation is not needed. In less than two months after the glorification of Valcartier, the Premier found himself challenged by the man who had already begun to act as though national headquarters were in the Militia Department. Sam Hughes was never unpopular in Toronto. The incident referred to might almost have taken place in Montreal.

Canada was beginning to understand, to heroize and to censure Sam Hughes. His measure was being taken here.

But the censure was unheeded. Hughes worked while critics talked. He was mobilizing, if not organizing, a nation. He still believed that he (*ipse*) could do it. The mobilization included everything needed by the army as well as the army itself. He wanted to get the nation behind the army : and himself behind the nation. He started everything—even to shells, high explosives and aeroplanes. Hughes knew what the army needed. He refused to admit that other men also knew how to get some of these things better than he did.

Cabinet colleagues were adjuncts. The motto punctuated by the smashing fist was, "I want to tell you !" No major on parade ever felt so overwhelming. Hughes was more than a martinet. He was a dilemma. The phenomenal was always about him. War was not even hell to Sam Hughes. It was more often a chance to show a civilian minister that he was a mere conventional ornament. Hughes may have hated the necessity, but he loved the spirit and the fire, of war.

Sam Hughes was probably wiser on what modern war demanded than many of the British command. Even Kitchener argued for shrapnel when Lloyd George wanted high explosives. There was no civilian in Canada to argue against Hughes, who aimed to do in Canada what the Minister of Munitions, Director-General, Headquarters Staff, and the Minister of Transports did in England. He was able from the first to get a realizing measure of the kind of mechanical hell known as modern war.

Start a force like that and you may expect abnormalities in the wake of it. We had "Sham Shoes". Hughes had nothing to do with those. He stated in Winnipeg that Wellington had once said that a contractor who made bad boots for an army should be shot. We had shell contracts—and the "friend" Joseph Wesley Allison ; the Kyte charges, which brought the Minister home from England to answer them in the House. Neither the answer nor the friend was characteristic of the kind of man we had supposed Sam Hughes to be. We had the Ross Rifle. Hughes knew that in actual warfare the Ross was the finest sniper's rifle in the world, but that in quick action it jammed so badly that often the Canadians furtively swapped them for Lee-Enfields whenever the chance came. There was no excuse for the Ross rifle, and Hughes ought to have admitted it. There never should have been a chance for any detractor of his to insinuate that the Minister had stock in the Ross Rifle Company. We had cellulose nitrate and Grant Morden, who has never had an equal over here for making sudden wealth out of next to nothing and getting popular credit for doing it. What the ex-Minister of Militia made out of that promotion was never stated. It never should have been necessary for him to have made a copper in any such way. On his retirement from the Cabinet Hughes should have had a big honourable endowment from the nation sufficient as an income for the rest of his life. The whole idea of such a character being even good-humouredly mixed up with any deal not absolutely foursquare is a paradox. The Sam Hughes that we knew best was as straight as a chalk line.

The exploits of Canada's army never surprised Hughes. He had always said they could do it. He boasted about the generals he had taken from desks and offices. But the generals were fighting. There was a cubist picture in the War Memorials at Ottawa thus described by a Canadian editor who went over the battlefields which it depicted :

"The canvas shrieking with its high hues was filled with Turcos in panic flight crowding one another in their terror, while over them billowed the yellow poison pall of death ; but in the midst of the maelstrom the roaring Canadian guns stood immovable and unyielding, served by gunners who rose superior alike to the physical terrors of battle and the moral contagion of fear."

That picture of St. Julien must have thrilled Hughes,

whose son was soon to be Brigadier-General. It was on the crest of the St. Julien wave that Hughes got his title and was given the freedom of London ; when some delirious writer in a London daily predicted that some day Sir Sam would ride through London at the head of his victorious troops. One writer called him the Commander-in-Chief of Canada's Army. None of these things moved Sam Hughes to humility. As well as any man he knew how small the greatest man was in the fury of that war.

Other Cabinet Ministers had to wait till the Peace Conference before getting such press notices. Even the Premier took nearly two years to convince London that he was much more than the civilian colleague of Gen. Hughes. Sir Sam was idolized from the beginning ; at times when generals at the front were baffled, discouraged and beaten, and when patient old Kitchener was enduring red tape and making perfunctory reports to the Lords, knowing that the war was bigger than his knowledge of it.

Hughes may not have been wise enough to estimate the real value of this idolatry ; but he was probably shrewd enough to know that it would soon be over. He knew that much as had been done to make Canada a war nation, the first two years had done less than half the work. 87,000 troops went overseas in 1915. That was natural. The majority of the men were in camp. In 1916 the number was almost doubled, from the enlistments of 1915. In 1917 the number sent overseas dropped to 63,536, proving that the enlistments of 1916 had been about half those of 1915.

Hughes knew this better than anybody. He knew that the voluntary system, in which he believed, was going to break down. We had no national register. A country as big as twenty Englands, with a population about one-fourth as big, had also Quebec—and the farmer. The Canadian census was five years old and useless for anything like a national register of resources of war. Camp Borden in 1916 helped to stimulate recruiting and to give Hughes something resembling in a feeble way the sensations of 1914. But Camp Borden was not Valcartier. General Lessard, whom he had ignored in 1914, was sent down to Quebec to encourage enlistments. He went too late. Wrong men had gone earlier. Hughes had never tried to placate Quebec. But in 1916 he himself went down to see Cardinal Begin. For an Orangeman like Hughes that was a desperate measure. He got what he expected—cynicism. Begin afterwards issued a letter to the press in which he tried to set the clergy above the law of conscription. No doubt the Cardinal came at Hughes with the twaddle invented by the Nationalists and later adopted by Laurier, about enforcing the Militia Act which provided for nothing but defence.

Canada had now four divisions in the field. The problem was how to keep them up, and how to send a fifth. The fifth never went. But it stands to the immortal credit of Sam Hughes that the four did, and that he had sent them.

The affair about the Chairman of Munitions was to Hughes a sore blow. He had started munitions as an arm of war. He did not want a civilian to take it over as a mere industry. Even that was a sign that the volunteer system was about done. Ottawa was full of experts now, each man taking over as a big business something started by Hughes. The one-man epoch was over. But Hughes refused to admit it. The man who had started everything was in no humour to admit anything. Yet in the darkest days Hughes never lost faith in the men who had gone. No man continued to say more heartening things about ultimate victory. And he played blind optimist against the cold, comfortless fact that the Canadian Army was wasting and the reserves were not marching up to mend it.

Hughes knew that conscription had to come. But he was the very last man in authority to admit it. Only a few days before Ottawa announced that compulsory service must be applied, and when Sir Sam knew it was coming, he said publicly to soldiers in Toronto that Canada, the free-man's country, would never need conscription. It was most pitiful to hear him. Sir Sam never seemed to pity himself. His egoism was game enough for anything. Bigger men than he had gone down. A big man here or there was nothing now. But what of little men that stayed up ? Hughes probably asked that in silent con-tempt as he saw the coming of Coalition. But he knew he would not be there when it came.

By this time the egotism that was so splendid in 1914 had begun to breed in Gen. Hughes rancours and envies and enmities. Some of the men he had sent overseas were now more potent figures than himself.

There was still a person at the head of the Militia Department known as Lieut.-General Sam Hughes, K.C.B. But there was no longer in Canada any such man as old Sam Hughes. The Fate chickens hatched in 1914 were coming home to roost. For two years the Government had carried on two wars, one with the Kaiser Wilhelm, the other with Kaiser Sam. It had to be determined that whatever defects government may have because it is a democracy—even such democracy as was left in 1916—it is bigger than any one man. It had to be conceded that the nation was bigger than any one political party, and war bigger than all the world's volunteer armies.

Sam Hughes belonged to the eternal Volunteers. The days of his glory were the days when Canada of her own accord went to war or stayed at home. The Force called Hughes dreamed that it was bigger than a machine called War. But the machine won. Hughes went down. He went down as he had come up—alone. His going down seemed more swift than his rising. And yet he began to go down when he stood on the rope ladder down the Gulf and watched the troopships drift out. If in that moment he had not dreamed that General Sam Hughes was above government, he might have continued his great work long enough to become Lord Valcartier. He might have helped in a second Capture of Quebec, made conscription less difficult when it came, and put the Fifth Division into the field. And in that case Canada's part in the war would have been even more magnificent than it now is.

The latter days of the General were characteristic of a man who never knew he was beaten. Musical geniuses have written tremendous scores to depict a man's struggle with death. None of them could have transcended the long battle which Sam Hughes put up to stay here. For months we had intermittent bulletins from his bedside when any morning we expected to read that he was gone. He was a hard man to conquer. And only his intimate friends are likely ever to know whether or not it was his own ultimate biting failure, after his almost super-human success, that turned this man of the shadow into a phantom before he let go.

And before he went the hard, bluff soldier, who has as much iron in his composition as any man of his time sprang one of those human surprises that even war fails to emulate—when he listened time after time to the record that he loved better than most music, "I know that my Redeemer liveth", from Handel's "Messiah".

THE STEREOPTICON AND THE SLIDE

LIEUTENANT-GENERAL SIR ARTHUR CURRIE

THE war was a great cosmic artist of infinite satire, making of humanity little stereopticon slides which he slipped in front of his calcium and flashed upon the clouds for a screen. When the war was done the stereopticon was smashed. The slides remain. What shall we do with them ?

One of the most world-interesting characters in the magic lantern of war was Lieut.-General Sir Arthur Currie. who in 1914 locked his real estate desk in Victoria, B.C., and in 1919 came back to Canada admittedly one of the ablest commanders in a war which made the exploits of Wellington seem like comic opera in simplicity.

Whatever partial, prejudiced or private opinions some Canadians may have about Sir Arthur Currie, it must be generally admitted that he was perhaps the most remarkable of all the slides slipped into the stereopticon of the war artist. To quote from "Canada's Hundred Days", by J. F. B. Livesay, concerning the secret strategy of Sir Arthur Currie for the great Amiens show in August, 1918 :

"That afternoon the Corps Commander had a talk with the two Canadian correspondents. Before him was a large scale map and the barrage map. It was all very clear and lucid. We take up our line here ; and our first objective is there ; 'zero' hour was named ; our final objective for the day over there—constituting a world record for a first day's advance. . . . .

"So at last all is ready. The story goes that the Corps Commander was asked how soon he could deliver the

Corps in fighting trim at the appointed place. 'By the
tent h,' he had said. 'Too long ; do it by the eighth.'
"And he did it. . . . .

"And it was all done secretly and by night. For an
entire week the men of Canada were passing south from
their old front, taking circuitous and puzzling routes. None
knew where they went. They sang as they marched—a
thing they had not done for two years.

"Foremost that night of nights was one's sense of
wonder at how it had been done ; how of many tangled
threads of railway and lorry and march, all that great and
intricate machine—more complex far than Wellington had
gathered on the field of Waterloo—had been assembled in
perfect order to the minute. . . . .

"Up the winding hill go all the impedimenta of war—
marching battalions, traction-engines towing great guns,
ammunition trains, long lines of Red Cross lorries ; everywhere the pungent odour of petrol. From every little
wood belch forth men. They march silently. They might
be phantoms, dim hordes of Valhalla, were it not for the
spark of a cigarette, a smothered laugh. There is no
talking. All is tense excitement. For miles and miles in a
wide concentric sweep every road and lane and bypath is
crowded with these slow-moving masses. Over the bare
hillsides lumber the heavy tanks, just keeping pace with
the marching men.

. . . . "Berlin thinks we are in Flanders ; London that
we are in the south. All is well. . . . .

" . . . . The watch hand is creeping round—half-past
three—four—ten past four—an interminable laggard. It
is to be the greatest barrage of the war.

" . . . . 'Zero' is set for four-twenty, and the pointer
has barely reached that figure when behind us there goes
up a mighty flare, and simultaneously all along the line
ten miles to north and south of us, other flares light up the
countryside. At the same instant there breaks out the
boom of our heavy guns, the sharp staccato of sixty-
pounders, the dull roar of howitzers, and the ear-splitting
clamour of whizz-bangs—a bedlam of noise. Shells
whistle and whine overhead ; they cannot be distinguished
one from another, but merge into a cataract of sound.

" . . . . The heavens are lighted up across their broad
expanse by a continuous sheet of lightning, playing relent-

lessly over the doomed lines. Now a faint light of dawn shimmers in the east and soon blots out the fireworks. A lark rises high, carolling. . . . .

"The fog lifts. It is eight o'clock. The cavalry, a wonderful sight, appear on the scene. They have come up from Hangest-sur-Somme and have lain overnight in the great park of Amiens. Like a jack-in-the-box they have sprung from nowhere—miles on miles of gay and serried ranks, led by the Canadian Cavalry Brigade."

On the 1913 side of this Wagnerian stage setting take a look at a real estate office in Victoria, B.C. The junior member of the firm is a pink-faced giant who had taught school and made no money, and having no other qualification for getting ahead in the world, went into buying and selling houses and corner lots. Victoria was booming then or he never would have done it He had maps of the city on his walls and could solemnly point out to some timid newcomer in 1913 what little house there or nice wooded lot yonder might suit her ; and the price—oh, yes, the price ; seems high, but the location is excellent, the neighbourhood fine, the scenery superb, and the city— well, it had been going ahead until the slump and then——

"Oh, yes, Victoria's all right," he insists heavily. "Got sleeping sickness, that's all."

Then he yawns, which is a relief to the lady client, who thinks that his face is less ugly that way. Such a huge, long, solemn face ! She glances at the office, wondering— if the agent is hard up ? If so, no wonder ; for he seems a sad salesman.

He closes his desk and locks up. Off to the rifle ranges, where he stays as late as the eye can see because—well, it's a joy to help the men get bull's eyes.

Sunday—marches in full Highland regalia at the head of the 50th Gordon Highlanders on garrison parade. On the curb a twinkling little Jap watches him.

"Nothin' like him in Japan, John," says a boy scout. "Wow !"

"Big—so big !" admires the Jap.

"Yah. Makes them big Macs. in the ranks look shrunk.
Knows artillery, too. Rifle—kick ! got a great eye. Look
at 'im right wheel !"

*   *   *   *   *   *   *

Then on the 1920 side of the Wagnerian stage picture
observe this same giant, less baby pink, thinner in the face,
clad in evening dress ; Inverness cape, crush hat, in the
rotunda of the Ritz in Montreal, beside an average athletic
citizen similarly dressed ; the superb civilian—and his
marionette.

"Er—I think the car's waiting, General."

"Oh, no. We'll walk. Only a block or two," booms
the giant.

He crosses the rotunda in seven swift, great strides,
while the marionette trots to keep up. They are off to a
function at McGill University. The new President—to
whom professors bow with frigid politeness and ladies ogle
in admiring awe, and university governors stand about
like a bodyguard as though to intimate,—

"Ridiculous ? Not a bit of it. There's no other university President like him. And what else could we do with
him ? The Government had nothing to suit him ; for
politics he's never meant ; for business never. Geddes
left us. We picked a greater man. Yes, it seems awkward,
but never mind. A year from now you will say—here was
the man that made McGill as famous in 1921 as Sir William
Dawson, the world geologist, made it in 1890."

Montreal that made a citizen of prodigious Van Horne
had here a character in a setting far more unusual. The
eminent soldier as head of a university. One of the last
surprises of the war ; almost as it seemed then a joker in
the pack ; when men had to remember how this man
leaped from an almost bankrupt real estate office in Victoria
to what he was in Canada's Hundred Days.

Of all men who seemed to have been absolutely created

by the war Currie was the first. He enlisted for active service in 1914, and Hughes made him brigade-commander at Valcartier. He was in the First Contingent that swung out of the Gulf the day that Hughes stood on the rope ladder, almost forgetting that he had shaken hands with Currie. He went to France as Commander of the 2nd Infantry Brigade. Within two months came St. Julien and the green gas when Currie held his part of the stricken line from Thursday till Sunday.

"And on Sunday," said Max Aitken, eye-witness, "he had not abandoned his trenches. There were none left. They had been obliterated by the artillery. He withdrew his undefeated troops from the fragments of the field fortifications, and the hearts of his men were as completely unbroken as the parapets of his trenches were completely broken." Much more was said in official despatches about the fine spectacular heroism of other officers of lower rank. Currie, the most picturesque physique on the West front, was no man for mere gallantry. Poor dashing Mercer, beloved of the ranks, later paid the penalty for the sort of bravery that inspires troops but does not win battles. Currie was no coward. But he was cautious. The Scot in him preordained that he might be a necessity higher up. He just flung his left flank around south and hung on.

We read on in the official record :

"Monday morning broke bright and clear and found the Canadians behind the firing line   But this day too was to bring its anxieties. The attack was still pressed, and it became necessary to ask Brigadier General Currie whether he could not once more call on his shrunken Brigade. 'The men are tired,' this indomitable soldier replied, 'but they are ready and glad to go again to the trenches.' And so, once more a hero leading heroes, the general marched back the men of the 2nd Brigade, reduced to a quarter of its strength, to the very apex of the line as it existed at that moment."

Five months later a party of Canadian newspapermen

visited the Canadian front when one of them wrote concerning Major-General Currie :

"English officers spoke of him with a curious mixture of enthusiasm and reserve as though he were some new sort of being. It was everybody's secret that this big, husky Canadian with the baby pink face and the blue eyes and the slow, smooth, bellowing voice was to be in command of the Second Canadian Division just then being organized. . . . . No place except Canada produces such voices as Currie's, or such tremendous easy-moving bodies. He met the newspapermen with a smile and a great outstretched hand. The gesture was something like that of a popular preacher shaking hands with the children on their way out of church. But the voice was the great thing. It seemed to come from illimitable depths. It suggested at once poise and unlimited balance. Cool judgment that could never be upset. Officers who saw Brigade Headquarters being strafed and who saw the roof blown in over Currie's head whispered among themselves that would be the last of Currie. But he emerged as calm and smooth and pink as ever. . . . . The day the newspapermen saw him a very junior officer who has since distinguished himself came to report breathlessly, 'That last one, sir, got my tent !' He was excited and just a trifle hysterical ; but two words from the General seemed to calm him at once. 'That so ?' he said, with the same quiet interest that a farmer might have received news that a certain hen had at last laid an egg. 'I thought that last one sounded a bit close.' "

Then there came to the head of the Canadian Corps a man named Byng, who could stroll casually into a billet or a training field to inspect "the muddy trench hounds" in canvas leggings and with three buttons loose. Until Byng came the Canadian Corps was a semi-disciplined and marvellous mob of men who could swear as hard as they could fight and fight like wildcats. Byng gave then the massive and complex mechanism of an army competent to conduct operations as a unit of modern war, dominated by the man of whom the boys sang to the tune of Three Blind Mice, "Byng Bangs Boche, See how they run !" Currie, commander of the 2nd Division, had seen this

Corps Commander stroll into a billet and hurl machine gun questions at the men who jumped like eager school-boys to answer. He must have silently envied this genius, who cared far less than he knew about what was wrong in a kit inspection, but had a shrewd eye for manœuvres. Not often in actual war does a man so personally popular organize a cross-section of a vast international country into a war machine called an army, and not seldom do men when they hear of such a commander being transferred look at one another in a sort of blank dismay and say, "Well, I'll be damned. Now who's it?"

Out of the army came slowly and ponderously the huge Highlander, with the "baby pink face" and the rumbling gong of a voice.

Sir Arthur Currie was much too honest to imagine that he or any other man could make the Canadian army. It was a heavy ordeal to follow Byng, just as it had been easy for Byng to succeed Alderson. But Currie knew the Canadians down at the root better than Byng knew them. He knew how that army had been made : that he was taking over a humanized machine that was to war in 1917 what the sword of Wallace had been in man-to-man combat seven hundred years earlier. He knew the weakness of men for idolizing a popular commander. They never would parody any nursery rhyme in his honour. Except the Anzacs, they were the most audacious army in Europe. They had become great in defiance of red tape, insisting on whatever is called Canadianism. They embodied all there was of Western independence on that Front. The Anzacs, great in fight and in ideas of personal liberty, had not been welded into such a machine as the Canadians, whose advertised national qualities Currie was expected to conserve.

"As soon as one lets the cheeky beggars, Canadians from America, have a bit of quiet, they get uppish," was the illuminating sentence in a letter found in a German trench near St. Eloi. Currie knew those "cheeky beggars". In his own elephantine way he loved them, when few of them could figure it out. He knew how hard those "beggars" could hit : how grimly they could stick : how madly they could raid and rush : how infernally they could scheme to "put one over on Heine "; how desperately they could abuse earth and heaven when they had time in the rest billets to smoke fags and write letters home. They were no army to go whacking on the shoulder.

It had been all right for Byng the Briton to go among those men with three buttons loose. Men like a touch of insurgency in a commander who has come up among the martinets. Byng was a professional soldier. Currie was not yet even a mild insurgent, or was not known as such to the ranks. He was almost a man of prayer. He moved in a large arc somewhat like his great resolute body ; an engine of might that never seemed weary ; who at "Molly-be-Damned" studied battle reports at two a.m., and was in the field at six. As he had almost come up from the ranks, the men knew him. Here and there in a British Columbia battalion may have been a man who had bought a corner lot from Currie in Victoria. If so, he liked to talk about the hard-up days of the Corps Commander when he was in real estate.

Currie knew that above all things he must keep the confidence of those men and that he could never do it by familiarity. Success was the only way. Not, anyhow, speeches. The C.C. was rather fond of talking aloud at first ; sometimes too religiously. It was a habit that he never quite abandoned, though he changed his style as he grew in experience.

There was work to do. No army had more ; few armies as much. Currie's was a mobile army ; needed as shock troops in rough places—a very good reputation if not too much of it. There was danger of the army losing its Canadianism by being shunted about. One of Currie's first objectives that he wanted above all things to achieve as a Canadian commander of initiative, was the capture of Lens. He had a plan for this. He was never allowed to carry it out. Says the author of "Canada's Hundred Days" :

"Thus when he is ordered to abandon his planned offensive at Lens and take the corps up the Salient, he refuses point blank to serve under the Commander of the Fifth Army. He is placed under his old Chief of the First Army, looks over the ground before Passchendaele and then protests against the whole operation as being useless in itself and likely to cost the Corps 15,000 men."

It was said by some who believed they knew, that the Lens preparation was nothing but a huge feint put up to mislead Heine for an attack in force elsewhere. This was one of the bewildering events of that baffling year when the French army was in a state of mutiny, the nation behind the army in a state of nerves, and the politicians, clamouring for victories—or at least a cessation of defeat. Something had to be done, not only by France but by Britain, whose Premier insisted that unless the Germans could be broken in the north he could not hold his country united at home. There was a Council of War—so, a few weeks before the writing of this, said a Canadian General in New York—at which Currie was present. Sir Douglas Haig unexpectedly arrived and was soon into an argument with the Canadian Corps Commander demanding that he abandon Lens and strike at Passchendaele. The two commanders were in violent disagreement. Currie refused to yield. The British Premier went to France and met Currie, who gave way to the Premier—as people usually did—and, against his own convictions, abandoned Lens.

The precise military significance is of less value here than the remark credited to Lloyd George, who is reported to have said in England after a subsequent War Cabinet meeting—that in the Canadian Corps Commander he had met "the biggest thing physically and mentally on that front."

What Currie was at the head of the Corps no civilian then in Canada has any means of knowing, except by what men say who were under him or about him. A brawny veteran infantryman, whom I met with his chum, said :

"Currie—oh, yes, he was a good general. But few of the men where I was in the trenches or the billets ever liked him."

"But did you see much of him ?"

"Too much, begad." His chum nodded agreement. "Too awful much, sometimes. Why, he used to come into a rest billet almost every day after we'd come there all shot to bits with only a corporal's guard o' the whole battalion, muddy and tired and sleepy ; yes, and what's the first thing we hear, but begad, we've all to shine up and get spic and span for parade because the O.C. says the C.C. orders it. Out we go, like a ragbag remnant and he looks us over, says he knows we're tired and makes a speech——"

"Oh, boy, them speeches !" sighs the chum.

"Tells us how well we've done and all like o' that, and at the end says there's such a devil of a job yonder that he's compelled against his will——"

"Oh, yes, dead aginst his will," pipes the chum.

"To intimate that he'd like us to trail back to the show and do it some more for the sake of the victory and the good long billet we'll get presently. Yes, Currie was a good General. He did the work, he got results. But never tell me he was easy on his men—becuz four years I was wan o' them."

One allows in this man's opinion for the tendency to "grouch" that always appears in veterans who know best how to fight. Men like this were "fed up" on the war, of which they never saw anything but the glimpse of their own sector. The war was over now, and between the armistice and getting home many such men had a chance to talk, as they wearily waited for a ship.

"Yes, and that capture of Mons," says the chum, as he sips a little drink. "Altogether useless and against orders. The war was over."

"No," says the veteran ; "that was a mere trifle, as I see it. Not one, two, three with the march into Germany. Begad ! if ever I was a rebel it was then on that 150 miles, says you. But—'twas so ordered by the C.C. and we went."

It was not likely that Gen. Currie believed his army to be rebellious against that march. He was too much of an insurgent to fear insubordination. He had packed many a pipe-clay parade officer home for inefficiency.

A machine gun officer, who had got a Blighty at Passchendaele and was asked by the writer what he thought about Currie, admitted that he knew very little about him because all he saw at the time was his own little corner of the show. He casually referred the question to two others, one of whom was a H.Q. staff officer, and saw Currie at first hand for months at a time. The answer was :

"I'll say that Currie always inspired me with absolute confidence in his genius for modern war. It was a pleasure just to see him revise a Divisional plan of action. He had a hawk eye for any weak spots and he pointed them out. No doubt some of the stuff that got through to the boys in some of the shows shortly after Currie took command was Byng stuff, and Byng sure handed over a fine army to Currie. But believe me, Currie had his own programme and picked his own men and developed his own machine shortly after. And I don't believe there was a commander in any of the Corps on that Front that had anything on him for what makes an army win."

The General's return to Canada was preheralded by a barrage of criticism that seeped through from men coming home. Some day we shall know how much or how little of this was politics inspired by Currie's enemies in Canada and by men who, jealous of his success and his eminence,

had no scruples about fomenting the criticism. But
Currie must be judged by what he did with his army. In
that last hundred days all the armies but the American
army were remnants of what they were in 1915. The
wonderful thing about the Canadian army is that in the
three months before victory it was an even more terrible
arm of war than it had been at Vimy Ridge. After a year
and a half of Commander Currie it was still the superb
fighting machine described in the extracts already quoted
from the battle of Amiens. For a few of the reasons why
it was so we quote again that same book the writer's
estimate of Currie :

"But according to the letter of the law he is not a good
subordinate. He cannot be popular with the powers that
be : he is always complaining about something ; getting
his own way or making it unpleasant for people if he
doesn't.

"In the panic of the following March (1918 after
Passchendaele) he finds the Corps is being torn to pieces,
its divisions hurried here, there and everywhere ; orders
given and countermanded and then issued again. He
protests strongly ; the Canadian corps whose value is
tested, must be kept together ; and he wins out." . . .

"Is all this insubordination ? If so, it is a quality that
makes for victory. The average Canadian is always
willing to "take a chance" because he has confidence in
himself. And the Corps Commander is very much of a
Canadian."

The author does not criticize Currie, though he had so
good an opportunity. In telling so well the wonderful
story of that last hundred days and so explicitly glorifying
the Commander whose best work of the war was done
during that period, he gives us no perspective. Is it not
just to admit that though the four reduced Canadian
divisions—with certain attachments—had defeated forty-
seven German divisions, they had conquered divisions
terribly more reduced than their own and absolutely without reserves in either men or materials and devoid of the

last vestige of morale ? The great bluff was about to break. It was due to have broken sooner.

When the armistice came all the armies but the Canadians laid down their arms. Currie had not finished his work. He had planned the whole hundred days, beginning with Cambrai, and the apex of that achievement after the breaking of the infallible Hindenburg line, was the recapture of Mons. He was once more "insubordinate". He did not seem to pay respect to the armistice. His men had often said that they wanted to fight Heine on German soil. Denied that, at least they wanted a chance to be part of the army of occupation, as far east as Cologne. Currie could never have ordered an unwilling army—not that army unwilling—to march 150 miles into Germany. He had an army of conquest, not of armistice.

But the stereopticon and the slides :

What was to be done with this soldier at home ? How could he be re-established in civil life ? Thanks to the Administration's predicament in trying to please both the General and his enemies, here was the worst D.S.C.R. problem of the lot. Thanks to McGill University, the predicament was removed.

A sagacious professor in McGill who knows by experience what it is to get the ear of the public, said when Currie was appointed President that almost the entire faculty were opposed to him because the idea was so ridiculous. That professor now alleges proudly that faculty, students and management are all convinced that Currie is a wonderful President ; that he has revolutionized all existing ideas about the headship of a university, that he understands even the academic mind ; that the *esprit de corps* of McGill is such as it never was.

In short, nobody is left to remark—

"I say, what a pity Geddes left us in the lurch !"

They are making a new stereopticon for that slide.

A COAT OF MANY COLOURS

SIR JOHN WILLISON

AFTER a life of wearing Joseph's coat, Sir John Willison, ex-editor of the *Toronto Globe* and of the *News*, finds himself President of the National Reconstruction Association. Programme—to reconstruct Canada, beginning in 1918, after fifty years of Confederation.

A supercilious editor once asked why on such an Association no farmer had been appointed. The answer was simple enough. Sir John was born a farmer. He used to wield a handspike at logging bees in Huron County, Ont. Why no Liberals ? But Sir John used to be the leading Liberal of unelected Canada. Why no professor of political economy to represent the great universities who are always supposed to be reconstructing a nation ? Simple again. Sir John himself once conducted a university of culture, economics and general information known as the *Toronto News*. In fact there was no need of an Association at all. Sir John Willison was sufficient unto the day.

One finds it tolerably easy to be sarcastic about Sir John Willison, because for many years he was to some of us the sort of man that compelled a sincere, almost idolatrous admiration. In this also he is more adept than the average man. He himself once idolized Sir Wilfrid Laurier in two volumes ; but a few years before he turned all his political guns on the French-Canadian Premier to get him out of power for good.

In all Canada there has never been a more versatile character ; never one who after a *volte face* in politics could

166

turn with such poise and dignity upon any critic cradled in the foundations of belief and ask, "Well, what's new?"

From his crisp manner of speaking and a certain austerity of manner, I used to think that Sir John was in a measure inscrutable. He had such a curt way of summoning a reporter, as once,—

"Never," he began when the culprit had got into the corridor facing the editor-in-chief, "never, when interviewing a man in his own home, say anything about the furniture."

Born a Conservative and a farmer, Willison became on the *Globe* Canada's greatest unelected Liberal. He conserved Liberalism. On the *Globe* he held the balance between the Free Traders who believed only in reciprocity and Erastus Wiman, who with Goldwin Smith made Taft a mere plagiarist when he said that Canada was an "adjunct" of the United States. It was Willison's attempt to consider commercial union on its merits that made the *Globe* seem like a mark for the annexationists, at a time when the high priest of the movement in Canada had the effrontery to remain a citizen of the nation which he was openly trying to sell at a bargain counter. The man who kept the *Globe* from becoming an annex to Goldwin Smith in 1891 had an experience that would fit any man to become a protection-tariff Chairman of Reconstruction, and to remember the sirens that tempted Ulysses.

Nobody could have predicted in those days that the great editor of the *Globe* would live to become first an Independent, next a Tory, and at the last a Liberal-Unionist. And perhaps none of these transformations would have been necessary if Sir George Ross had not tried the trick of "32 years in the saddle" from the days of Mowat; to do which and to remain politically virtuous was an impossible feat, even though the Premier of Ontario was a director of the *Globe*. Ross remained director, and also Premier. But it seems that Mr. Willison saw in such a dual role a greater inconsistency than even he deemed to be worthy of so brilliant a man. As he could not remove the director, he took what seemed to be a providential opportunity to remove the Premier.

The reconstructed *Toronto News* was the opportunity. The elimination of Ross was the first result. The removal of Laurier was the necessary sequel. The first was a pleasure. The second must have been a pang. Because of the first, in place of Sir George Ross, Willison had as frequent visitor to his sanctum James Pliny Whitney, the new Premier of Ontario, "honest enough to be bold and bold enough to be honest." From that to Toryism was merely opening a door. It took the new Tory editor eight years to remove his old idol Laurier, the result of which was a sort of intense and bigoted animosity to the Province of Quebec which Sir John is now learning to overcome. When the Tory *News* became a Northcliffe Imperialist organ it was inevitable that Sir John should convert his common hostility to the western Laurier-Liberals into a polite suspicion of the Radicals who were becoming Agrarians.

When finally, weary of mere politics in which he was our greatest journalistic expert by instinct and experience Sir John left the *News*, he was free to engage in work of a more practical character than writing, and to become Chairman of the Government's most important branch of active agenda outside of professional politics.

In all these Protean changes of makeup, if not of character, Sir John Willison has never abandoned two early habits ; lawn bowling and reading the *Globe*. He is an expert in both. Bowling vexes him least, because its rules never change. The *Globe* gives him pangs because alas ! it is now engaged in the unpardonable effort to merge the Liberals with the National Progressives as a greater Liberal Party.

Inconsistency may be the evolution of greatness. Inconstancy never. The *Globe* of a certain date in June, 1921, contained a front page display of the Agrarian bye-

election victory in Medicine Hat On another date there
was an editorial once again advising the Agrarians to make
common cause with Liberals against the common enemy,
Meighenism, or as it might be said, Willisonism.

Perusing the *Globe* in his Reconstruction office, Sir John
glances up—leisurely at a spot on the wall, next to the
portrait of Sir John A. Macdonald Like Macbeth's dagger,
he sees a cold, organizing face smiling like Mona Lisa,
fair at Sir John ; the face of T. A. Crerar.

The Levite of Reconstruction shakes his fist.

"Down with you," he mutters. "Avaunt ! I'll have
none of you. There's nothing under Medicine Hat—except
what Kipling said, 'all hell for a basement,' Natural gas,
Crerar, not a test case at all. Oh, no. Too near the border."

Sir John yawns and peruses a proof of the 745th pamphlet issued from Reconstruction, total of nearly seven
million copies paid for not by taxation of the people, but
inferentially by tariffs. Probably a very patriotic minority
read these Willison bulletins aiming to reconstruct the
country by putting a crimp in the exportation of the Canadian dollar, looking after welfare work in factories, women
and children, grappling with unemployment, helping to
change over industry from war to peace, aiming to "stabi-
lize" the nation, to curb that team of wild horses, Bolshevism and Agrarianism, and generally to keep Canada
from going to perdition.

In spite of Sir John, in 1919 and 1920, people bought
Canada almost bankrupt on the exchanges. Hence among
the items in the cheapening list may be placed the Canadian dollar which is now worth about 89 cents in New York.
That is what happens to the dollar when it goes away from
home and plays prodigal son. What Sir John works to
see is Canadian commodities crossing the border and the
Yankee dollars coming back in exchange.

Here is one of the greatest moral issues of the age for
this nation. Even the preachers, if they could see us
put up the barriers against luxury imports from the United

States—said to be such a wicked nation—would breathe more easily. People so often buy sin done up in dutiable packages. For the fiscal year ending March 31, 1921, Canadians went into debt to the United States over a million a day—adverse exchange. Nearly $400,000,000 in one year spent for Yankee goods more than Yankeedom spent buying goods from us.

And now comes the need for the rationalizing philosophy of Sir John Willison, truly our most versatile expert on tariffs from the *Globe* reciprocity down to the Reconstruction. Beginning in 1917 with Foster's "economic unity" in North America, a friendly Democratic tariff had let Canada send certain natural products into the United States free of duty. Private interests found it profitable to handle Canadian trade, much of it in transit to Europe in a state of high demand. The democratic element in Sir John must have approved that. Grit as he used to be, Sir John must believe in letting the great United States practise free-trade if it be so disposed. Those good Democrats ! Had they not enacted the Underwood tariff, what a mountainous load must have been imposed upon the Atlantean shoulders of Reconstruction !

Which brings us to the eve of Dominion Day, 1921. Sir John was not bowling ; he was reading the *Round Table* for June—at least if not he should have been—an article on the meeting of the "Imperial Cabinet".

"Mischievous title !" he mutters. "It's an Imperial Conference of Premiers. John S. Ewart will be sure to make a kingdom article out of that. Very ill-advised. Er—Come !"

"Evening paper, Sir John," says the boy.

Sir John takes up the paper and is at once confronted by an item which convinces him that if ever Canada needed protection from the United States, now is the time. The item is the repeal of the Underwood tariff. Accustomed for life to unpleasant sensations from printed pages, his face gives no sign of emotion. Swiftly he reads through, flings the paper down and looks up. At once he rises, glaring coldly at the Crerar palimpsest on the wall. Again that Mona Lisa exporting smile, as the lips seem to say :

"Well, Sir John—what will be the Republican Reconstruction price of the Canadian dollar now ?"

"Bah !" Sir John snorts into a handkerchief, like a Tory squire. "That tariff, Sir, is not a menace, nor a prophecy of agrarian victory at the polls. It is a challenge to this nation. Canada will not let down the bars. We shall put them higher ! Keep the Canadian dollar in Canada. Sell our natural products to Britain. Build up our towns and our industries. Utilize our great water powers, the cheapest power in the world. Use our raw material ; our manufacturing experience gained in the war. Develop the home market. Sell more to ourselves and spend our incomes in countries that do not put up economic barriers against our products. Without some adequate protection, sir, we are economically as extinct as the Dodo. There's but one alternative—commercial autonomy from the United States or commercial annexation. Nobody but a lunatic or an Agrarian would ever doubt which of these we shall choose—eh, what's that you say ?"

The portrait chuckles. An uplifted hand appears in the unframed picture.

"I said, Sir John—put the repeal of the Underwood tariff under your Medicine Hat."

In sudden fury Sir John flings the *Round Table* at the place where the picture vanished.

This may be a whimsical conclusion to the study of a personality so perplexing and vagarious as Sir John Willison. But he himself, having a high sense of humour, will appreciate its psychological justice as much as he regrets its historical inaccuracy. Sir John has always aimed at being a big Canadian, and he has usually succeeded. He did his share of contribution to right thinking about the war, as he did in vicarious action when he lost one of his two sons in that struggle. He could not do otherwise, because in spite of his bewildering superficial changes of coat, when even his detractors almost admired the dignity with which he changed it, Sir John, the Tory at heart, has always been a loyal servant of his country. Without him the story of political journalism in Canada would be a thing of shreds and patches.

He has at various times wielded an immense power usually in the direction of shrewd, sane thinking about national affairs. No Canadian editor of his time so thoroughly mastered its intricate problems. He has a faculty of clear, constructive thinking and a fine style of writing. With no college education he became a cultured journalist—which is sometimes an anomaly—though he never showed any zeal for the "humanities" and never knew much about that peculiar sociological phenomenon called the proletariat.

Since he drew away from the farm Sir John has never had a desire to return, even in sympathy. With a fine sense of humour he has never relished reminiscences of the backwoods and the smoke of the log heaps. His published "Reminiscences" are a fine contribution to our political history, but they show no real sympathy with the rude pioneer life from which the writer came and to which he owes a debt that he could very well discharge, if he would write a book about the social and craft life of the Canadian farm as it was in the Victorian Era. There is more national vitality in the story of that than there is in the programme of the National Reconstruction Association. Sir John has a true sympathy with that life, because he knows it has been at the root of all his own big Canadianism in all its forms. He is one of the kindliest men alive and he writes with great discernment and dignity. Let him stop writing Reconstruction bulletins and do something of more value to the country, so that the older enthusiasm of men who used to think he was Canada's greatest editor may not althogether die.

WHATSOEVER THY HAND FINDETH

Sir Joseph Flavelle, Bart.

"Whatsoever thy hand findeth to do, do it with thy might." I have forgotten whether it was Paul or Solomon who said that. But Sir Joseph Flavelle, Bart., will be sure to remember. From the time he was big enough to carry in wood for his devout Christian mother near Peterborough, Ont., he was living out that text.

The Flavelle family afterwards moved to Lindsay, where the future baronet went into business. Queer little town—to be the home of three such men as Flavelle, Hughes, and Mackenzie.

A man who has had years of business intimacy with Sir Joseph said to me once—under suggestion—"Yes, you never miss a word he says to you, because he puts everything so clearly, and you admire the big things he does, because he has such a genius for action after he thinks—but somehow you are so exasperated when you leave him that you feel like giving him a big swift kick."

Another man who was under him in an organizing position for years during the war said : "Well, the higher critics can say all they like against his methods and his personal peculiarities, but I tell you—I like the old boy."

One of Britain's foremost financial experts in the war said to an interviewer : "Ah, you know Flavelle ? Clev-er man ! Clev-er !" That was nearly twenty years ago.

In 1918 Sir Joseph Flavelle had in his Munitions Office at Ottawa a staff of 360 accounting clerks working upon thirteen ledgers, each representing a separate department of the Board, which up till that time had placed orders in this country for war material aggregating $1,60,000,000 in value.

At that time an editor wrote Sir Joseph asking for a statement of what his Board had done. Within a few hours of receiving the letter Sir Joseph forwarded an itemized statement a column long, of which one paragraph read :

"Upwards of 56,000,000 shells have been produced ; 60,000,000 copper bands ; 45,000,000 cartridge cases ; 28,000,000 fuses ; 70,000,-000 lbs. of powder ; 50,000,000 lbs. of high explosives ; 90 ships built, or under construction aggregating 375,000 tons ; 2,700 aeroplanes have been produced. "

He stated also that 900 manufacturers had taken contracts in all the Provinces except Prince Edward Island. The great ex-Minister of Munitions himself, reading that report, might have said : "Flavelle ? Yes—he is mighty clever." And Flavelle had been for one year then a baronet. That also was clever ; and just in time. The man who happened to be in England when war was declared and sold war bacon in August, 1914, was not to be caught napping in 1917 ; neither after he had got his title was he to be found slacking in his marvellous work in 1918. Flavelle earned a title—even after he had taken it.

"Whatsoever thy hand findeth to do !" Yea, verily.

I have been fairly well acquainted with Sir Joseph for a good many years. I do not know him. Yet his altogether uncommon personality has almost frozen itself into my memory. Whenever I see that thick-shouldered, whitening-whiskered man of sixty-three hastening afoot up the street, or driving his little runabout, or wiping his glasses every minute in some office, or coming becaped and crush-hatted to a concert, I can hear that high-keyed, slow voice, the calm dispassionate utterance with never a syllable misplaced, and feel the energy of a nature that of all men I ever met is the oddest compend of clear thinking, cool judgment, strength of grip and juvenility of impulse.

The story of his struggle to affluence is not much
different in basic outlines from that of any average, self-
made man ; differing vastly in the character of the man.
A year after he was forced out of Lindsay by boycott
because of his Scott Act campaign, the freezing of a car of
potatoes on a Toronto siding almost wiped out his business.
Frankly and modestly, yet with a sort of fatalistic assurance,
he discusses the kind of man he thinks himself to have
become since he lost those potatoes. He denies that he
has ever been interesting ; rather bewildered that at one
time or another people have taken such a peculiar interest
in him. He talks of his early struggles, the economy of
bacon, and the bigotries of Old Testamentarians in the
same concise language set to the same unvaried monotony
of voice. If you should fail to follow him, he would almost
chide you for not paying attention.

Nearly twenty years ago I met a preacher keenly interested in Flavelle. He told me a story repeated to him
in a sort of admiring deprecation that very day by a Methodist preacher from Toronto who had a gift for elevated
gossip. This story was probably out of the Apocrypha, as
it concerned a very worldly episode in the joint experiences
of Mr. Flavelle and another Canadian financier on a visit
to Chicago, when the latter got a wire stating that a certain
conditional donation of his to a small church in Ontario
had been unexpectedly covered by the congregation with
the stipulated equal amount, and that it was time to send
the money. It was said that he showed the wire to Flavelle;
that the two financiers took joint action on the Stock
Exchange ; and that the money was wired immediately.
The little details about the transaction I omit, partly out of
deference to the preacher who bandied the yarn—wherever
he got it. He probably only half believed it himself. Even
ministers will gossip.

Much has been said about Sir Joseph's religious affairs.
He has had many. He has been in publicity over a few,

such as the controversy between the late Dr. Carman, his old adversary, and Rev. George Jackson, his then pastor, whom he defended. Flavelle has never concealed his enthusiasm for the church. He has entertained many a celebrated minister. He has been prominently identified with Missions, with the Methodist Book Room—that sadly unecclesiastical corporation—with debates in Conference on amusements and other things, with Methodist education. In all these he has practised the text, "Whatsoever thy hand findeth to do." The church needed Flavelle's organizing hand. He generously lent it. He could not do otherwise without being untrue to his own prodigious and inherited passion for a certain kind of organized religion.

The personal faith of a public man is no business for the critic, except where that faith becomes public works. Sir Joseph has been conspicuously aligned with the militant work of the Church. It has been the belief of those who know him, casually or intimately, that his philanthropic works were inspired by his faith. But many men have had as much faith with less works, because of too much dissipating emotion. Sir Joseph with all his juvenility of impulse had a way of hitching his emotions up to a job. The church needed organization. Other wealth-getting Methodists were prominent in pews, public donations and conferences. Flavelle believed in the seven days' work. He had a programme of action for the Sabbath. Church, social work, business, were to him very much one thing; all in need of organization to get results. He had no use for the idle church and less for what he called "the dead hand"— referring to the influence of his old adversary, Dr. Carman, who thought it presumption in a wealthy pork-packer to regard himself as a critic of clerical authority.

It is tolerably certain that had Flavelle made less of a business of religion, the public would have had less business condemning him on the bacon inquiry evidence. Here was a man who all his life had been a tremendous organizer of the church and a professor of a peculiarly active faith, president of a company which in one year had made an alleged profit of $5,000,000 on a capital investment of less than $14,000,000. Bacon at that time—1917—cost the consumer 50 cents a pound. The price was considered outrageous. Bacon afterwards went to 80 cents at a time when nobody blamed Sir Joseph ; and when he had disposed of his interest in bacon altogether. But the alleged extortion of this powerful and baroneted Christian stuck in the public mind. Bacon was the pioneer in exposed "profiteering." O'Connor's report was made public at a time when it was yet the private property of the Cabinet. There was politics here. And the Premier was away. Other men afterwards made much more amazing profits that never were mentioned in the press ; men who never went to church ; who had never in public said such words as "let war profits go to the hell where they belong."

It was not the actual profit, but the alleged hypocrisy of Flavelle that roused the detestation of a large section of the public. And to the end of his life this man will never erase from the minds of many people the notion that he was of all profiteers the worst, because the most hypocritical.

Then there was the baronetcy. For a man who had preached Christ so much this seemed a thin business. A man's Christianity, if he works hard at it, becomes advertised without posters. The world that mistrusts the church on principle, that only waits the chance itself to profiteer and to get social preferment, is quick to anathematize the man who in a big way seems to corelate church, profits and society.

The public are no longer concerned, neither did they understand at the time, whether the Davies Co. made 5.05 cents a pound on bacon or 5.05 minus overhead charges, 4.1. Here was the first "sinner" caught ; sentimentally lynch him. It made no difference then what had been the man's serious work in philanthropic organization and in public service ; or that for war production he had offered the Wm. Davies plant to the Government to operate at so much percentage to the company ; or that Flavelle himself had no connection with the management and at the time concerned knew very little about it. The public appetite did not want extenuating facts. It wanted a victim. Certain other interests, curbed by Sir Joseph in the matter of prices for munition contracts, wanted revenge. Under the old system of contracts these men had made a fairly good start at plundering the nation in its extremity. Between the long-suffering public, who thought they had a reason for hating Flavelle, and the profiteers who really had such a reason, Sir Joseph had an experience that would have tested any man's Christianity.

However, he made no protest ; did not resign his post or leave the country, but worked on. The time came when he could have said, "Et tu, Brute !" to men who with no record for helping the church or organizing to help humanity had profited far more prodigally than the Wm. Davies Co. But he kept silence. He believed in his conscience that the company buying hogs at competitive prices, and selling in a protected market was ethically A1 at Lloyds. He still believes so. His enthusiasm for the company has not waned. He admires it even to a point of emotion. The company was not his, but he had made it. From the day that William Davies drove to Flavelle's house in an old open buggy and asked him to sell out his provision business to manage the company, till the day it produced about 100 million pounds of bacon alone, in a year, he had been its energizing head. The Wm. Davies Co. was but the main thing from which he made his money. Its stock was not sold on the markets. There was never any need of capital except what came from the business conducted by Flavelle. There was no wit and philosophy in "The Letters of a Pork Packer to His Son" that could have instructed him in the shrewd business of making a great commercial concern out of a little business. His success in Canada was relatively equal to that of any Swift in Chicago. Multiply it by the ratio of population and see. In one year during the war the Wm. Davies Co. had a bacon output of forty million dollars.

But Flavelle never can be judged by bacon. He could have done as well at railways or banking or law. He did even better at munitions when there were no profits, not even a salary. He did as well at any other form of public service. No man can justly judge him by commercial success. He invested—himself—in everything to which he set his hand, with the one exception of the now defunct *Toronto News*, which he left to the management of other people. He invested the same self capital in the commercial concern and in public service.

Any patient who has been in the Toronto General Hospital will tell you what a wonderful institution it is. He may not know who made it possible, or whose genius for order and perfection of mechanism it expresses. Without Flavelle, Toronto, instead of one of the greatest hospitals in the world, would have had just a good hospital. Almost a village was pulled down to make room for it, on a site that would suit the medical needs of the University. It needed a strong will to put it there, against the opinions of other people ; a great hospital on the end of a slum ! The same will put the great "Methodist Book Room" where it is—against the wish of a majority.

Flavelle was Chairman of the Commission that reorganized the University of Toronto. He had no desire for the work. The late Goldwin Smith was already chairman, much disliking Flavelle for some editorial about him in the *Toronto News*. The old professor was feeble. The Commission asked Flavelle to replace him. He consented. If they thought he was the man, he was willing to do the work. And it was thoroughly done, so far as a business brain could direct the reconstruction of a concern in which business system is the anatomy, not the life.

No man could sit at a conference with Flavelle and not think hard ; or accept a duty from his committee and not discharge it. He demanded on behalf of the public—service. No man ever sat on a committee with him who had time for badinage. That man with the slow, high voice and the steady look was judging other men by results. Men came to believe that when there was a public task to perform, Flavelle was the man to take it. He was almost forced into service, often by the public indolence of other men. Canada has always played the professional grandstand method of getting things done for the public. Before the advent of Rotary and Kiwanis Clubs our two chief cities systematically advised the humble philanthropist without pull to go to such men as Flavelle, Edmund Walker, one of the Masseys, E. R. Wood, J. C. Eaton, Thomas Shaughnessy, Herbert Ames and F. S. Meighen—because these men were in the habit of doing or giving or organizing for the public interest, which is supposed to be a game for experts, not amateurs.

Flavelle's investment in things that made him no money was one of great ability, hard work and conscience. His returns on such capital were in the efficiency and usefulness of things which he had helped to create ; the need for which he had observed as clearly and calmly as ever he had foreseen the scope of a great business.

Yet for much of his life he has been a creature of impulse, powerfully attracted by things not in business. He left his seat once in a great Buffalo hall to stand at the door that he might judge the effect of a certain decrescendo from a choir. To a group of musical enthusiasts in Chicago he suddenly suggested a trip to the Cincinnati May Festival. Speaking to the boys of Upper Canada College, he drew from his pocket a piece of putty to illustrate the plasticity of character. Standing amid heaps of luggage at the docks in St. John, he looked at the immigrant sheds and said, "What a very human picture !" Pocketing the proof of an hospital article, which as proprietor of the *Toronto News* and Chairman of the Hospital Board he had withdrawn from publication, he said to the reporter, "Old man, a place of suffering should not be described in the language of the racetrack." When Pastor Wagner, author of "The Simple Life", was in Toronto, he was the guest of Mr. Flavelle, who for a time was as much absorbed in the peasant philosopher as he often was in the "Meditations" of Thomas á Kempis.

Considering these impulses to express himself, it is not hard to understand how Sir Joseph came to say to the Toronto Board of Trade that war profits should go to the hell to which they belonged. He was speaking under a sense of emotion. All through his enormously successful career he had been energized by a sudden enthusiasm to take hold of something, and afterwards to make it go. "Whatsoever thy hand findeth."

Flavelle's hand found many things. Among them was the *Toronto News*, his one recorded failure. This also was an impulse ; precisely the same as had led him years before to subscribe $5,000 to a fund for the better education of the Tory party. The *News* cost him one hundred times as much, for much the same reason on a larger scale ; and he lost it. But he has never regretted the loss, because he gained the experience. The *News* did a valuable work. But its rather Utopian resurrection had a sad sequel in Toryism such as Flavelle never could have endorsed, and its ultimate extinction seemed to prove that newspapers cannot be operated by ideals.

Again, reconstructing enthusiasm followed him to Ottawa. He went there at the instigation of the Imperial Government. Whether he himself made the original suggestion of the need, I do not know. But he obeyed the need when he saw it. Impulse drove him to meet it in

the greatest work of public organization ever done in so
short a time in this country, except the sending of the First
Contingent.

Flavelle had never liked Ottawa.   Ordinarily he had a
sort of contempt for its waste of time and its dissipation
of morality.   It is not conceivable that he would have
taken Munitions under any Canadian department.   Nor
was it necessary.   Canada was to produce munitions for
much more than the Canadian Army.

The work was vast and varied ; the man at the head
of it capable, exacting and impartial.   His sole aim was to
produce and to export munitions at a price high enough to
attract industry and low enough to prevent profiteering.
For three years he was the superman of Canada's industrial
fabric.   The C.M.A. and the Department of Trade became
mere annexes to munitions, at a time when Davies' bacon
clamoured for ship-room needed by Flavelle munitions.

Official Ottawa had never known a man like this.   He
was not popular.   The Government had no control of him.
Ottawa had never cared for super-men.   Flavelle was there
without politics.   He had a department greater than any
in the Administration.   He was never responsible to Parliament.   Ministers to him were not necessary.   He had
no favours to ask of members.   He never even looked in
at the Commons which he would like to have reformed.
People sometimes ask why such a man does not go into
Parliament.   Impossible.   He regards government as sheer
business, when it is often a passing show.   Foster's Business Conference that never met would have caused him to
discharge the department for incompetency.   Sir Thomas
White had no desire to lift his eyes unto the hill Flavelle,
the super-Minister who for years had been a critic of his
own party, and now believed it more inept than ever in
spite of the great work of the Finance Minister.   Sir Sam
Hughes had never wanted Flavelle.   There was a good
reason.   Sir Sam had started the munition industry in

Canada as a branch of war, not as a department of mere business. Flavelle was all business. War was business. There was the rub. The nearer the war came to a climax, the more men like Flavelle at home became part of the machinery. Foster never could have salaamed to this super-man of trade and commerce. Did even Sir Robert Borden ever feel comfortable with him ? Back from Europe in a fit of impulse more powerful than he had ever known, impressed by the success of Coalition in England, Sir Joseph wanted to see it established in Canada. The nation was united for munitions ; why not for national business ? The Premier was away in the West. Sir Joseph wired him asking permission to urge coalition at a certain public dinner. There was no response. Evidently the Government wanted no advice from a man who had nothing whatever to do with it and represented merely big business.

Something must have caused the Premier to treat Sir Joseph coolly. Afterwards at the bacon investigation there was cause for a change in temperature. The Premier had been negligent about some documentary evidence extenuating to the Flavelle presentation of the case. The two had warm words. Sir Joseph told the Premier one thing which, as it was repeated to me without reference to use in publication, had better be omitted here. But it was scathing. Sir Joseph is no mean master of the kind of language that hurts. But he has the Christian spirit— which in this case he laid aside. I should like to know what the Premier said to Sir Joseph ; and precisely what were the Premier's opinions, before and after, concerning the baronetcy.

In his quiet moments Sir Joseph does not rebuke himself more than he regrets the moral myopia of other people. I think he is somewhat disillusioned as to what it is worth to gain a good deal of the world at the risk of a lot of people thinking he has lost his soul. He does not believe that his soul was ever in danger of being lost. Often he goes to

rugby games. In this he sees again the virtue of struggle.
probably wishing he himself had played rugby in youth.

"When a man gets old," he said lately, "he loves to
sit at home."

But Sir Joseph, for all his whitening whiskers and his
impatience with the shortcomings and animosities of the
world, is not yet old. He has the strength of two men,
and a power of administration possessed by few men in
public office in any country. He has lost some of his
bubbling enthusiasm for the humanities. The last thing he
will lose must be his faith in himself : and that is very far off.

"Whatsoever thy hand findeth to do . . . ."

Sir Joseph Flavelle has yet a strong hand. What
remains that he will do with all his might ? If he so
desires, more of service on behalf of the public good in the
ten years he has left than many men accomplish in a
strenuous lifetime.

It is time we learned the difference between a public
pirate and an organizing servant of the public. Take away
from this man his public church business, his power to
make money, his human vanity over an hereditary title,
and we still have left the story of a big life, much of it spent
in doing good for the sake of other people. You cannot
efface that strange personality ; that desire after all the
admiration of his wonderful ability to administer him
mentally "one good swift kick." But you will never
mentally kick a man of such powerful good to his country.

NO FATTED CALVES FOR PRODIGAL SONS

HON. SIR HENRY DRAYTON

WERE I a novelist sketching a character for Henry Herbert Drayton I would have him, except in one item, just about all that he is not. He should be unmarried, live with his maiden aunt, most of his time make very little money and depend for his income upon winning about three good criminal prosecutions a year ; the rest of his time to be spent reading up criminal psychology and taking his aunt to see pictures. The commonplace scene-shifter who places behind people the scenery of real life has bungled Sir Henry, thereby robbing him of much interest. What a net a man with his classic patience and enormous ferret instinct for minutiæ could have woven about some cunning but once too often embezzler ! Instead we have Drayton, K.C., pushing himself methodically through a series of legal metamorphoses, at each change getting one convolution higher, by public corporation solicitorships and county attorneyships, burrowing into hydro-electric affairs for Toronto until he becomes Dominion Railway Commission chairman—seven years at that—and at last steps out into the full glare of undramatic notoriety by taking office as Minister of Finance in 1919.

Well, in that capacity he has rubber-stamped millions of people in the region of their pockets whom he would have missed altogether had he been taking his maiden aunt to the picture galleries between detective cases. Besides, he has three or four children, and I'm sure that when some lady writes the cinema of his life she will portray him as a hugely devoted papa with perfect young geniuses of children who yearn to spend papa's money upon the very luxuries against which he is warning the parents of other young people.

Once,—it was something to do with Niagara power—I heard Mr. Drayton weaving a dull dry web of apparently trivial evidence about some very important people. It seems to me that one William Mackenzie was a particular object ; if not he should have been. Once you admit that Drayton belongs to corporation instead of criminal law— though sometimes there's precious little difference— Mackenzie and Adam Beck are just the sort of audacious public-interest performers that a man like him should be after. He seemed to have an insatiable capacity for picking out little filaments of dry-as-dust technique from which on behalf of an impersonal client like the city of Toronto he could manage to inveigle a web of silk about any anti-civic despot who regards a city as a thing to be worked for dividends, and people merely as common economic dots and carry ones.

He impressed me then as a born Englishman. He had the neat, chiseled accents and the imperturbable air of a perfect gentleman, with a touch of nonchalance and the suggestion that if at the time of adjournment he had just got to the up stroke of a small "i", he could leave it there and come back to-morrow, beginning precisely where he had left off. But he was not born in England ; only educated there—which is something. A few more of our public men would be the better for a little Harrowing.

Once into public finance, Sir Henry does not propose to be a mere reverberation of Sir Thomas White. Never have we had two such drastic highwayman budgets as those which Drayton flung at the people in 1920 and 1921. From the tone of any supplementary remarks which he feels like making in order to amuse us while he lightens our pockets, it may be worse next year and thereafter unless we have a care. This man has never uttered a soothing phrase since he took office. He has made no attempt to furbelow our finances. He is not even concerned about the precise political effect of his taxes and tariffs. We never had a Finance Minister who so disregarded the Gladstonian principle, that if figures cannot lie they may at least make interesting romances of the truth. In the two years that he has been budgeteering, this dapper, tailored man with the sailor hat and the truculent jaw and the heavy outskirts to his eyes has treated a budget as though it were a Santa Claus stocking to be talked about a long while in advance, so that when it comes it may be all the more significant.

Such budgets as he gives us are not the work of a true Conservative. They bear no interesting bigotries of the party. They deal only secondarily with tariffs. I believe Sir Henry knows that most people regard a tariff as a very oblique way of reaching the pocket. People compute tariffs and argue about them. Only the farmers can make them into frightful realities. Nobody understands a tariff any-way when it comes to the schedule. Its chief use is for winning and losing elections.

But Sir Henry's admonishing finger goes up, and we are hushed to see what is the really cruel thing he intends to show us next, that will hurt just like a thumbscrew. He smiles and flips down a long scroll of—direct and drastic taxes quite shocking to contemplate.

"This is going to hurt you all, good people," he says. "But I may as well be honest about it. I am not a financial Christian Scientist. You will all feel better after you are properly hurt."

Thus far we remember chiefly how it hurt. We are still hoping to feel better.

Drayton had some grounding in practical finance long before he took any of the detail jobs that have had so much to do with computations and costs. We are reminded of a little episode of his early youth in Toronto.

Harry Drayton and Frank Baillie were schoolboys together. They lived on the same street. A neighbour was about to have an auction sale of his goods, but looking over the lot he made a present of a punching bag to Harry and Frank, no doubt because he foresaw that they would both have strenuous lives. The boys thanked him and took away the bag. On the way home Harry said to Frank :

"Do you really want a share in that punching bag ?"

"Not so keen as I might be," said Frank. "Why ?"

"Because he had something else I'd rather have. Remember that little printing press ?"

"Oh, what he uses to print calling cards on ?"

"How would you like to go snooks with me and get that, Frank ?"

"Well, it certainly would be swell to print our own calling cards, Harry."

"He wants $6.50 for it, though."

"Oh ! That's different. Here, let me sell the bag, anyhow. That'll be a start."

Frank, already budding into finance, sold the bag for one dollar and twenty-five cents.

"Well, we're still shy $5.25, Frank," said the coming Finance Minister of Canada.

"Yes, and it's your move, Harry."

"All right, I've got an idea. You wait."

Next day the sprouting financiers met, when Harry had a fine steel trout rod.

"See that, Frank ? Got that from dad. Made me a present of it—at my own suggestion. What is she worth ?"

"Don't you want to fish, Harry ?"

"Not if you can sell the rod."

Frank took it and looked it over.

"Sure !" he said. "I'll sell that for the company."

There being no guile in either of these young men, the sequel is that Frank sold the trout rod for $5.25 and Harry proudly took the entire $6.50 to the neighbour, paid for the press and had it taken home to his attic, where it must be presumed the two of them spent rainy days printing calling cards for Draytons and Baillies.

Canada took very little interest in Drayton till he came to be Chairman of the Railway Commission. But by that time the said Commission was no longer the grand court it had been in the days of J. Pitt Mabee. It settled more disputes than ever and settled them as well as ever. Drayton had almost twice the mileage to cover that Mabee had in 1903. He did it with tireless exactitude. He was less concerned with the ethical issues at stake in decisions between railways and communities than with the unethical fact of such a prodigal lot of lines having been built at all to give trouble to the nation We were just getting to the end of the race of the railroads, when thousands of foreigners had been dumped into the country with shovel and pick, and thousands of miles of new railway built that would shortly be a charge on the country.

An able writer a few years ago wrote a series of articles in a Canadian publication headed, "Is there a Railway Muddle?" Being himself a railwayman he seemed to think that the muddle, if any, was chargeable to conditions over which the railways had little or no control.

Mr. Drayton, shrewdly traversing the network of those prodigally built railways, felt no need of asking any such question. He carried on into the slump in business, and on into the war when the Railway War Board, practising a sort of church union by cutting out competition and re-routeing traffic for the sake of getting war haulage done as quickly as possible, left very little for the Drayton court to settle. But there was a bigger settlement to come later, and Drayton was to have a hand in it.

As Chairman of the Commission he never made a statement that was good for a headline, or coined an epigram, or lost his temper, or spluttered into print. But on a certain occasion, before retiring from the Commission, Sir Henry put on record a number of things that the people of this country read with acute and sustained interest. This was the report of the Smith-Drayton-Acworth Commission for the purpose of finding out whether the Canadian Northern and the Grand Trunk Pacific could ever manage to pay their own debts, including interest on multi-millions borrowed from abroad, or whether, debts and all, they should be handed over to the people of Canada ?

During the war this nation had many commissions. Their very names are mostly forgotten. Most of them committed themselves to nothing. This commission to investigate railroad bankruptcy was fated to be very different. Much of the difference was in Sir Henry Drayton who, had he been asked the question, might have saved the country the cost of the Commission.

But of course he was prejudiced, and against the roads. He knew those roads. The minority report of the chief of the New York Central made no difference to the grim bulldog judgment of the Chief Railway Commissioner— that the two secondary systems of Canadian railways were alike and for much the same causes constitutionally bankrupt, and should therefore be given the nationalizing cure.

What more disagreeable qualification could a man have for being made Minister of Finance ? The air holes that White had skated around, Drayton proposed to go right over and to take the people with him. What the common stock of these roads might be worth was for Sir Thomas to find out. By the time Sir Henry went to the national ledger that matter was all adjusted and the thing left was to raise the money.

There's a divinity that shapes our ends even when they do not meet. The little Houdini of calculations was at last into a predicament where it seemed that he never could figure himself out. One fancies him gazing intently over the Finance Department of whose precise technique he knew nothing as yet, and saying to himself :

"Well, White did a wonderful turn. I don't believe the

audience will like mine half as well—at first. No audiences ever do. I'm bound to be more or less unpopular because I don't know how to act a bit like Tetrazzini."

The great organized orgy was over, when the dollars followed the drum and the drum thumped at every cross-road ; when a Victory Bond in every top commode drawer was more necessary than a bottle in every cellar. The whole nation, four times tagged for Victory, was once more tagged for reconstruction. Done with credits to England for purchase of war material in Canada, we were invited to extend credits to war-swept nations in Europe who would be sure to want things made in Canada to help put them on President Wilson's new map of self-determination. Even profiteers now admitted everything to be abnormal. The whole country was like a milkfed pumpkin at the fair. War wages inclined every man to become a profiteer. The land was teeming with war money and denuded of necessary goods. People who used to be content with good wages, a plain rented home and a bottle of beer, went out after short hours, high wages, French heels, $300 coats and motor-cars. It was part of the emancipation of people for which soldiers had not died.

"Er—if you need me, telephone, old chap," one fancies Sir Thomas saying as he carried Sir Henry's luggage to his room. "But I'm sure you are the man for the job. I really have to go back to private finance. However, the super-tariff on imports of luxuries is one thing with which you will feel at home, I am sure. Quite suited to your temperament, Sir Henry."

In one of Scott's novels a gentleman named Front de Boeuf pulls out a Jew's tooth every time he wants more money. Both our national dentists knew that a super-tariff on anything is the very thing that makes a large number of well-to-do people want it. People bought luxuries in this country and growled at the high cost of necessities. Most folk feel rather proud of a big price for a coat or a gown or a Chesterfield, if they can get even by skimping on the price of butter and potatoes. Low-value money and visions of Utopia had played far worse havoc with the people than legalized liquor had ever done. And one of the worst features of the situation was that the bulk of our luxury buying was done in the country which had the only remaining standard of value on the exchanges. Canada had convenient access to the country which alone had a surplus of factory goods. Our tremendous buying average in the American market was even used as propaganda in the interest of keeping the peace with Britain.

Hence the devil of exchange and Drayton's dilemma. The things Drayton said to this country even before he presented his first budget were as comfortable as what the doctor prescribes when you are overfed. On went the unpopular luxury tax and sales tax. The general principle was that the more people bought, the more they got out of living, and the more they should pay for the privilege. It was not merely a tax on improvements, but an impost on being alive. Accustomed as we had been to war taxes which never came off, this was a sanctioned way of "passing the buck" such as we had never known. The advantage is that when we pay 14 cents for a box of matches that used to cost five cents, we can read "5 cents War Excise Tax Paid" on the wrapper.

Sir Henry Drayton had no superb suavity with which to beguile those who made complaints. He heard the howlings of all the babies in the national dormitory and went ahead. He did not impress us as a financier, but as a plain doctor of homely common sense. He said in public many things which threw much instructive light upon our buying and selling. He spoke some blunt but kindly truths even in the United States at whose supremacy in our markets his policy was aimed.

"The men who save the world," says *The Onlooker*, "are those who work by rule of thumb ; who do the day's

work by the day's light and advance on chaos and the painful dark by inches ; in other words, the practical men."

Such a motto might be Drayton's crest. He is very
practical ; too much so to be an interesting personality
to the average man. But by his dull and diligent practi-
cality he has done rather more than his bit in helping to
re-establish Canada. He would, if he could, cut our
imports from the United States in half in order to rectify
exchange. Whenever he dies the Canadian $ par on
exchange will be found graven upon his heart.

Drayton's tariff tour was one of the most characteristic
things he ever did   In this, however, there may have been
an element of politics. A travelling tariff commission
taking evidence in almost every village with a smokestack
from coast to coast must have had some real object. But
Sir Henry had cleaned up most of the possibilities in direct
taxation ; it was time he tackled the tariff, even though he
knew it was largely a show to satisfy the people that the
most patient investigator in the world at the head of a small
court had taken evidence on what every Tom and Dick
had to say for and against in any part of the country outside of the Yukon. Had it been practicable to hold a session
on Great Bear Lake, to determine the trade relations between the copper-kniving Eskimos and the meat-swapping
Yellow Knife Indians, Sir Henry would have done it.

Such vast patience is phenomenal even in Drayton.
One almost fears that he is becoming interested in a Federal
election. If so, the end is in sight. The day we partyize
Sir Henry we shall lose one of the oddest and rarest personal
identities we ever had. But we can better afford to lose
his personal identity in his party service than to lose both
in putting into the Finance Department in 1922 some
idealistic experimenter in the efficacy of Free Trade.

M

THE PERSONAL EQUATION IN RAILROADING

EDWARD WENTWORTH BEATTY, K.C.

THE main thing that E. W. Beatty, K.C., did to help win the war was to become President of the C.P.R. And he did it well. A glance at this polished pony engine of a chief executive suggests that he has never done anything but well, and that he is the kind of man likely without preachments to stimulate well-doing in other people.

I first met this self-controlled master of executives not long after he became President. He was most cordial ; as Shaughnessy had been austere. Under such a direct impression it seemed that I had at last found a man who would make the inexorable old C.P.R. become a golden door to humanity. Of course I was mistaken. That kind of man is born often enough, but he seldom stays with his birthright. I knew that the railway of railways was no school for the humanities ; but this university graduate, Chancellor of Queen's, distinguished counsel and potential eminent judge, bachelor, Canadian born, every inch an athlete and as rugged as Carpentier, seemed to my aroused imagination one who would be as much bigger than the stodgy C.P.R. as that system was greater than others of its kind.

Beatty has not been at his new job long enough yet to prove what I suspect—that I was wrong. But he has been long enough with it to know that the surging ideals and aspirations of a young, healthy man in his own office are pretty rudely shaken down by the practical operation of a great system in a time of financial difficulty.

194

We talked for nearly an hour. He seemed to have the time and the interest. His big office was as quiet as a library. His desk was almost devoid of signs of labour. Not a paper to be seen that required immediate attention ; every item neatly disposed ; himself smoking—a fairly strong pipe ; scarcely a telephone call to interrupt. He seemed the sculptor's embodiment of strength in reserve ; a man who never could be tuckered or peevish or unable to detect either the weakness of an opponent, the penetration of a critic or the need of a man who came to ask him for advice. There was a big instant kindliness about him that would have won the cordiality of the stolidest of interviewers, as we talked about railways, government ownership, the needs of journalism and the value in business of the personal equation—his own phrase which he repeated so often that it seemed to contain something of prophetic intention. He paid his venerating respects to the founders of the C.P.R., but he seemed to have more enthusiasm for Lord Mountstephen than for Van Horne.

I heard him say some strong, sincere things about the uselessness of rich men who would sooner use their money on the gratification of vanity than upon public service. He meant that. He repeated such things at various interviews. In doing so he proved that he himself had always made a god of very hard work, discipline and self-denial, for the sake of giving his own personality a square deal, without regard to the money he could make. He had the strength and he used it. As solicitor and chief counsel he became almost a machine to win cases for the railway. He must win, and know how to lose. Fighting a corporation's battles is a good way to believe that the system can do no wrong. But I don't think Beatty was ever blind to the native defects of the C.P.R.

Railroading is a great university of character. Nothing else in our practical affairs attracts such a variety of men. None of our railwaymen have climbed to the peak of the railway operation business quite so successfully and so Canadianly as E. W. Beatty. Most other transportation magnates we have imported from either Scotland or the United States. This one is Canadian from his cradle up. He embodies the best characteristics of the average Canadian in a very high degree. He is an amateur athlete whom hard work has never been known to make weary. At the end of any perfect day of hard work he has as much strength in reserve as he had in the morning when he came to it. Even in his talk he wastes never a word, states everything clearly and in forcible language, but is seldom curt at the expense of courtesy. He does not talk like any big American executive whose equal or superior he may be in administration. He copies nobody. The day's work has always been his exemplar. He has no desire for mere personal success. Years ago he could have made more money by exporting his brains to the United States. But he preferred Canada where he has made less money, justly earned more fame, and where he can continue to do more work that counts for efficiency in himself and in other people. He is the kind of man—like Arthur Meighen—who inspires other men to go in with him on a heavy task to get it done in a big way.

Beatty's type of mind, though somewhat dry and legal and at times judicial, is also capable of an immensely quiet enthusiasm that transmits itself to other people. He invites discussion, but not familiarity. Not personally careful just to maintain traditions, he profoundly respects the men who created them—and goes ahead to transact business now, and to hand out decisions immediately, that get to-day ahead of yesterday and as near as possible to the day after. He believes in the square deal in action and in the high common sense of a decision. There is no public question upon which his opinion might not be sanely valuable, though one would never expect him to succeed as a leader in politics. As a business reorganizer of McGill

University he is bound to consider a college as a "going concern". As Chancellor of Queen's, he upsets all traditions as to the dignity of pure scholarship.

It seemed like a long stride from being Chief Railway Counsel to becoming Chief Executive. But to his practical personality the stride was only a step. On an average this is no lawyer's job. Judges in the United States can preside over big corporations. The chief executive of the C.P.R. works. He must know the system, its men, its technique. Railroading is a complex of specialities. A good president must enter into the spirit of the man who builds a locomotive and of one who constructs a timetable.

It fell to this first Canadian President that the road ever had to shoulder a load which would have made the wizard Van Horne read up Hercules. Beatty holds the record for getting through with a programme that would have puzzled either of his two eminent predecessors in that office. Shaughnessy at the same age might have done it. Van Horne never. Yet Beatty never could have built the C.P.R. His brain has no wizardry in it. He is a co-ordination of facts that knows not the meaning of magic. He is the most matter-of-fact man in any high executive position in Canada. The task he undertook was all cut out for him. Fate decreed that he should take it. He never dreamed of refusing. And what a task !

The greatest trouble Beatty had to face when he became President was too much traffic, too little rolling stock, an almost tragic scarcity of labour and the McAdoo award in wages. Railroading costs were at an apex before even munitions costs began to be. The collapse of railways in the United States drove a vast amount of traffic over Canadian roads. The two younger transcontinental systems were on the verge of receiverships. The brunt of the burden fell upon the old C.P.R., which at that time, in spite of the McAdoo awards was making a heavy profit. The cash value of traffic handled was colossal. War work

was wearing the railways down. New locomotives and
cars were hard to get. Orders could not be placed outside.
Canada's railways had to depend on Canada. Ships could
not wait, though submarines could. Freight must move.
Two hard winters nearly paralyzed all the systems. No
new lines were being built. The old lines were wearing out.
Canada had the longest hauls of any nation in the world.
Our systems were built for the long haul. The railway
systems of other countries were demoralized with wastage,
low repairs and enormous traffic. Even in short-haul
England of the easy climate, there was railway paralysis.
But England had great gasoline highways and coastal routes
when Canada had neither. It is said in a report of that
period, "General Superintendents in charge of some of the
"key" divisions of the big roads have had to work from
12 to 20 hours a day to keep roadbed, rolling stock and
crews up to top mark." 22,000 Canadian cars were "lost"
in the United States in one winter. What war left of the
railways winter did its best to debilitate. Industry stole
transportation labour at high wages and rolled out vast
quantities of material that had to be moved, when even
C.P.R. efficiency seemed to be just about obliterated from
the chart of the world's work.

This was no time for any man to pray that he might be
made chief executive of the greatest transportation system
in the world ; nor a time for Lord Shaughnessy to continue
in that office. The work was now too heavy for the
autocrat and for a man whose eyesight was bad. A successor had to be found. The directors did it almost automatically. There was but one man to consider ; and he
had no experience in any of the mechanical departments.

Beatty was the man. The old autocrat himself had
said so ; and he knew. Shaughnessy had taken the road
from its wizard creator, and made it the size and efficiency
that it was. There was almost apostolic succession.
Stories that the Montreal directors favoured one man, the

Toronto directors another, and that Shaughnessy gave the casting vote, were mere fabrications. Yet Beatty stated that never in his long years of experience with the system had he a clear ambition to climb up its ladder. He never wanted anything but a large day's work—and he got many. But, when he was made Vice-President, he must have known that he was the man. Vice-Presidents on the C.P.R. are not necessarily presidents to be. One of Beatty's friends travelling with him up from Three Rivers once bought him a picture postcard with the legend, "No mother ever picks her son to be a Vice-President." Beatty smiled it off. He probably knew. This was one of the rare bits of humour that illustrated the Shaughnessy regime. His lordship, fond enough of Irish jokes outside, was never humourous inside the system. All the humour in Canadian Pacific was supposed to have died when Van Horne left it.

But now and again a gleam of human insight came from the grim efficiency of the great system, and at least upon one occasion it flashed from the legal department. When the Railway Commission was almost a new thing under that remarkable square-deal chairman, Joseph Pitt Mabee, the town of Trois Rivieres, Que., had a suit, through its Board of Trade, against the C.P.R., involving discrimination in rates. The counsel for the plaintiff was a French-Canadian who could read, but not comfortably speak, English. The further he went the more bewildered the chairman became, until he ventured to interrupt :

"I have a suggestion to make to my hon. friend who is having difficulty in getting me to understand the case."

The suggestion was that the solicitor for the railway, who had made a special study of the Board of Trade's argument for the sake of demolishing it, should himself present that side of the argument in the clear, concise English of which he is a master ; that wherever necessary the French counsel should correct the statement ; and that afterwards Mr. Beatty should proceed to demolish the argument which he himself had put up. The counsel was agreeable. Mr. Beatty rose to the occasion. His statement of the case was so satisfactory to the counsel for Trois Rivieres that he afterwards wondered how Beatty was ever able to demolish it and win the case.

Beatty has no hobbies. He cares for no art, collects no curios, has no great house, drives no big cars ; cares not at all for society ; thinks more of the Amateur Athletic Association and the Navy League and the boys of the Y.M.C.A., the athletic equipment of Queen's University and the success of Sir Arthur Currie as President of McGill. He never travels for pleasure. When he goes over the C.P.R., expect results. The average Montrealer does not even know where he lives. He is said to spend forty minutes a day, indoor weather, at basketball. In summer he camps. Snapshotted in a sweater he looks like a compromise between Babe Ruth batting a home run and Hofmann playing the piano.

When Beatty was first a young lawyer in Montreal he was so lonesome for the city he came from that he used to go down to the station to see the Toronto train pull in. He did not dream then that some day he would be the man that pulls all the trains in ; that from his desk he should have a periscope on the world—every day—the greatest intelligence department in America. When he was a school lad in Thorold, afterwards at the Upper Canada "Prep." (where he got so bad a report that his father was advised to take him out of school), he had no idea that he would be Chancellor of Queen's University.

The system and the man. Determining which most affects the other is like the old problem of the hen and the egg. But here, anyhow, is a great system. No man venerates it more than Beatty. He does not even consent to call it a corporation ; prefers to think of it as an association, imbued with enthusiasm and loyalty. Now and then he publicly discusses national ownership ; none can do it better. He did it at Thorold soon after he was appointed. He argued it in Ottawa with Cabinet Ministers. He did it in Winnipeg. One suspects that Beatty's ability to do this was one of his qualifications for the presidency.

A year before Beatty became president a man high up in the system predicted that the C.P.R. would spend a million dollars to campaign against Bolshevism. He failed to foresee that the stolid old bulwark of things as they are would never need to do any such thing. All it needed to spend was Beatty who, within six months of the time he changed the sign on his door, had convinced the system that a sort of new optimistic vitality had got hold of it. There was once a cynical proverb around those offices : "It's cheaper to buy editors than newspapers." One hears very little of it now. The annual meeting of the Directors may be fine copy for the *Montreal Gazette*, but the yearly banquet of the officials is a matter of real public interest, especially to the young President. There is a psychology in this—"association"—that is not a corporation. How does he gauge it ? From the officials. He does not visit the Angus shops ; though if he did he would be welcome. It was an old axiom of Van Horne that what the head is, so also will the system be. Beatty extends the axiom—to include the officials. He would have them radiate optimism, not particularly caring that they get it from him.

For the past two years optimism has been needed. C.P. reports are not what they used to be. Even the stock exchanges tell the tale. But in comparison with American lines, with other Canadian systems—ah ! here is always some comfort. Trust Beatty to miss no chance of intimating that he would much prefer to have real competition from Government roads. He fervently hopes for Government ownership to succeed. C.P. cannot thrive on weak competition. He has no fear that any sane Government will try absorbing the C.P.R. Even farmers, he thinks, would soon settle down to a sense of responsibility. The old pioneer is a hard organization to make into a tail that does not wag the dog. Steadily he has advertised to the public that the system is still the handbook of efficiency ; let Government roads imitate. National ownership, being impersonal, somewhat Bolshevistic, and very vague, cannot develop the intensive "super-loyalty" of the big private system vested in a board of directors, and the chief.

Since ever he became chief Beatty has made this clear ; for a purpose. Did I omit to say that he is the first C.P.R. president without whiskers ; the first with a college degree ; the first Canadian born, the first lawyer, the first bachelor and the first man from Toronto who had occupied that position ; the youngest of all the presidents ; that he used to be an expert at college Rugby ; that at Upper Canada "Prep." he was much addicted to pugilism ; not to mention the discarded tilt of his Fedora? If so it is because the man himself sets no value on these things. His faith is in the collective personality, called the Canadian Pacific, built up on the Personal Equation.

But Ottawa—what of that ? Almost ever since Ottawa was, the C.P.R. has been said to own it. Governments of either party have never been inhospitable to the benign octopus—centipede it became—that had its origin in the Parliament of Canada and wrecked one Tory Government. The penalty of transcontinental railways is that they require to have mortgages on governments. Presently the worm turns. But that usually costs more money than the mortgage. We are now paying off the mortgages of two great systems. The C.P.R. mortgage was paid long ago. The President of the C.P.R. is usually regarded as second only to the Premier in point of national management. But Premiers and governments come and go ; the President stays on. Suppose that in the year 19—— there should be a Cabinet mainly of farmers. Alberta has a farmer government. Saskatchewan with a "Liberal" government has a Cabinet mainly of farmers. Manitoba sometimes has to remind herself that Premier Norris is a kind of farmer.

Ontario has a farmer Premier and more than half a Cabinet of farmers.

This is the age of the farmers' innings. Suppose that a Cabinet of super-Agriculturists at the Capital some day should not agree with Mr. Beatty that farmers when they get responsibilities measure up and settle down to conservatism. Such a Cabinet might not remember that the C.P.R. had really done so very much for the prairies in comparison with what it has got from the West. It might decree that a lawyer President should be called upon to elucidate why he judges that so efficient a Personal Equation as the C.P.R. should not be "nationalized", if not government-owned, for the good of the whole people, and especially of the people whose traffic creates most of the revenues ?

This is merely supposing. In any case Mr. Beatty would be master of the occasion. The lawyer who argued against himself and won at Three Rivers might be able to put up a more convincing argument to Ottawa Farmers than Lord Shaughnessy did to the Union Government when he offered to amalgamate the C.P.R. with the Government roads providing the management should be C.P.R. and the dividends guaranteed.

But of course this is a merely hypothetical argument. There may never be a Farmer Administration in Ottawa. And if there ever should be, we may trust to conservative and progressive old C.P.R. to do its share of injecting a "sense of responsibility" into a Farmer Cabinet to help it measure up and settle down, even if some farmer should buy C.P. shares enough to get himself elected as a director. As it stands to-day in the estimation of the travelling public, who may or may not care a copper about the personality of its rugged and efficient lawyer president, the Canadian Pacific is the one greatest proof that Canada needs no revolution which will interfere with the morale of that system. In fact so long as the C.P.R. holds its own an economic revolution in Canada is impossible.

A BOURGEOIS MASTER OF QUEBEC

Sir Lomer Gouin

Early in January, 1917, a remarkable dinner was held in
Toronto, the first of its kind ever held in that city of
Orange Walks. Protestants and Catholics sat side by side.
They applauded the same sentiments. Orator after orator
dug into the mines of national idioms. They cracked
jokes and told stories and worked up climaxes. The three
hundred rose again and again with glasses of orangeade,
and Apollinaris, toasting—Quebec, Ontario, and United
Canada. They waved napkins and cheered and sang again
and again "For he's a jolly good fellow". A Methodist
minister sat at the back of the room next a Congregationalist
preacher and pretended to unwrap a *de luxe* cigar. Orangemen sat at the same table with Catholics. Macs hob-
nobbed with 'eaus. They autographed one another's
menus. The books of songs were bilingual—French and
English. "God Save the King" was sung in both languages. "O Canada" was done in French. Methodist
orators vied with French speakers. Col. George Denison
sat next Gen. Lessard. They fraternized as soldiers. The
Methodist local-preacher Premier of Ontario sat with the
Roman Catholic Premier of Quebec. Sentiment ran high.
But no French-Canadian was so emotional as N. W.
Rowell, who glorified the heroes of Courcellette ; and no
Anglo-Canadian was quite so stolid, serious and impressive
with homely common sense as Sir Lomer Gouin, the Premier
of Quebec. This man spoke slowly, massively, almost
gutturally like a Saxon, in fluent but accented English.

He was far less excitable than the Premier of Ontario on the same subject :

THE RACE UNITY OF CANADA

PREFIGURED IN

THE BONNE ENTENTE

Three hundred public-spirited men of whom eighty came from Quebec were as one family on this.

At one in the morning the concomity broke up. Not a drop of *vin* or *liqueur* in any form had been served. The enthusiasm was, therefore, as natural as the tide of the St. Lawrence, which in the form of the great lakes and Niagara does its best to put its arms round the neck of Ontario before it cuts through the heart of Quebec. To the pure imagination it was somewhat as though a procession of St. Jean Baptiste had suddenly dreamed it was an Orange Walk.

This unusual Entente was held between the rancours of the bilingual dispute of 1916 and the Quebec revolt against conscription in 1917. Those present who doubted the sincerity of passionate speakers anchored a timidly steadfast hope to the practical, broad-angled Premier of Quebec, who, had he sat between Mr. Bourassa and the Premier of Ontario, would have inclined his ear to Ontario.

Nothing is more certain than that four French-Canadian leaders, had they been given or had they asked for the opportunity and had acted together, could have put a different face on Quebec's relation to the war. Four men namable in that capacity are, Sir Lomer Gouin, Sir Wilfrid Laurier, Ernest Lapointe, and Cardinal Begin. Of these, Gouin was at that time the most able. For ten years he had been uninterruptedly Premier of Quebec with a moral guarantee that he could occupy the Premiership by an overwhelming majority until he should be gathered to his fathers.

Again and again rumour slated Sir Lomer for Ottawa. He wisely declined. He had a peasant's attachment to "le pays" and its white villages. In Quebec he was the Chief of Ministers, the little elected father of his country. In Ottawa he would have been perhaps a grand Minister of Public Works building docks in Halifax, customs houses in British Columbia, post-offices on the prairies, armouries in Ontario and court-houses in Quebec. Yes, there would be surely armouries in Ontario.

I met Sir Lomer but once, in his office in the Parliament Buildings. There was no particular reason for seeing him except the pleasure of encountering a descendant of the people who so gallantly fought under Montcalm so that posterity could enjoy a city in part exclusively English and for the most part idiomatically French. A few evenings previous I had talked on the Terrace to a glowing National-ist, a young expert in cynical idealism, who spoke very curtly about the Premier. An ardent patriot, he talked freely and interestingly, as we gazed out at the blue-hazed domes of the noble hills that mark the valley of St. Lawrence. The roofs of Old Lower Town were sizzling in heat. Drowsy, lumber-laden bateaux and ocean-liners crept and smoked about the docks. Beyond the grey-scarped citadel the vesper bells of parish after parish clanged a divine discord into the calm of the great river.

"What do you think of Gouin ?" I asked him.

A cynical smile flicked over the Nationalist's face. For a moment he did not answer.

"Pardonnez-moi," I mumbled. "I am Anglais."

"Oh !" he said, sharply, laughing. "Have you seen the Montcalm suite in the Chateau here ? Do so. The C.P.R. discovered an old bed and some creaky chairs said to have been used by the great general. They placed them in a suite of rooms which they rent to curiosity-hunting Americans who sentimentalize over history at twenty-five dollars a day. Such is Quebec when she is commercialized into a highway for tourists."

"But what has that to do with Sir Lomer Gouin ?"

"Directly—nothing. Sir Lomer is not even a director of the C.P.R., or of the Bank of Montreal, though one never knows what he may do with his money and his talents when he gets tired of manipulating elections."

"Oh, you mean that Gouin—does not reflect the idealism of Quebec ; its love of the land that bore our fathers, its poetic isolation among the provinces——? "

He blew a shaft of cigarette smoke.

"Sir Lomer," he said, "is Chairman of the Board of Directors of the Province of Quebec. His chief duty is to go about inspecting and improving properties and to sit at directors' meetings declaring provincial dividends instead of deficits."

I remarked that since Quebec is so prosperous and so large and populous with so many cradles, the Premier need not perhaps vex himself deeply about ideals such as the French language in schools outside the province.

"What !" was the reply, as a glass banged upon the table. "Would you cage us in here like Indians on a reservation ? Has the French-Canadian nation no rights outside Quebec ?"

"What would you do ?" I asked him. "What could you do ?"

"Secede !" he exclaimed. "Become the Sinn Fein of Canada."

"What about the Pope of Rome ?"

"Has as much to do with Quebec," he laughed icily, "as the President of France. If the Pope should issue instructions to the bishops of Quebec, asking the clergy to educate the people of Quebec on their duty to go to war or to vote for either of the old line parties, the people would openly disregard them. We would as much resent the interference of Rome in our affairs as the American colonies did the tyranny of George the Third."

Here was the superb inconsistency of the French mind wedded to a single magnificent idea. This Nationalist admitting the possibility of secession, made sure that it would not be to the United States which puts the French language on a par with Choctaw.   When I suggested as a recipe for national unity that French and English be learned by both English and French all over Canada, he flouted the idea of French-Canadians learning more English than they needed in business, and of English-Canadians learning French at all.   He fervently held to the Keltic notion of making a preserve of the French-Canadian race, language, literature and customs whatever may become of the religion ; yet he objected to penning the race into a reservation like the Indians.   He observed that in 1911 the Nationalists bucked reciprocity with the United States.

"I think we should become an independent republic," he said as he plopped a fresh cigarette.   "We have the main part of the St. Lawrence.   No, you will not find Gouin say so.   Gouin is a Tory prefect.   He plays politics, not nationalism."

I observed that the band was about to play.

"Ha !" he exclaimed, stretching his legs with a yawn. "And the concert will conclude with that amiable farce, 'O Canada,' followed by 'God Save the King.' "

This Nationalist interview is given at some length because it illustrates much of what Sir Lomer Gouin is not, and if he were would not openly say so, because he stands for a majority the watchword of which is "Stop, Look, Listen".   I went at once to see the Premier.   He was closeted with confiding—perhaps confederate—priests, and with simple habitant folk who stood, not in awe but in affection, of the Premier.   He might have been himself a father confessor.

Talking to him I found Gouin peculiarly on his guard ; broad-faced, heavy-jawed, slow of speech, almost devoid of gesticulation, he was as unamiably dispassionate as a bank manager.   There was no militant passion of the

minority in this man ; no heroic tilting against windmills ;
no expression of ideals ; no suggestion of a delightful
outlaw. He was amazingly practical, with no inclination
to discuss freely the native peculiarities of either race. He
understood Ontario—as a politician only ; England as a
democracy and a form of government. He had no absorbing
idiosyncracies and made no attempt to pose or even to
be interesting. After the bounce of the young Nationalist
he was as tame as a grandfather's clock.

I felt that Sir Lomer was asking himself—what did the
stranger want ? He would have been infinitely more at
ease discussing with a bishop how to prevent a strike in a
cotton mill ; or with a political outposter what to do to
keep some seat for the Administration. If I had made
to him such a statement as once I had made with such
volcanic results to Bourassa, that nine-tenths of the population in a village like Nicolet could speak no *Anglais*, he
would have been eloquent. Had I observed that 70 per
cent of the operatives in a great Quebec industry cannot
read and write French, that Ontario has a policy of good
roads comparable to that of Quebec, that Orangemen do
not dominate Toronto, that the Ontario farmer is a better
producer than the habitant, or that Protestant clerics do
not interfere in politics, he would have bristled with information to set me profoundly right. But he created no
atmosphere of free discussion with a stranger. He was
coldly aloof, yet earnestly endeavouring to say something
worth while.

What I really wanted to tell Gouin was that he was
personally very much like the late great Tory, Sir James
Whitney. But he did not warm up to personal comment.
The bilingual question was too complicated. The atmosphere of the Bonne Entente was lacking. Gouin and myself were in different envelopes. He was the Premier.

From what is said of him I am sure most of the fault
was my own. I did not understand him. He was too

much the Premier ; the master executive. The Nationalist
was almost right ; Gouin suggested the dividend and the
census.   He was the chief executive of a Province larger
than almost any country in Europe but Russia, and with a
population about half that of Roumania, of whom about
one-sixth are the Anglo-Saxon minority.   He seemed to
know Quebec from Montreal to the edge of Labrador
almost by telegraph poles.   You recall that the French in
Canada evolved the modern census with its intimate penetration into the affairs of the people, some time before the
Germans did it.   The Premier of Quebec was a handbook
encyclopaedia of Quebec.   He knew the precise location by
the roads of almost any white village, pulp-mill, water-
power, mine, timber limit ; knew as much as a man can
about the number of horses and cattle and cradles to a
township ; could talk with enthusiasm about the pioneer
arts of the habitant—the rugs, the baskets, the furniture,
the hand-made churns, the open-air bake-ovens. He
could give the address and the full name of many and many
a priest.

But beyond this there is a Quebec which Sir Lomer
Gouin did not know, because he himself with his *bourgeois*
excellences and his great good citizenship has not the
Gallic sparkle in his mentality.   He never deeply knew the
soul of Quebec.   He was too much concerned with its
practical and useful politics to be conscious of its passions.
From the shrug of his shoulder, and a certain twinkle in his
eye when he mentioned diplomacy with clerics, one surmised
that among the clergy he was the master among politicians
who must walk warily.   But he was too stout, too thrifty,
too much of a high type of budgeteer to be spiritually
informed of the crude but basically beautiful passions that
undercurrent all peasant communities.   There was no
poetry in Gouin.   No fire.   Little imagination.

"Those Nationalists ?" he repeated shrewdly, slowly.
"Yes, I know their talk.   Oh, they are not so dangerous,

but a troublesome minority. I think—I know Quebec
better than they do. You have, I daresay, Nationalists
in Ontario ?''

What he perhaps expected was some statement about
Orangemen, who of course are nearly all Imperialists. Yet
these very Orangemen represent an intense phase of Canadian life ; the backwoods era, the simple industries, the
old villages, the quaint settlements of the U.E. Loyalists
as picturesque on the Upper, as the dormer-windowed
villages of the French are on the Lower St. Lawrence. To
these men the Empire is as visual, as to the intense Quebecker it is nebulous. And as the politician in Ontario
has to regard carefully the Orange vote, so the Premier of
Quebec had to be wary of the franchises of his emotional
friends, the Nationalists. He was somewhat afraid of the
minority as all masters of majorities are. Clearly—it was
Gouin's main business to continue being elected. Had he
gone out on behalf of enlistments, to educate his people,
even to speak for France, he would have been in danger of
converting Gouin Liberals into Nationalists.

Ontario cannot fail to make an asset of Gouin's anti-
Nationalism. He was never for any of the violent doctrines
propounded by my friend on the Terrace. He would not
oppose Quebec going to war. I am sure he God-speeded
the 22nd who died at Courcellette. He was the Premier
of a free Province. Those men had freely gone. Others—
the majority—had freely stayed. But an election was
coming ; where everybody would be free to vote.

Then there were the clergy ; most of them friends of
Gouin. The Cardinal at Quebec had been interviewed by
Sir Sam Hughes on aid to enlistments. Gouin could have
told Hughes that he would fail ; that Begin, though not a
Nationalist, was a reactionary. The bilingual controversy
was still acute. Gouin could not have gone out or sent
emissaries out, to reason with French-Canadians about
marching with a Province which had denied the French

language rights in contrast to the Government's own claim that it had given rights to the Anglo minority in Quebec.

Conscription was coming. It was a precarious time. The master of Quebec had to move cautiously. His loyalty to Britain was never questioned. His faith in a United Canada was never doubted. Had Quebec been all for Gouin instead of Gouin all for Quebec, the Premier's way would have been easier. Better let well enough alone ; encourage those to enlist who really wanted to go—because Quebec was a free country.

Then there was the Laurier influence. Had the old man gone in with the Premier to help the Ottawa Government— Impossible. Neither of them was asked before Coalition came on the heels of conscription. And when conscription came, the minority of Nationalists opposed to the war became the majority of Quebeckers who preferred not to comply with the law. From disregarding the law to rebellion, to Nationalism was not far. Gouin had the balance to hold.

The Cardinal's attitude on conscription made Gouin's position still more difficult. His letter to the press bluntly put the Roman Catholic Church above temporal law. One heard of no rebuke from the Premier of Quebec to the Cardinal. A Cardinal may be above politics.

Sir Lomer was playing the game of safety, when from his own temperament and position and unbacked by other leaders he could do little more. He stood for the law and did not hinder its operation. But if there was a chief executive in Canada who wished the war were righteously over, it was Sir Lomer Gouin. No Premier had such a predicament ; so much at the end to lose ; so much at first to have gained—if only he could have foreseen, as nobody did, that conscription was coming and that law would be more awkward than liberty.

The Premier of Quebec had experience in keeping his Government immune from agitators. It was not alone the Nationalists who had made him uneasy. On the other extreme there had been for some time one Godefroi Langlois, former editor of *La Patrie*, and later founder and editor of *Le Pays*, whose platform was compulsory State education away from control of the clergy and in defiance of the Archbishops. Gouin did not endorse Langlois. How could he ? *Le Pays*, when it condemned clerical schools, attacked the Administration. Politically Gouin was right in opposing Langlois. Nationally he was playing provincial. Langlois had a mission, in line with a broader, nationalized Canada ; the same mission which is now being reflected in the National Council of Education.

So, between the reactionism of Bourassa and the radicalism of Langlois, Gouin was the compromise ; and Langlois was conveniently given an official post in Europe.

Gouin has compromised his whole political career. With the leverage of enormous success in elections and administration, he never had the vision to declare himself in favour of a bigger Quebec than could be got by extending its boundaries to Ungava.

He was too old to begin. Quebec to him was a vast prefecture to be administered ; not a vision to be realized. Ontario—except politically—was almost as far away as British Columbia. He was seldom in Toronto. Montreal was as a rule the last west for this voyageur. He seldom or never went to the Maritimes. He knew the people down there regarded the *bloc* Quebec as a denationalizer. He had little or no desire to see the prairies. He wanted Quebec to prosper. He delighted to see pulp mills and cotton factories and power plants and railways and trolleys vibrating along the St. Lawrence. He loved to dream of the great unpeopled hinterland—all Quebec ; of the other hinterland—all the rest of Canada ; of the transcontinentals converging at Montreal ; of the steamship lines terminating there ; of a land where there are few empty cradles or idle factories or wasting farms.

All these things Gouin, growing stout and somewhat heavy of face, loved to behold ; and out of that grew all the vision he seemed to have.   In this enormous prefecture within the Empire he beheld a far more comfortable State than the Nationalist dream of a separative Quebec ; glad when he could find time to motor grandly and amiably out among the villages and be greeted as *le grand seigneur* of politics, even when he lacked the grand manners of the eminent patrician.

At any conference of Premiers in Ottawa he held himself somewhat aloof, studying the lot, respecting them all, cordial with all, anxious to do all that constitutionally in him lay to further co-ordination.   But Gouin always sagaciously knew that there was no Premier in the pack who already had so much, with so little to ask, from Federalism as he.   His was the pivotal province of Confederation, the grand compromise of Old Macdonald with Cartier ; the basic sixty-five members of Parliament, unchangeable except by ripping up the B.N.A. Act, an instrument of Empire.   He could wink the other eye and reflect that from the political concessions of the Act in official bilingualism and a fixed representation, in the outlet of the St. Lawrence, in the possession of the historic city, in the control of ocean navigation, in a solid clergy, in fundamental virtues of thrift and an established peasantry—he and his had more than any of the others could ever ask.

"Ah !" he said eloquently, with a fine twinkle of his eyes to the interviewer at Quebec, "you have not seen our Province ?   Then you must come down again, when I am not busy, and let me take you to see—all we have down here !"

A POLITICAL MATTAWA OF THE WEST

JOHN WESLEY DAFOE

FIRST impressions are always tyrants. The first time I heard John Wesley Dafoe talk he was in his large sanctum of the *Manitoba Free Press*, in the summer of 1916. He was without a collar, his shirt loose at the neck, and his hair like a windrow of hay. He reminded me of some superb blacksmith hammering out irons of thought, never done mending the political waggons of other people, and from his many talks to the waggoners knowing more about all the roads than any of them. The wheat on a thousand fields was baking that day, and the 'Peg was roasting alive. Since that I have always pictured Dafoe sweltering, terribly in earnest, whittling the legs of the Round Table and telling somebody how it is that west of the lakes neither of the old Ottawa parties has now any grip on the people.

Dafoe talked that way in 1916. He was beginning to lisp a little along that restless line of thought in 1910. And in 1940 he may be sitting in that same sanctum with walls of heavy books on two sides of him, telling somebody just how it came to be that an economic cyclone on the prairies once caught up all the Grits and Tories and nothing was ever heard or seen of them again.

When Kipling wrote, "Oh, east is east and west is west, and never the twain shall meet," he had never met Dafoe. Some directive angel planted him at Winnipeg shortly after Clifford Sifton crowded the gate there with people going in that they might choke it again with wheat coming out ; and while people went in and wheat came out through this spout of the great prairie hopper, Dafoe dug himself a little

215

ship canal which as it grew bigger sluiced the political
rivers of the West into his sanctum before he lifted the
lock and let them on down to the sea at Ottawa.   The
West as he saw it was a place of coming mighty changes.
His own party was pushing the transformations.   The
prairies were due to become the mother of great forces.
You could not be always herding people into a land like
that from south, east and west and not come within an ace
of fostering some revolution.

And of all cities west of the lakes, Winnipeg was the
clearing-house, as much for policies and programmes as for
wheat and money and people.   No political cloud ever
gathered on the prairies that did not get blown into Winnipeg before it burst.   Dafoe stood ready for them all.   He
believed that no change had happened yet to the Liberal
party comparable with the changes yet to come.   He saw
that party chaining itself to tariffs and big interests and
he said :

"Believe me, that won't forever do.   There's something just short of a revolution going to happen to this
party before the West gets done with it ; and if the party
isn't ready for the West, so much the worse for the party."

Just to get ahead of mere chronology, the bane of many
a good man's life.   In 1919 the most complete imitation of
a little Moscow ever seen on this continent was set up in
Winnipeg.   For many weeks it looked to some hopefuls as
though the Wheat City would reconstruct the whole economic structure of the nation to suit the ideas of a violent
minority.   The main recorded issue was "collective bargaining".   The real issue was direct action in the form of
the sympathetic strike.   By its expected control of urban
centres the Soviet organization aimed to throttle big
utilities, finance, shipping, railroads, telegraphs.   The
United Grain Growers were to be but a helpless giant in the
hands of Jack Proletariat.   Parliament was to be super-
seded by Direct Action.   The A.F.L. was to become

obsolete. Trades Unions were to be taken over and painted red. Citizens in starched collars were to become comrades in shirt sleeves, or enemies. Political parties would be reconstructed. The "workers" would own the country. The British Empire would be shaken into Soviets. The Army and the Navy would be internationalized. The real Capital of Canada outside of Winnipeg would be, not London, but Moscow. The International would supplant national anthems. Public opinion would be exterminated except as revised by the Red leaders on the Red River at its junction with the Assiniboine.

In the unfolding of this Great Adventure we pause here to observe that it was a newspaper which behind the Citizens' Committee administered a black eye to this attempt to make Winnipeg the Soviet headquarters of North America and 120 millions of people. The name of the paper was the *Manitoba Free Press*.

And the *Free Press* was seeing Red. What business had the Red Flag in a city like Winnipeg at all ? If anywhere in Canada, why not in the industrial, big-interest East—in Montreal or Toronto ?

"One revolution at a time, please," we almost hear the *Free Press* saying. "Now the war is done the West has to settle the fate of Government at Ottawa in its own way. And the way of the West is not with the Red Flag ; not with Direct Action. This city is a headquarters of evolutionaries, not of outlaws. You people of the Strike Committee are trying to get the spot-light when you've no business anywhere except right at back stage."

A perfectly straight argument, though not couched in those words. Dafoe and his associates were profoundly busy with what to them was a ten times greater issue than any form of Soviet anywhere in Canada. As a matter of record the paper did admit that the metal workers had a right to strike for collective bargaining.

"But no other Union here or elsewhere," it thundered

"has any right to a sympathetic strike to help the metal workers. This city is not going to be throttled by a thug minority, who want to exercise governing power as a revolutionary usurpation of authority."

A minority always leads. Majorities follow. The position of the *Free Press* was, that it is only a minority able to command a majority that should rule ; and the Soviet was no such minority—while the *Free Press* was.

A clear grasp of this is necessary in the business of judging Mr. Dafoe and his coming influence upon Canadian affairs. What Dafoe enunciated about the strike will have a strong bearing in the case upon what he thinks about the Agrarians. The judge must get a fair judgment. But of this later.

Dafoe was, so far as we know, the first editor in Canada to advocate from the beginning of the war a Coalition Government. This was natural. The *Free Press* had no faith in the Borden administration of Bob Rogers, owner of the *Winnipeg Telegram*. By the summer of 1916 it was into a Coalition campaign. A year later when the Premier came back from England declaring for conscription and inviting Laurier to join in a Coalition, the *Free Press* supported him.

Why this anxiety ? We must pull off a bit of the makeup to find out. The *Free Press* was a Liberal paper. It supported Laurier in the West. But the older it grew the more clearly Dafoe and his associates saw that the man who had created the two new Western Provinces could not hold them. Other gods were now arising. Their organ was the *Grain Growers' Guide ;* their parliaments were in grain growers' conventions ; their policy was radical Liberalism. The Liberal organ of a Wheat City could not consistently antagonize this radical movement. The farmers must be studied. So far as they could strengthen Liberalism by becoming a Radical wing, they must be encouraged. At the point where they developed an extreme left away from the party they must be checked. The *Free Prses* which was yet to fight an economic revolution must not itself be revolutionary.

This leads up to policy in Empire. The paper had gone against Borden in 1911. It was against the taxation Navy of Borden even though it could see the danger of war ahead. It was opposed to the whole super-Tory idea of a centralized British commonwealth of nations. It "hung the hide" of Lionel Curtis and his Round Table propaganda clubs to the Canadian National fence. It argued for "a progressive development in Canadian self-government to the point of the attainment of sovereign power to be followed by an alliance with the other British nations", who it was assumed would do likewise. For years before the war the *Free Press* had talked of this evolutionary Empire, deeply regretting that Mr. Bourassa had coined the word "Nationalist" and made it obnoxious..

Winnipeg seldom does things one half at a time. In the summer of 1917 J. W. Dafoe was one of the most astounded men in Canada. The other one was Sir Wilfrid Laurier. That was the year of the famous Liberal Convention. Had such a Convention happened in Chicago with such a man as Roosevelt as the centre-piece, its doings would have been cabled the world over. In its small way the Winnipeg Convention was more sensational than the Big Strike two years later. Mr. Dafoe was in Ottawa that summer. He was needed there. The Premier had come back from England primed with a policy of conscription to be enforced by a possible Coalition Government, an offer of which was made to the Opposition leader. Since early in the war the *Free Press* had argued for coalition, but opposed conscription until after the United States entered the struggle because of the inevitable exodus of slackers across the border.

There was a strong conscriptionist group of Liberals in Ottawa. We must assume that Mr. Dafoe, though not a member of Parliament, was strongly behind them ; his presence in Ottawa indicates that his counsels were needed in view of the attitude to be taken by Western Liberals. It was the conscriptionist group of Liberals in Ottawa that decided upon the Convention, whether on the advice of Mr. Dafoe is not generally known. The intention was to create a Western Liberal group free from Laurier control, prepared to consider coalition—involving conscription—on its merits. So far, the policy of the Convention was in line with the previous programme of Mr. Dafoe. But the Liberal machine in the West—which was not Mr. Dafoe's party at all, because for some time he had been working on the principle that both the old parties as such had lost their grip on the West—went out and captured the delegates. The Convention was suddenly stampeded for Laurier, a result which Mr. Dafoe never expected but against which he had strongly urged the Liberal Unionist leaders. The *Free Press* thereafter thundered against the Convention as entirely misrepresenting Western Liberalism. The subsequent South Winnipeg convention shewed that the *Free Press* was right. Almost the entire strength of Western Liberalism swung into the Union movement and the Coalition, and the *Free Press* became a temporary, though independent, supporter of the Union Government for the purpose of winning the war.

Now for the larger front stage view ; how does Mr. Dafoe's attitude in the defeat of the Winnipeg Soviet idea of government and his former campaign against Laurier Liberals match with his attitude towards the Farmer Movement as embodied by Mr. Crerar ? The leader of the Agrarian movement is a friend of the *Free Press* for much the same reason that the strike leaders in 1919 were a foe to it. Crerarism in the West looks for the support of that paper in its drive upon Ottawa. From his experience outwardly to the public, and intimately behind the scenes, always concerned with building up a new Liberalism on

the wreck of the old, Dafoe endorses Crerar and his movement. When Crerar went into the Government the *Free
Press* favoured his going. Mr. Dafoe clearly states that,
"if the Union movement could retain its Liberal elements
and produce an economic and taxation policy acceptable
to Western opinion, we could continue to support it." In
contemplating such a miracle, did he expect that the ultra-
Tories would lop away from the Union, making a "rump"
party to match the Laurier Liberals, and leaving the Union
Government free to make an alliance with the Farmer
Group ? This we do not profess to know. In a political
age like this almost any sort of alliance may be made for
the purpose of capturing Parliament. But a permanent
alliance between Western Liberalism represented by Mr.
Crerar and the Government by Coalition looks now as
fantastic as a Coalition between Lloyd George and de
Valera. Mr. Dafoe probably knew that the Government
and Mr. Crerar would lock horns over the tariff—since
any species of protection and free trade never could sleep
together. When Mr. Crerar left the Government on the
budget issue, the *Free Press* ceased its active support of
the Government and moved its guns to a detached position.
When Meighen became Premier and in his programme
speech at Stirling outlined his policy, Dafoe definitely
declared himself as no longer in support of the Union
Government. As he could not support the Laurier Liberal
party, which he had formerly opposed, the only thing left
was to make an active and open alliance with Mr. Crerar.

Such a mobile course of action is incomprehensible
unless we keep in mind the fact that Mr. Dafoe has long
found it impossible to support either of the old parties.
The Coalition was a new one which he consistently supported on its merits and up to a point. The point was
reached. Unionism and Agrarianism were incompatible.
Therefore Unionism was a Tory institution ; and the only
Liberal programme left for the *Free Press* was to form

an alliance with Mr. Crerar and his great group of class-conscious Agrarians.

By this time, if he reads this, Mr. Dafoe will have observed that we are trying to corner him on the question :

If you were opposed to a Labor Soviet which aimed at making a little Moscow of Winnipeg, what are you going to do about a Farmer Soviet that aims to capture Ottawa ?

Already he has begun to answer. He uses a label for the party led by Mr. Crerar and evolved with the aid of Mr. Dafoe :

The National Progressive Party.

A good name, even if not new. What is behind the label ? That the party so named has now taken over all the Liberal economic traditions in the West and after the next general election will become the real Liberal Party of Canada. In the opinion of Dafoe, Mackenzie King should keep out of the West in the coming election in order to let Mr. Crerar romp home with three-fourths of the entire representation in Parliament. He alleges that Laurier destroyed the old Western Liberal party in 1917 ; that King has not revived it—though Mr. Fielding might have done so ; that Western Liberals have become Progressive except in the cities, where some have become Unionists. In making this statement he probably reckoned on Michael Clark becoming a Progressive. But Michael Clark has turned out to be one species of even Free Trade Liberal which Crerarism cannot absorb.

Let us concede that here is one of the most absorbing problems in Canada. If Dafoe backs Crerar in the effort to get that preponderant majority away from Meighen and King, then he is afterwards committed to Crerarism. Dafoe cannot afford to take Crerar and abandon the traditions of the *Free Press*. If he is so keen about real "nationalism" in this country as to regret that Bourassa made the word obnoxious, he has surely decided that the policy of the N.P.P. must be to build up a true national life in Canada. And the man who was Canada's press representative at the Peace Conference, with such exceptional facilities for focussing Canadian national sentiment among other nations, will not dare to countenance in Mr. Crerar and his followers any policy that will open the gates for the United States to walk in and walk over this nation as twenty years ago his *Free Press* associate, Clifford Sifton, opened the doors to let Europe inundate us with a polyglot, un-national flood.

No Canadian journalist has shouldered so perilous a responsibility. Dafoe knows what a struggle it is to preserve national identity on a basis of one to twelve against us. Born in Ontario and experienced in the East as few editors have ever been, he surely knows the value of not surrendering our national birthright for a mess of free-trade pottage.

If he knows this as well as we think he should, will he uphold the *Free Press* as the constant critic of Mr. Crerar if he attempts to denationalize this country ; or will he accept a portfolio of Minister of the Interior in the Cabinet dominated by Messrs. Crerar and Drury, and in his haste to establish the new Liberalism of the National Progressive Party help to strike out the meaning of the word "National" in the label ?

Can a man who fought a Direct Action Strike because it aimed at revolution, consistently endorse, lock, stock and barrel, a movement which aims at a revolution by Indirect Action through Parliament ?

Is government by a "National Progressive Party" Agrarian Group with a business-farmer Premier and a farmer-dominated Cabinet any less of a group government in principle than the One Big Union, even though it does not tie up the nerve centres of the country by a minority general strike, but merely throttles Parliament, which is supposed to be the national brain, by the use of the group minority in voting ?

Mr. Dafoe has already begun to answer. Again we see him sweltering in his sanctum, his hair like a windrow of hay, as he dictates something like this to his stenographer :

"Your logic is good except that your major premiss is a case of being off to a bad start. The National Progressive Party is not a group ; it is a business majority. It contains the people who produce the majority of the nation's wealth for consumption and export and therefore enable the nation to pay its bills. It is Liberal because it advocates free-trade and is opposed to big monopolies, and there is no other Liberalism in Canada left worthy the name. The N.P.P. is the new Liberalism, not for the West alone, but for the whole country. It depends upon the franchise of the people, not upon the strike action of revolutionary groups. Agriculture, not industry, is the basis of Canada's economics. Even labour as embodied in the Trade Unions does not aim at revolution. Only the Reds want that. And the Reds are a hopeless minority. The farmers are not as yet a popular, though they are an economic, majority; but the future of this nation depends upon a voting as well as a producing majority of farmers."

This may not be the exact way in which Mr. Dafoe would state the case, but it expresses the fact that sound economics are at the root of all ideas which have to do with fair government. And it suggests that J. W. Dafoe with his *Free Press* has more to do than the *Grain Growers' Guide* with what the people think about the N.P.P.

For this reason we hope that Mr. Dafoe, the judge and the advocate as well, will always stay "behind the scenes" to keep Mr. Crerar on the right track if ever he gets the right of way.

HEADMASTER OF THE MANCHESTER SCHOOL

MICHAEL CLARK, M.P.

THE eminent headmaster of the Manchester School in Canada is one of the few M.P.'s who know how to build a wheat stack. He farms in the spot north of Calgary where the poplar bluffs begin to mark that you are in the black loam of wonderful crops at a maximum distance from Liverpool. It is an art to build a wheat stack. Michael Clark—so we believe—knows exactly how many tiers to lay before he begins the "belly" ; how to fill up the middle so that the butts of the sheaves droop to run off the rain ; and how high to go with the bulge before he begins to draw in with the roof. All day long as he worked on his knees, not in prayer, he had mental leisure to think about one vast, fructifying theme ; which of course is Free-Trade as they had it in England ; unrestricted trade according to the Manchester School. And when he got his stack done he could tell to a ten-dollar bill how much tariff the railways and steamships would levy on that stack by the time the wheat got to Liverpool.

During the War, Clark was a win-the-war Liberal. He broke away from Laurier on conscription, which he openly supported. In July this year he was scheduled in the press—another of those wish-father-to-the-thought news items—to join Messrs. Drury and Crerar in an anti-tariff tour of Ontario. He did not go. He probably never had the slightest intention of going. Michael Clark had other wheat to stack. An Alberta election was coming. It came. When it was all over Alberta was in the grip of the Agrarians. Liberalism by constituencies was swept

225

out as clean as a barn floor at fanning-mill time. And Michael Clark sat down to think it over. He had half expected that tornado. But he refused to like it. The farmers had stolen his own programme of free trade and by means of it had stampeded his Province for the sake of using it as a spring-broad to make the grand jump into the Federal arena. The apostle of free trade, himself as good a farmer as any of them, was now regarded as a chip on the Agrarian stream at high tide.

Wherefore Michael Clark, after certain "conversations" with Mr. Crerar, wrote the letter which, if Mackenzie King is as wise as he is hopeful, will be used to flood the country. Hoardings and electric signs in the interests of true-Liberal ism should blazon abroad such sentences as these :

"The House of Lords, the Family Compact, the Manufacturers' Association and the junkers and militarists of Germany are each and all examples of group government."

"Class consciousness is none the less class selfishness, and therefore doomed to die, because it suddenly appears in Farmer and Labour parties."

"The apostles of progress must unite upon common principles, sincerely held to resist reaction, which is ever present like a dead weight to drag down the aspirations of the race for freedom, justice and democracy."

"These were the things for which sixty thousand Canadians died in the recent war. . . . . I have been fighting 'class' for forty years. It would be quite impossible for me to turn my back on my past and the right in this election."

Our political history contains no declaration of independence more significant, manly and sensational. Repudiation of the Free Trade, group-governed, National Progressives by Michael Clark, the farmer and the apostle of Canadian Free Trade, is the first truly emancipating note that has been struck in all this pre-election barrage of group against group. Michael Clark may be no bigger

as a Canadian for such a stand, but he is true to his own
form as one of the rarest and manliest Radicals that Canada
ever had.   And his declaration should be of immense value
to the Government, which confesses that its real fear is,
not of Liberals, but of Agrarians.

The headmaster of the Manchester School in Canada
has had a multitude of pupils ; none more brilliant than
Mr. Crerar, who seems to have made Free Trade a species
of bondage.   In no other land could Michael Clark so well
have demonstrated the virtues of Free-Trade.   On those
plains, buffaloes worth multi-millions of dollars in trade
annually migrated across "Parallel 49" into Montana
and back again into the Territories.   The prairie schooner
trekked northward over the border carrying migrants in
search of homes when there was no government official to
turn them back or to question the terminus of their travels.
The freight wagons creaked up from the south into Mac-
Leod and past it into the valley of Saskatchewan, carrying
goods made and bought in the land of the Western Yankee
long before the great antidote to Free Trade, the Transcontinental Railway, put those crooked trails out of business.

Clark was spouting free-trade on the prairies at a time
when many men in the West scarcely knew that trade had
any restrictions except in the matter of beverages.   He
was an apostle of Cobdenism almost before the Territories
were baptized into party politics at all ; when Regina was
the home of a Territorial County Council that had neither
Tories nor Grits.   He was farming and prophesying commercial union before James J. Hill began to compete with
the protective C.P.R. for trade north and south instead of
the long-haul east and west.   Before ever a real Agrarian
began to head out on the plains he was contending like a
tribune of the *plebs*, that unrestricted reciprocity between
two halves of a great productive continent, of which one-
half contains nine-tenths of the people, was not a prelude
to annexation away from the grand old Empire.   And when

he got into Parliament the voice that had been so mighty in the trail-side school houses and the little town-halls became more potent than ever as "Red Michael" went full tilt in the House against the high protectionists.

High courage was here. Bucking bronchos from the West who had gone to Ottawa were duly corralled, haltered, hobbled, surcingled and thrown, finally harnessed and driven by either of the old parties. In breaking a political broncho the Liberal party was as good as the other. But the House is full of insurgents now, lining up into a tyrannized and tyrannous group organizing as a party. In Clark's inaugural days, and for years after, there was but one real solo voice calling like a trombone from a high tower for Free Trade as the Kingdom of God which, if they would first seek it, all other things would be added unto them.

French psychology traces certain forms of insanity to the fixed idea. There have been times when Parliament has regarded Michael Clark as a melancholy victim of this big idea that warped his whole political mentality. But it was a grand form of insanity. Nobody ever heard Clark in the House who did not realize that here was a fine British rebel whose brain should be a great hope to his party. The old chief knew that. He kept his ear towards Clark when he was sometimes deaf to his ministers.

Clark was the mountain peak which the party had left for its fleshly sojourn in Egypt. The Liberal party in Canada had once been a free trade party—somewhat before Clark's time. In free trade and the universal franchise had been its life. But Liberalism before 1896 was one thing ; afterwards another. Laurier in practice knew that Clark was magnificently wrong ; in theory superbly right. Therefore he indulged and admired him ; sometimes playing with him, conscious that Liberalism was the only show in which Clark could be a national performer.

In truth Michael Clark was for long enough a man without a party. But from the benches of the Liberals he could stand and preach his Manchester doctrines to Hansard and the nation, even when the party yawned and held dangerously on to the tariff.

It was always a tonic to hear Clark in the House. Like Carlyle he breathed a certain inexorable vitality into public affairs. To meet Clark in the corridors was to get a breeze that swept like a chinook across the frozen waste of old-line politics. In the gloom of the lobby this apostle of red hair and rubicund visage was a beacon light. I have met him so, of a Saturday afternoon when the House was out of session, and when the member for Red Deer was ripe for a free talk to any stranger. A great friendliness possessed him always. He could laugh at the besetments of party and the tyranny that opportunism imposes on great minds. He himself was free. He wanted others to be free. He could stand for half an hour in one gloomy crypt of those corridors in the old Parliament and talk of the power of being that kind of Liberal.

It was the wheat that helped to keep Clark where he was on the outpost of Liberalism. When his old leader became enswathed with election bandages, Clark looked out upon the landscapes of the wheat, not so long ago the limitless pasture of the free-trade buffaloes, and felt again the vision of the life that is Liberal but is sometimes called another name.

Alberta was leaping to a great life. Almost in the middle of it north and south is the town of Red Deer. All about it were the settlements of "nationals" emancipated from bondage in Europe. What was the use, quoth Clark, of bringing such people to a country of free homestead land, of alleged free institutions and making them the slaves, first of political machines, second of protected interests in the East? If enslaved people were to become free in a new land why should the wheat and the oats and the cattle which they raised not be made free to move for a market as naturally as the wind blows across the borders?

This may not have been the precise order in which such ideas generated in the mind of Michael Clark ; but it is the way those ideas confronting such a man strike a contemporary. I have lived in the land where Clark lives, though not at Red Deer, and remember well the burning desire of twenty years ago in that far northwest for economic emancipation. Then at any meeting, no matter what, any little dinner to a citizen no matter whom, men rose to talk about the need of conquering the isolation of the country. They remembered the tyranny of the old Trading Company into Hudson's Bay. They clamoured for more people, more farms, more towns, more railways, more life—from the East. And when it came they said the East was a tyrant, an economic monster to bleed them white. Clark, as one remembers him best, has not been so much a foe to the East as he has wanted to be a friend to the South.

But a new oligarchy was arising on the great prairies. As official Liberalism got its grip on the three Provinces and became itself a tyrant, while unofficial Toryism in league with the big railways got a stranglehold on British Columbia, and when even "Honest" Frank Oliver ceased to be an independent Liberal and became a red-taped Minister of the Interior, Clark the Free Trader in Parliament found himself striking hands with a sect mainly of Liberal Radicals first called Grain Growers, next Agrarians, and by some the very devil. With official Liberalism as expressed by Scott, Sifton, Cross, Norris and Martin he had only superficial sympathy. These men were more or less on masquerade. The Agrarians were barefaced, one-faced Radicals who would open the borders, and abolish the customs houses, and set up a sort of Western political autonomy whose root idea was that trade should be as free as grasshoppers. These people were not raising Old Flag wheat.

How far Clark fell in line with all the doctrines of the United Grain Growers, I do not know. But one thing clear about this insurgent is that he has always stood four-square for the British connection—and for all that it means to Canada. Clark is a Britisher. He still has his English accent. You would spot him at once as a transplanted Englishman. He is prouder of being a Briton in Canada than he ever would have been in England. Clark never forgot—Manchester and Cobden. He stood among the wheat and saw the Empire.

When the War came and his adopted Province of Alberta for a long while held the lead in enlistments for war, no man was happier in the grim outlook than the member for Red Deer. The War to him was a great emergence of Liberalism the world over when Peace should bring Free Humanity, Free wheat, Free trade. Why not? His son went to the war—and he lost him. His speech on the Military Service Act was in many respects the best of all in that debate, not in rhetoric, but in logical virility. It was a howitzer broadside, slow, deliberate, but every shot a hit. His old leader had already declined a belated offer of Coalition and was now opposing conscription and arguing for amemdment by Referendum. In all his life he never got from a political foe such a searchlight on his soul as his once devoted follower gave him in this speech.

Laurier had previously executed the Nationalist dodge of taking refuge behind the Militia Act, asserting that it was right to enforce that Act calling out the Militia for the defence of Canada ; to which Clark replied :

"England is fighting this war wherever she sees the turban of a Turk or the helmet of a Teuton. She is fighting it in Egypt, Mesopotamia, in Macedonia, in Belgium—most of all in France. . . . . America, whose independence had been fought in a struggle of blood for sound fiscal ideas was now immortalizing her reunion with Britain, her old enemy. . . . . If organized labour was opposed to conscription, so much the worse for labour, whose own trades unions were a form of conscription ; in England he had never

named either lord or labour with a capital L. . . . Canada
should be in the war to her last man and her last dollar. . . . .
As to the referendum amendment, it was fathered by the
man who down to his attitude on this question had gone
into history as the greatest of all Canadians, but who had
applauded Pugsley when he argued against extending the
life of this Parliament, and who in the matter of sending
men to fight, in organizing the whole nation for war, in con-
serving national unity, and in making an election a smaller
matter than the honour of a nation was opposed to the
Government. If the amendment should carry, and the
Referendum show a majority against the Government
measure by omitting the soldier vote and piling up the vote
from the Province which had given birth to the Referendum, then when the author of that measure should be
returned to power on a no-conscription issue what chance
was there for Canada to win her part of the war with the
lion Laurier and the lamb Oliver lying down together—and
a little child—Macdonald from Pictou—leading them ? ''

Not as a climax, but as a mere personal note midway in
his speech, he had said :

"I have a little toddling grandson on my farm out West
to-day whose father was killed with a gunshot wound in his
neck two weeks ago. I say to you, sir, on my soul and
conscience I support this Bill, because I believe it to be a
part of the necessary machinery which can save that little
fellow, born a Canadian, and thousands of others like him
from ever going through what his father and his uncles
have gone through."

Parliamentary debate has risen to much higher levels
of oratory, but seldom to such a height of accusing vindication and personal affection for the accused from whom an
insurgent is driven to sever his allegiance. Clark can
always make some sort of big human speech with a natural
knack of getting at the vitals of a subject in simple, dignified
language and a searching logic—once you admit his major

premiss. That one speech flung into bold relief, almost as the No Man's Land under a flare of a great barrage, the issues between men who for so many years had been political confederates.

A couple of years later I again met Clark when he was speaking guest at an Empire Club luncheon. His topic was—the Empire. His brand of political ideas was vastly different from those of the average man in his audience, and he knew it. The Club had invited him, because he was Michael Clark. He said not a word about trade. He uttered no propaganda. He talked simply and strongly about the race that had made the Empire which to him was a commonwealth of neither trade nor conquest but of liberating ideas.

I don't think that any of the Chamberlain-Foster school could have uttered quite so broad and noble a tribute to the inner vitality of the British League of Nations. And not even Mr. Rowell could have surpassed it for breadth of view on that subject. Clark looked at the Empire from within outwards. He saw in it the expression of a great race of people working the leaven upon other races ; a mighty confederacy of free nations.

Red Michael has been a great informing Liberal, and a big illuminating Canadian. Whether grandly right or magnificently wrong, he is never uninteresting ; a man who could come off a stack of wheat, wash himself up bare-armed, and in Sunday clothes but seldom well-dressed and never groomed, step on to a platform over in the school-house or the town hall and make a great speech to men who believe in the simplicity of a big mind that thinks hard on the welfare of the majority. John Bright would have loved such a man. Even John Macdonald might have loved him. And the one regret among those who value the power of a big free nature in a nation is, that owing to some fatalistic streak in his genius, Michael Clark has not risen to the inspiring height from which the country might get the best that he has to give. Never cured of his insurgency in Parliament, he has become an uncompromising conformist to one big and bigoted idea that universal Free-Trade is the need of the world, and especially of Canada. He persists in the delusion that what has been good for Britain must be good for Canada ; not only is Canada at war when Britain fights, but when Britain has no tariff Canada must have free trade.

All which is freely forgiven this stalwart on account of his challenge to the group who took his Free Trade luggage and attempted to label it National Progressive. The Free Trader who could watch that caravan of adventurers going down the trail and stoutly tell them all to keep on going to the devil, deserves well of his country. Michael Clark's advocacy of Progressivism might have got him the promise of a Cabinet position. His rejection of it is the proof that the free-man who believes in great parties can never be bound by a class-conscious group. "Better a dinner of herbs . . . ." Michael Clark, whether M.P. or not, is free to consider himself if need be a party of one man— without a platform, but not devoid of a cause.

Whatever Michael Clark knows about the benefits of Free Trade and its effect upon the exchanges, he knows peculiarly well the danger of unrestricted reciprocity in sentiment between Canada and the United States.

THE SPHINX FROM SASKATCHEWAN

HON. J. A. CALDER

THE Hon. J. A. Calder has never seen the Sphinx. But he has a looking glass. He has never been in Egypt. But he has lived a long while in Saskatchewan. A man who can continue to know as much as he knows about the confessional side of government, and who can say so little, has some claim to be considered—Canada's political Sphinx.

Such a reputation is sometimes enviable. The average public man babbles. Often he talks to conceal thought or as a substitute for action. The mental energy needed to turn end for end what some of these garrulous people say, in order to decipher just what they mean, is usually more than the wisdom is worth. Calder spares us. He tells us nothing. His silence may be golden, or it may be just a habit ; but from the known character of Calder it is never the omniscience of stupidity.

A Sphinx in action may sometimes give himself away. It is not usual for a Sphinx to do anything except to conceal the riddle. Calder has all his life been a busy man. He is still in middle age. All but fourteen years of his life up till 1917 he spent in the West, most of it in the part now known as Saskatchewan. Ten years ago he was furtively discussed as successor to Laurier. He is now a Unionist-Liberal. To give him work in the administration commensurate with his ability—or somewhere near it—a new department was created in Immigration. Now he is slated for the Senate !

Little was heard about Calder's department. He had a publicity bureau which did not spend vast amounts of money on diffusing information. The department is said to contain a moving picture section, some of whose films probably creep into Canadian movie houses. But nobody ever saw a picture of J. A. Calder on a screen. He had a Canadian novelist as chief of publicity. That novelist might have yearned for the chance to immortalize his chief in a story, but so long as he is in the pay of Mr. Calder's department he will continue to yearn. And not even he has been given to understand why when a reconstructed Liberal like Mr. Rowell left the Cabinet at the appointment of Premier Meighen, the Minister of Immigration stayed on. One might surmise that the man who, a decade ago, looked to some people like an Elisha to Laurier, would run again in Moosejaw as a National Liberal Conservative with the expectation of re-entering the Cabinet, probably as Minister of the Interior. But he was suddenly and humdrumly designated for the Senate.

Apparently the Sphinx is not a great deal concerned over the fact that his action in the case would throw some light on the sort of government we may expect, and the kind of man we are privileged to conjecture Mr. Calder to be. He seems to take very little interest in what any one thinks about him. He accompanied the Premier on his Western trip. Now and then he made a speech. He was heckled. He was in the land of his critics, where he was unofficially known as "Jim". What did he mean by staying in a Government which was supposed to have finished its work in 1919 ? Was he coming back as a Liberal ? Had he no longer any fellow-feeling for the farmers among whom he had lived for so long ? The Sphinx did not directly say. He was publicly and conventionally endorsing the Premier, who was well able to speak for himself on behalf of the administration.

Calder was headmaster of Moosejaw High School when he was twenty-three, in the year 1891. He must have learned reticence then. Up in Edmonton, a few years later

one heard considerably of Goggin, the speechmaking
educationist of the prairie; rarely or never of Calder, who
about that time was Inspector of Schools for the Territories, not yet provinces. The silent young inspector must
have looked like the reincarnation of Socrates as he drove—
sometimes a four-horse team on a buckboard—through the
sloughs of the Northwest No prairie doctor with a radius
of fifty miles, none but a pioneer missionary like McDougall
or Robertson, ever had so glorious a chance to study what
the life of a new country was going to be, as this inspector
toiling hundreds of miles over a land, where, if he stopped at
three school-houses a week, he was doing a good average
in bad weather.

Regina had no party politics then. All it had was the
mounted police and a leg-boot legislature. Every man
was then a trailsman. In Calder's time as Inspector, there
were only 400 miles of railway north of the C.P.R. main
line—the two branches to Prince Albert and to Edmonton.
It was only in the last year or two of this buckboard and
broncho inspectorate that there were even any Doukhobors
in that part of the world to bring back the days of Adam
and Eve. He saw all the "nationals" beginning to arrive.
He could put his finger on a gaunt anemic map of the Territories and point out just where there was beginning to be
some nucleus of a foreign settlement. He could talk a
little Cree and he learned the jargon of several countries in
Europe. He saw the farmers arise, and railways begin,
and little villages dot the skyline, and here and there an
elevator, when a box car was looked at by a trailsman as
a small boy gapes at a circus parade.

Calder lived in Regina when politics was born. He
shares with Frank Oliver the memory of the day when
Nicholas Flood Davin was the wonder orator of the West,
and when freight-carters from Winnipeg to Edmonton via
Saskatoon, which was then a temperance colony, carried
demijohns of whisky on traders' permits to make every-

body at home ingloriously drunk, including the mounted police. He recalls the day when the first lieutenant-governor was inaugurated in Regina and what Frank Oliver said about it. Four years he was Deputy Commissioner of Education for the Territories up till the inauguration of two new Provinces when, travelling on a thousand miles of new railway and over the old main line of the C.P.R., Laurier paid his first visit to the Great West and discovered as one of its greatest potentialities J. A. Calder, who under Premier Scott became Provincial Treasurer and Commissioner of Education.

To people outside Saskatchewan—even in Alberta, he was very little known—Calder has always been a somewhat nebulous figure ; to some critics, a rather suspicious character ; but always—clever. Being a Sphinx he never courted popularity and seldom got it. Scott was brilliant, popular and impulsive. His chief executive in Education, Railways and Telephones and Premier *de facto* during more than half of Scott's term, was cold and calculating. The West prefers warm-blooded politicians. Calder succeeded in spite of his manner, or his mask, or whatever it may have been ; and he did it by a penetrating knowledge of the country, a superb capacity as administrator and a talent for keeping out of trouble. He was no man for prima donna scenes. Even the Education Department, a witch's cauldron of troubles over the Separate School question in the new provinces, never entangled him in theatricals. He was unpopular with the Opposition as soon as the new Government began, because he was regarded as a Civil Service interloper. What business had a school inspector in politics, and in a Cabinet ?

Calder demonstrated that best when he handed over the educational cauldron to Scott and became Minister of Railways and Telephones. Here was a department of utility administration in which he shone. He had great political executive ability. When Scott was absent more

than half his time through illness, Calder was Premier.
There was no other man to choose. The liquor problem
was more his to handle than the Premier's. Calder did
not share the popular enthusiasm for Government-dispensed
liquor. He knew the weaknesses of officials and the historic
thirst of the prairie. The Opposition constantly accused
him of being in league with the liquor men. Calder made
no denial or affirmation. He was Mephisto enough to let
people wonder whether he was one thing or the opposite.

A man who knew Calder twenty-two years ago gave,
not long ago, some impressions of the Minister in connec-
tions with the liquor administration.

"About two weeks after Saskatchewan went dry," he
said, "I was spending a night in one of the larger towns in
the Province. Among the other guests at the hotel was a
member of the Government. In the lobby an interesting
argument waged throughout the evening, the Minister of
course, defending the action of the Government in closing
the bars. Among other things he told us about the relief
work carried on by the Dominion and Provincial Governments in certain districts where there had been crop failures,
in order that the destitute settlers might earn or borrow
enough to keep themselves and their families through the
winter. He emphasized one mistake the Government
had made in not first closing every bar in the districts
affected, because there were many instances where every
dollar that had been earned or borrowed had been spent in
the bars on the very day that it was received, by the men
whose families it was intended to save from freezing and
starvation.

"I was telling this afterwards to one of the leading social
reformers of Saskatchewan, and a smile played over his
face as I was speaking. When I had finished he said :

" ' He didn't tell you the whole story. We recognized
the necessity of closing those bars before that relief work
was started, and urged it so strongly on the Government

that they agreed to do it. The Orders-in-Council were drawn up and ready to be signed when Calder, who had been absent from the Province on business, returned and immediately it was all off".

Calder has a sister who is one of the leading social workers in Regina. She has a profound regard for her talented brother Jim.

The liquor did more than even Separate Schools to disrupt Government forces in Saskatchewan. Calder was no hypocrite to weep over the moral issues in prohibition. He was not a profound governmentarian or a champion of enforced morality A Government might own and operate telephones, but not so well consciences. The liquor administration turned out to be a mess in Saskatchewan, largely because the administration did not unanimously believe in the thing that the majority seemed to want. Calder was no more to blame than anybody else, except that he was highest in the Government when the Premier was away.

The reformers said that Calder was pro-liquor in the administration. He seemed to have no opinions about that—at least for publication. Ideals often run away with communities. If he had only spouted a little now and then he would have given people a chance to bring something home to him, and himself a chance to get near the people. Two or three scandals came up in departments over which he had control. Commissions were appointed to investigate ; they always exonerated Calder. Even in the search-light on liquor—as many as four, one after another—no technical blame attached to the silent Minister. Calder may have had a contempt for either commissions or public opinion. A Sphinx is as a rule not much of a burning avenger of wrongs to the community. Besides Scott was continually running into emotional trouble. The Premier *de facto* had the balance to keep. He must work while other people talked.

A German-born but thoroughly loyal detective engaged by the Borden Government to report upon seditious activities of the German element who were so badly disgruntled over the Wartime Elections Act, repeated to the writer more than once with great vehemence that Mr. Calder had a special interest in the *Regina Leader,* which was used to get votes for the Administration, particularly among the German element. Governments had been known to own newspapers before Calder ever began. *The Leader* was naturally a Government organ and may have needed pap. This is a form of patronage hard to uproot.

When Scott finally retired the chief administrator did not succeed him. Martin was picked, a safe, genial and popular man. The Sphinx , it is said, might have had the post ; but he preferred to stay behind the scenes. Before that he had been much talked about as a possible successor to Laurier—but with not much hope of succeeding. There are probably a number of reasons why Mr. Calder did not take the Provincial Premiership. Dig them out of Calder if you may. He has never explained. He leaves it to his commentators.

We are privileged therefore to conjecture that :

Mr. Calder was pretty well sick of Saskacthewan politics and was looking hard in almost any direction for a good way out;

Mr. Calder could see far enough into the near future of prairie politics to know that Liberalism was becoming a label for something else ; and he was not disposed to come out as an Agrarian Liberal ;

Mr. Calder wanted a chance to begin politics all over again, because with all his practical success he felt that he had travelled some wrong trails.

Possibly all of these had something to do with the case. At the Winnipeg Liberal Convention in 1917 he was a coalition-conscription Liberal. He worked against the Liberal machine that captured the Convention by a fluke for Laurier. Before that he was known to believe in Union Government. It was only common sense to make him one of the Prairie triumvirate—Calder, Sifton, Crerar, who carried the West into the Union. Cloudy as his career has been, for no reason that anyone specially cared to name, he might in Ottawa be a big force for the Government. He was a behind-the-scenes actor. He knew something about the art of winning elections and converting immigrants into voters. He was practical. He would be needed in Ottawa—more than he could see any use for his talent in Saskatchewan with its farmer-dominated Cabinets.

Alberta has gone Agrarian. All Saskatchewan needs is a change of label. Some psychological morning Premier Martin will get up and rub out "Liberal" after his name, buy a big farm and set up as a National Progressive. Provincial Legislatures are things to be captured. The old parties shrewdly used them in the Ottawa game. The new ones are just as apt. Too long these Western elective bodies have been on the switch. It is time to shunt them, once more, on to the main line that leads to Ottawa—with a different company label on the cars.

By no exercise of the imagination can one behold Jim Calder becoming a Grain-Grower Progressive. The thing is anomalous.

On the other side of the Sphinx he is credited by those also who know him well in Regina with going to Ottawa purely as a patriotic duty. He wanted some work to do for the whole country bigger than any he had done in Regina. The authority formerly quoted in this article had this to say about Calder in 1917 when Calder took office in Ottawa :

"About the time of the Winnipeg Convention I was talking with the same man whom I have already quoted, and we were discussing the enigma which Calder's character and public record seemed to present. I knew that my friend was not especially a friend of Calder's, so his words seemed to carry greater weight.

" 'There is no person in Canadian public life,' he said, 'who has been trying more conscientiously and con- sistently to be good than Calder. I will not say that his motive may be higher than that of political expediency ; but he has been and is more scrupulously careful to do nothing that may reflect in any way upon his honour and integrity. I believe that he has set before him the highest possible ideal of public service and that he is doing every- thing he can to live up to it.' "

A prominent citizen of Regina who has seen a good deal of Calder, both in his home city and in Ottawa, has the same opinion ; adding that Calder never bamboozles a deputation with suave words or false hopes ; what the Cabinet thinks about any particular programme of a deputation he already knows and suggests that a typed memo, which he will present, will be as good as waiting days for a personal appeal. In 1919 he informed the writer that he proposed to enact much-needed reforms in immi- grating Canada, especially as to the quality of new-comers.

Why has Mr. Calder never made a big study of this absorbing question ? When the Premier went to the Imperial Conference with his mind pretty well made up on the Anglo-Japanese Alliance, why had he not in his grip, to show the Conference, one common sense, powerful little book signed by Hon. J. A. Calder, Minister of Immigration, giving a complete exposition of Japanese life in Canada ? When we are all talking about the good *entente* with the United States why can't we get from the Immigration Department in Ottawa a hand-book giving a complete picture of what Americans have done in the West ?

However, the Sphinx may have the best of reasons for not doing these simple things. But there is scarcely a Department of administration that does not regard itself as a machine for winning elections as much as for serving the people who pay for it. Apart from all he has not told us, I have no doubt Mr. Calder is doing a big reforming work on immigration in Ottawa.

The Immigration Minister should be our leading socio-logist. He should be able to diagnose communities. He might easily begin upon Ottawa. What a study a cross section of the Smart Set would be, especially upon the arrival of a new king at Rideau Hall ! There's nothing in other democracies quite like that. Washington has a White House, but the inmate is merely an elected servant of the State. Rideau Hall is an endowment, a gift of the gods. The 30,000 people of greater and lesser degree in Ottawa who normally or abnormally live by the Civil Service are profoundly affected by the arrival, sojourn and departure of the Governor-General. They are vitally influenced and entertained by the Parliamentary restaurant, even without the bar. The social show provided by Ministers' and members' wives and their visiting friends is itself a subtle study in the art of getting on in the new world, which is at the root of all immigration. Bridge for money and dining out with your friend's wife are within the reach of any ambitious immigrant. The Smart Set in Ottawa is an exotic colony all by itself. Montreal and Toronto and Winnipeg can merely copy it. Some of the farmers have their eye on the Set ; no, not to abolish it. Women must have their share in the Government. Petti-coats and politics are affinities. Farmers are no more necessarily immune from what is said to have corrupted the Roman Empire than Tories or Grits. Farmers in fact, as Mr. Calder knows, are not the hope of the world ; neither are lawyers nor manufacturers.

Suppose we ask the Sphinx about this. Listen in imagination to this once Liberal, as with an astounding burst of candour he says :

"My friend, your description of my make-up may be as right or as foolish as anybody feels disposed to think.

None of it bothers me. What does bother me is the law of compensation. Agree with me that the manufacturer had his drastic innings with Canadian governments ; that tariffs and protected industries are the result ; that lawyers —yes, I'm a lawyer—have had a big day in our affairs because they had the talent for schemes and speeches. Admit that and conclude—that the very human farmer thinks his turn is coming, and rather soon. But—somebody who was never educated as a Tory has got to help the National-Liberal-Conservative Government to get an even chance to administer this nation after the upheavals of war, Somebody who moves silently while others are talking their tongues loose may be needed to manipulate——"

Before the Sphinx could complete his statement of the case he was politely asked if he would care to inter his talents in the Canadian Senate, and he suavely answered that such a thing might be a good way to solve the conundrum, even though it would make a thoroughly stupid last act in the play.

A TRUE VOICE OF LABOUR

MR. TOM MOORE

MANY years ago an Irish poet visiting Canada and voyaging down the Ottawa wrote a poem of which may people recall only the lines—

"Row, brothers, row, the stream runs fast,
The rapids are near, the daylight's past."

The Tom Moore about whom this article is sketched is not a poet. He is, in fact, one of the prosiest public men in Canada. But we may leave it to any of those who have known him during the past three years when he has been President of the Trades and Labour Congress, if many and many a time he has not felt some such sentiment as—

"Row, brothers, row, the stream runs fast,
The rapids are near, the daylight's past."

Since Mr. Charles Draper first became Secretary of that Congress he has never known a period when so much was expected of a President by way of limitless patience, statesmanship and self-control as has been shown by Tom Moore. The rapids were always close to this man, and there were rocks under the rapids. It took steady piloting by the captain to keep the crew of the labour ship from getting holes in her bottom and going down.

So far as one has been able to follow the career of Moore at the head of the Congress, and as reported in the public press, he stands now and always for adherence to the principle of Union in evolution. He believes in labour getting ahead ; but not by the method of upturning everything that is established just to see what kinds of crawling things there may be underneath.

246

When we reflect that Canada is not primarily an industrial so much as an agricultural country, it is startling to remember that two years ago it was the home of the only organized attempt ever made in America on a scale of efficiency to establish something closely resembling a Soviet government. The big Winnipeg Strike was a lurid menace to the solidarity of labour in Canada. West of Winnipeg, once the Red River Soviet had been set up, there was a chain of inflammable centres to link up with the revolution. Calgary was the scene of one convention which had sent a cable of sympathy to Moscow. British Columbia was full of seething susceptible elements, regarded by some of the Reds across the border as the real centre rather than Winnipeg, of the One Big Union idea. The mines of Alberta were dominated by swaggering foreigners who owed no allegiance to the British or any other flag except the Red emblem. Long ago under the influence of the clergy and the Archbishop of Montreal, Quebec had created a Canadian Labour movement intended to cut Canadian labour away from the American Federation. This was a phase of the Nationalism that had its headquarters in Quebec, but had spread in various strange guises to other parts of the country, when none of the clergy or intellectuals behind the movement dreamed that the One Big Union insurgent against the A.F.L. would be the most theatrical result. Once get the O.B.U. idea rampant in Quebec with its scores of big industries and its thousands of poorly educated workers, and the Red movement was due to spread faster than the United Farmers' programme had ever done.

In the propagation of the Red programme Ontario, and especially industrial Toronto, was regarded as the buffer state. But if the Soviet had succeeded in Winnipeg and further West, then the whole weight of that success marching upon Ontario, with Quebec bringing up the eastern end, would form a sort of nutcracker device from which Ontario would have had a hard time to escape.

This was the dazzling formula propounded at a time when every nation in the world was in a state of ferment, and when the vast loose-jointed nation known as Canada was in a condition of instability unknown since it became a Confederation. The apostles of the Red programme had all the advantages of being able to sling the paint on to the canvas of the future without caring overmuch about the drawing. Men in large numbers everywhere seemed ready to grasp at and embrace the unusual. People who for years had been ground down by high prices for the commonest necessities, considered seriously the question of the "salariat" joining forces with organizing labour under a banner that might be red. Civilization, physically shattered by the war and hysterically stampeded by the doctrine of self-determination of peoples—a high form of Bolshevism—stood ready to inquire whether the theories being tried in Russia were not, after all, right, no matter what butchery might be perpetrated in working them out.

Revolutionary ideas were everywhere.

Everything prepared the public mind.

A barrage of propaganda had been set up—and kept up.

Legitimate Trades Unionism itself in Britain had subscribed to The Aims of Labour put forth by Arthur Henderson, who foreshadowed barricades and bayonets in London streets if the proletariat did not get their "rights".

Canada did not surely escape. We had the Winnipeg flare-up, which was watched by legitimate labour across the border. The A.F.L. was challenged for authority in this country. It came to the peculiar pass, that in order to maintain the solidarity of Canada as constituted by Government under the Old Flag, the legitimate leaders of labour had to fall back upon the one continental organization which makes brotherhoods, not across the seas, nor so much across Canada, but across the border.

It was Ontario's opportunity ; the steady old Province of some bigotry, great industry, many labour unions, and more or less fixed ideas regarding the function of Government. The office of Tom Moore is in Ottawa. There the President of the Trades and Labour Congress is in close touch with the Labour Department, with the *Labour Gazette*, with the Government in Council. We shall never know just how much of the steady conservatism of Moore at the first Congress following the Winnipeg strike, as well as at other Congresses later, was developed and held steady by association with Government.

But whether or no, even though it was nothing but loyalty to the established brotherhoods of the A.F.L. or a deeper loyalty to his own ideas of the case, the rock-steady influence of Tom Moore at the conventions was the one biggest hope of the indirect action element winning out. He was not opposed to Socialism. He has to work with Socialists—of many sorts. The whole basic idea of the Federation of Labour is a degree of Socialism. But it was the Marxian brand of Socialism born in Germany and transplanted to Russia to which Moore was opposed. He saw no field for this in Canada. He believed that Canada had a right to freedom of action. At least if it came to a choice between authority from the Gompers organization in the United States, and the Lenine tyranny in Russia, the course was clear. Time and time again he was bombarded and machine-gunned by the Red elements in Congress and Convention. As often he solidly stood his ground, based upon the older idea of labour getting its rights through negotiation and later through the ballot.

"Row, brothers, row, the stream runs fast,
    The rapids are near——"
But the daylight was not yet past for this Tom Moore. He could see ahead.

"I have seen Moore," says a close observer of him for two years, "faced by labour opponents in a number of Western cities. In all the howling he has never lost his temper or his dignity."

It would have been so much easier for this man to lose his temper, except that he knew it would be harder at the end when he had to face his own steady rank and file accusing him of poor chieftainship. It would have been so much easier to compromise with the preachers of glittering formulae, except that in the settling up he would have to justify himself to those who suspected him of defection.

Moore stuck to the commonplace business of wages and hours and agreements. He had no head for the poetry of Utopias. He knew, as he knows, that wages are the chief item of cost in all commodities, and that no matter what form of capitalism you choose, whether embodied in a Soviet or in a close corporation of dividends, wages of labour must be paid. He knows that prices of living and of labour are almost convertible. Amid all the howling and pæaning for a better day, for the new life, for the heaven upon earth, for the glorification of the proletariat, he could stand hard and fast by the common necessity of sticking to an agreement and as fast as possible bettering conditions.

We have heard independent observers say that the Reds have always shown a grasp of the new life, while the Trades Union men were crawling along with the uninspired programme of wages and hours ; that the Reds were the sacrificing idealists and the Unionists the selfish Tories who wanted nothing more than to slowly improve their condition. Well, the logic of events seems to show that in the long run the Moores have the gospel. One scarcely cares to think what might have happened in Canadian industry and common living had Tom Moore given way to the Reds who came at him from almost every quarter.

At the 1920 Congress Moore had the old-fashioned courage to ask the new Premier of Canada, Arthur Meighen, to address the delegates. Of all men, the man who prosecuted the leaders of the Winnipeg Strike was the last to say anything to organized labour about milleniums or about anything more Utopian than a common agreement between labour and capital for the good of all. Moore had no fear. He believed that he was right. Had he invited Mackenzie King he would have got a speech with more in it about the philosophy of Industry and Humanity, and perhaps more to the point in the practical study of the labour question. By inviting the Premier, Moore paid respect to government. Even Mr. Crerar might have made a more sympathetic speech. But in the Moore philosophy there is no radical connection between Crerar and Labour. In the organization of the Drury coalition between Labour and the Farm he can see one way of getting the rights of each incorporated into legislation.

But the Government is the final thing. Statesmanship is bigger than programmes painted on the clouds. There's a vast deal to be done yet in this country for the enfranchisement of labour in industry as it is franchised in government. There are pig-headed Tories of industry who will have to illustrate tombstones before some of the old spirit of repression of labour will die out in the nation. But the die-hards are fewer every year. Some wages had to come down to get everything else down. But we believe also, as Moore probably does, that wages which are the chief item of cost in all commodities ought to be as high as production will stand and pay reasonable profits on investment ; that collective bargaining is sound as applied to individual industries, but a form of bigoted tyranny when extended to the whole group or to the sympathetic strike ; and that the slogan, "Union is Strength", does not mean levelling efficiency to the lowest common denominator.

The day may come in the recorded minutes of Trades and Labour Congresses in Canada when a man of broader and more constructive vision may be needed to build the brotherhood out into labour statesmanship. But for the past few years, and for the few to come, Canadian labour and common weal may well arise to thank Tom Moore, who, when the rapids were near and the rocks were under the rapids, kept his craft rowing into safe water. Tom Moore of Ireland was a poet. Tom Moore of Canada is not. The play on the names is only an accident. The parallel holds. May we never again need such a man in this country to be sure that Labour does not run us all on the rocks under the Red rapids.

A MAN WITHOUT A PUBLIC

Sir William Mackenzie

A FEW years ago, before Stefansson reported on the blond Eskimos, the first Eskimo movie ever taken was shown in Toronto to a small audience who waited an hour for the film, which did not begin until a thick, grizzly man with shrewish, penetrating eyes came in with his party.

"Sir William Mackenzie, late as usual," whispered one. "He never arrives on time at a public function, often sleeps at a play, and sometimes when his family invite musicians to his home he plays bridge in a distant room so as not to hear the music."

"Oh, yes," nudged the other ; "but Sir William, you see, owns this film. It was taken by his own exploration party."

"Oh ! Then the last scene will probably be Eskimos laying railway ties."

"Oh, no. Digging up mineral deposits. Iron—Sh !"

It was a wonderful film full of epical energy and primitive beauty ; picturing one of the few kinds of people in Canada that Mackenzie had never been able to link up to civilization. The room was hung with costumes, curios and weapons of these folk, all of which were afterwards presented to the Royal Ontario Museum by Sir William, who was never enormously interested in ethnology. And that exploration of the far North was the last act in the complicated drama of William Mackenzie's great discoveries in Canada.

A study of Mackenzie is useful under the head :

WHAT DID YOU—NOT—DO TO WIN THE WAR ?

He was appointed in 1915 on an "Economic Commis-

253

sion" which seems to have practised a rigid economy on
what it did for the country, because it was never heard of
again. However, it was No. 1A of the 46 war-time commissions, and because Mackenzie was a member it should
have a memorial.

There is one man in Germany something like William
Mackenzie, who makes money almost by magic out of
utilities and buys up concerns in other countries with
money which he made in his own. His name is Hugo
Stinnes. Mackenzie is a bigger man and a higher type
than Stinnes ; but each man regards his country as a
commercial asset to be developed ; each is a wizard of a
species of applied finance. For years Mackenzie was of
speculative interest in Canada to people who had never
even seen his photograph. He was the man who had a
second headquarters in Ottawa and a branch office in every
provincial legislature except Prince Edward Island. We
almost had Provincial Premiers lullabying to their Cabinets:

"Hush ye, hush ye, do not fret ye,
The Black Douglas shall not get ye."

Mackenzie seemed to arise about twenty-five years ago
from some magic mountain and to stride down upon the
plains with the momentum of a Goth army. He was a
contractor who became for ten years a demigod. Sometimes before the war when people saw him on the street
they paused to watch him walking as though a black bear
had suddenly wandered down from Muskoka.

"By Jove ! Mackenzie's back again."

"And is that William Mackenzie ?"

"Did you never see him before ?"

"No, sir, I never saw him before."

"Well, take a good look. He's just going to lunch.
That man brought back sixty million dollars this time
from Threadneedle Street. A gang of reporters met him
at Montreal to get the good news—more money for Canada.
Great game ! He got forty millions a year ago or so."

"Who's that benign man with him ?"

"That's a Provincial Premier. His province wants more railways and the Government has to guarantee more bonds——"

"Oh, then he sells bonds with Provinces for security ?"

"That's the big idea. Why, what's wrong with it ?"

"Oh, I guess it's all right."

"Of course it is. Railways can't be built out of earnings of lines built last year. Traffic's too thin ; has to be developed. Mackenzie's building lines for a real population Canada, my boy, is a terrific country to railroad. The C.P.R. got land and cash grants. Mackenzie takes Government-guaranteed bonds. The whole country is on the same road. We import people on to homestead land and we have to borrow money to set the people up so that they'll become real Canadians——"

"Yes, especially at election time. But tell me—who finally owns these railroads ?"

"Well, you've got me. Nobody has figured that out yet. Everything is too new. All I know is that Governments are behind Mackenzie, and the people elect the Governments, and the people want the roads, and if they don't get 'em the Government probably goes out. Anyhow I take off my hat to Sir William Mackenzie as a great man."

Nine-tenths of Canada used to think that Mackenzie was a great man. The more he borrowed in England on Government-guaranteed bonds, and the more he invested in Mexico and South America, and the greater number of street railways, power plants, transmission lines, ore mountains, new towns, smelters, docks, ships, whale fisheries, coal mines and land companies that he and his able partner Mann were able to octopize, the greater the country thought both these men were—and especially Mackenzie.

Toronto Board of Trade once gave a dinner to these

men to celebrate the fact that by the building of the new line to Sudbury at a cost of about fifteen millions, Toronto was at last actually located on a Mackenzie road and had a right to be made the headquarters of the system. A deer in some places could have jumped from that line to the new line of the C.P.R. built at the same time—and about the same cost. There was no farmer in Ottawa to prevent the C.P.R. from getting a charter to double-track this line. It was the same year that Mackenzie inaugurated the Canadian Northern line of steamships, the two Royals, and for lack of tidewater was compelled to dock them at Montreal under the shadow of the C.P.R., who of course did not join in the civic welcome. And in the same year people were talking—as they are now again—about Toronto and Port Arthur becoming ocean ports. The wonder was that Mackenzie did not see to it. But he was fairly busy, tying Halifax to Vancouver by the Yellowhead Pass, and giving Provincial Cabinets new ideas about government.

Without a doubt William Mackenzie had a mandate from this country to do a great work—and he overdid it. Bankers and other financiers agreed that he had found new ways of investing creative money. Scarcely a teacher of geography but admitted that Mackenzie was changing the map of this country so fast that a new one became necessary every three years. New towns sprang up at the rate of a mile a day of new railway built by Mackenzie. Every new town became a monument to this man's faith in the future of Canada. Even the old city of Montreal, preserve of the C.P.R., lent its mountain to Mackenzie for a tunnel and a "Model City" on the hinter side.

There was always money to be had. A map of Canada in Mackenzie's satchel when he went to England to see money lenders seemed under his talk as big as the whole British Empire. It was not common Empire patriotism to refuse either the money or the guarantees for the bonds. The whole of Canada backed Mackenzie's notes. It was

he, not Sir Thomas White, who invented the principle of
Victory Loans whereby the nation becomes your banker.
Between building a new line and operating a line built last
year, there was no system of accounting that could audit
his books. The centipede became so vast and complex
that no banker could begin to understand it. Mackenzie
never made the effort. He was developing Canada.

The Saskatchewan valley was the one great trunk
Eldorado, the greatest discovery of natural resources ever
made in Canada. The settlers in that valley wanted more
people, the people wanted the railways, the Government
needed the voters, and Mackenzie wanted settlers, people,
voters, Government and all. If a Government was ob-
streperous, Mackenzie might lend a heavy hand to help
turn it out at the next election. It was not proper for a
Government to obstruct him. He was the over-man.

In no other nation has there ever been a man who could
play such a prodigious and prodigal game with the resources of the whole country. Mackenzie mobilized the
nation before the war. Millions of people in Canada used
to regard him as a sort of magnified Daniel Drew—the father
of Wall Street and watered stock and corrupt-contract railways. But Mackenzie was a broader man than Drew, with
a much higher sense of honour. Drew admitted that he
was a wonderful Methodist, that he had been a profiteer of
the Civil War, and that he had starved a railway of rails so
that it killed a large number of people in an accident.
Mackenzie was no Methodist ; and he never was a profiteer
from any emergency of the people. He wanted Canada to
prosper. All his profits must come from greater wealth in
Canada, which he did much to produce.

Mackenzie had more faith in Canada than most of the
politicians had. He wanted a great Canada, chief Dominion
in a great Empire. The best way to conserve a nation's
wealth, he said once, is to develop its resources. We never
had such a developer. He never was a born railwayman,

Q

any more than he was a pure financier. He was a colossal exploiter of national resources by means of borrowed money. In the era before Mackenzie we had Clergue at the Soo. Clergue was a pigmy forerunner of Mackenzie. What Clergue did in Algoma the other man aimed to do for the whole country, And he almost did it.

Asked once why he gave so much leeway to men like Mackenzie and Mann, Sir Wilfrid Laurier is reported to have said :

"Well, what other kind of men could you have to do such remarkable work ?"

Beaverbrook said at a dinner in Canada not long ago :

"I never was a William Mackenzie. I created nothing as he did."

The debacle of Mackenzie railways was never contemplated by Mackenzie. He did not even imagine that it was possible—except that he was prophetically troubled by the ambition of Laurier to create a third transcontinental. He had the right of way in this. He and Mann had developed the Canadian Northern out of a little stub line in Dauphin, Manitoba. The thing grew because it served the people, and the people lived in a fertile country that needed a road to market. The whole basic idea of the Mackenzie roads was to give more and more people a road to market. The original idea of the Grand Trunk Pacific and the National Transcontinental was to rival the Canadian Pacific monument to John A. Macdonald by erecting a railway monument to Wilfrid Laurier.

The race of the railways just about broke the nation's neck. It was not all the fault of Mackenzie that the race ever began, or that it was carried on to insanity. He was a practical philosopher to perceive that a Government is an elective corporation capable of manipulation in the interest of an all-Canada enterprise needed and wanted by the people. He was a master cynic to surmise that when the future came to balance the accounts, Father Time would be a very bewildered assignee.

The war was very ill advised. Mackenzie had no use for war. He never could see in the predicament of a nation any chance to profit for himself. He wanted perpetual prosperity. It never occurred to him, perhaps, that some day critics would arise to say that the country called Canada had done more for William Mackenzie than he had ever done for the country ; and that when the parent utility of the cycle which he had helped to create was declared bankrupt, he had no rights in the case whatever and never should have been paid a dollar of indemnity for the common stock.

But as the country had submitted to Mackenzie's system of building railways, so it was compelled to be content with the Royal Commission method of adjudicating what the builders should get out of the wreck.

Financiers and politicians and common citizens may wrangle till doomsday about the ethics of this debacle. They will never get anybody to understand it. The thing is an economic outlaw like its author. Mackenzie as a common storekeeper would have been sold for taxes. As a railway builder he staged the greatest pageant of industry ever known in Canada, and when the show went off the road because it was no longer able to pay its bills, took what he could salvage of the properties and left other men to wrestle with the reconstruction.

We shall never have another Mackenzie. Bigger men may arise. More unusual characters may stalk out of obscurity into places of eminence and power. But there never again can be an era like the Mackenzie epoch, because that kind of experience is suffered and enjoyed but once in a nation's lifetime. He still has big interests, some of them gradually being taken over by governments and municipal corporations. But he has shot his bolt, and it was a Jovian big one. No doubt he is enormously rich. That does not

matter. Canada no longer cares whether he is rich or
poor. Once a demigod in our national ledgers, he is
now a grizzled relique of his former energy. He used to be
a despot feared by those who had to work under him,
admired for his superhuman audacity and power to get
what he wanted just because he knew why and when he
wanted it, and capable of inspiring an almost insane loyalty
to a man-made system that never was anything at all but
an economic mirage. He is now just William Mackenzie,
more or less a citizen, now and then interviewed laconically
by a reporter who never can extract anything but arid
commonplaces from what he says to the public.

Because, to William Mackenzie there never was any
real public. What he cared about was the prosperous
nation upon which he could build and build without limit
till he died. When the nation came to a crisis in the war
he did nothing to help it, except to let the Railway War
Board pool his lines for traffic and the Government com-
mandeer his ships. The man who years before had been
regarded as the greatest doer in Canada, when the country
and all Mackenzie's works along with it came to the great
test, never so much as lifted a personal finger to help in
the work that had to be done. Mackenzie had done his
work in prosperity. In the great predicament he had no
function. The nation paid him his ducats and let him go.

This, if we are concerned about the man value of Canada,
is a tragedy. For there was in William Mackenzie somehow, with all his ruthlessness and audacity and semi-pirati-
cal creed, the element of a kind of great man. There is in
his uncommon face the look of a man who with less excess
of one quality might have become a wonderful citizen.
Nature made him vastly selfish on a scale big enough to
devise a totally new scheme for over-capitalizing Canada.
She denied him the commoner human qualities that
make a man a constructive citizen whether his country
is in weal or woe.

The epic which Mackenzie and his partner achieved in this country out-bid in dimensions, variety and the use of practical imagination, even the work of Rhodes in South Africa. It was a feat of economic and financial engineering which but for its peculiarly selfish energy and ruthless characteristics, might have become a monumental contribution to the human welfare of Canada. No man of common brain or conventional ethics could have been the dynamic head of such a work. For years, decades, this astounding adventurer exercised his precarious despotism over the country that he might make its prosperity a factor in his own success. In gambling with its securities he hoped to multiply its wealth without diminishing its happiness. The constructive imagination and tireless energy that he expended on his great cycle of utilities, had it been spent by a poet would have produced epics and dramas. But in all the things he did and the words he said, there is no record of any sentiment of sacrifice for the good of a nation.

William Mackenzie had his day, while Governments rose and fell. His day is done. The public which he dazzled and outwardly despised has no credulity left for any further hero-worship of such a man. "Well, what does Mr. Mackenzie want now?" was the oft-repeated query of the bewildered Laurier to Mackenzie agents in Ottawa. No Canadian Premier will ever ask such a question again. Ottawa has no further possibilities for William Mackenzie of any interest to the public. The kind of prosperity created by such men as he is played out in Canada forever.

The forecast than Mackenzie and Flavelle might form a new two-man junta to operate National railways was too absurd even to merit denial. Such a partnership would merely revive the old Schoolman debate of the Middle Ages—What happens when an irresistible force meets an immovable object? The two mentalities are incompatible. For twenty years the chief common ground between them was the Canadian Bank of Commerce, of which Sir Joseph is a director, who long ago discovered that the total assets of the bank were but a turbine in the Niagara of Mackenzie finance.

And William Mackenzie who built the conspiracy of enormous interests with which his name is identified, was never meant to be a railway operator at all. One might as well expect Lloyd George to be a successful manager of Sunlight Soap and of Lord Leverhulme.

THE IMPERIAL BRAINSTORM

LORD BEAVERBROOK

LORD Beaverbrook could stroll into an Arab camp and in five minutes be psychologically *persona grata* as the man who could make something out of almost nothing. He could learn the Arab language, adopt their customs, interpret their ideas, transact their tribal business, and go away without an Arab to admit that the strange new chief—or whatever they might call him—would ever learn to be a true Arab.

This man without a congenial country has an unlimited talent for adapting himself to the necessities of time, place and opportunity. He has little or no power to assimilate himself to the real life of the people. He trailed like a comet through the land of his birth and left it in a mirage of finance before Canada had made him a citizen. He went to England where in a few months he had made himself intimate with public affairs ; and in ten years, "with all his honours thick upon him," he has not yet become an Englishman.

Once only I met this extraordinary man, at close range, for a number of hours. He was a most absorbing study ; and he knew it. There never was a moment when Beaverbrook could not consciously estimate the effect of his actions upon some other man, or group of men. As an actor he is not a mediocrity.

A personal friend vividly describes meeting him at a small semi-private dinner in a Canadian city. The ostensible occasion was a mere complimentary affair to his lordship. The psychological objective was—something else. There began the conjecture. What was it ?

It must be inferred. There are some men who study the effect of themselves upon a group. The group method of psychology is essentially Beaverbrookian.

A number of speeches had been pre-arranged for this dinner on behalf of various interests. At the close of the talks Beaverbrrok was asked to respond to a toast of his own health. He did so in a perfectly amazing confessional of a speech, saying things which he said he felt sure no journalist present would publish. He was asked questions. Each question meant one more speech. He made four in all, occupying much more than an hour of time in a most graphic and humanly interesting account of things that had happened behind the curtain in British politics, shrewd estimates of the signs of the times, forecasts of coming events and vivid delineations of great men whom he had intimately met in various parts of Europe.

In all this there was not a trace of embarrassment or of suspicion. The little dynamo with the prodigious head and the baby mouth and the intense, deepset, restless eyes stood by his chair, and with knuckles on the table much of the time, talked down into the flowers directly in front of him. He spoke sometimes in a husky, low voice, now and again in a smothered shriek, again in a tragic whisper. He was in a small gathering and he seemed to know that though the dingy, mysterious room was somewhat high, he had no need to lift his voice to the shrill impetuous discord that is said to characterize his speeches in Commons or Lords. He was carried away by some indefinable atmosphere. What it was he scarcely knew. After the dinner he shook hands with people, delivered himself of a number of snappy brusqueries, laughed a good bit and, almost the last to leave the charmed precinct where he had unbosomed himself among "congenial" souls, he wandered out.

Next day, lying poseurishly on a lounge in his room at the hotel, he said to a confidante who had been with him at the dinner :

"Bunting !" (that is not the true name) "Will you kindly repeat to me some of the things I seem to have said last evening. I know I talked an unconscionably great deal. What on earth did I say ?"

As it had been a perfectly abstemious occasion, one imagines that Beaverbrook at the dinner was sincere, though playing the actor, and that in his room he was both theatrical and insincere.

This man has a confusing, but in his own mind seldom confused, orbit of his own. He was a conundrum in Canada. He is an enigma in England. That he still considers himself a Canadian, because he was born here, fortuned here and voluntarily exiled from here after he had completely mystified a large number of people as to his working psychology, is proved by the fact that he continues to come back here. He also professes to be manning the *Daily Express* with Canadians. He has been for ten years the intimate of Bonar Law, also a distinguished Canadian of sorts. And a few months ago there was a rumour, which no one remembers him to have refuted, that he was a likely candidate for the Governor-Generalship of Canada. Of course if ever Rideau Hall should take Beaverbrook for a tenant, it will be time to take refuge in a Canadian republic.

It is easy to think disagreeable things about Beaverbrook, because he is so enormously interesting, so pathologically unusual, and altogether so brilliant and resourceful a phenomenon. I have called him the Imperial brainstorm. A dozen other titles would fit him as well. There are times when one almost imagines himself mingling an element of real liking for the man with one's unfailing admiration of his remarkable ability. But always when you feel like that cordial handshake and talking to him with brusque familiarity, there is the intuitive feeling that one of the two, perhaps both, might live to regret it.

You cannot absorb the atmosphere of such a man. Whatever the sterling qualities of his character, the approximate miracles of his achievements, the warlike strategy of his career, you judge him at last by that indefinable but inexorable law of common congeniality. To live at close range with Beaverbrook, to become part of his daily scheme of vibrations, to work either with, or for, or even over him as a regular part of one's programme would be to a normal man a penalty almost amounting to a crime.

Though of course tastes differ, even in companions. There are people who rather like hobnobbing with Beaverbrook. Some are interested in his idiosyncrasies, as though he were a good subject for a novel. Some enjoy the sensation of playing moth to a social flame. Others—perhaps—have a deep respect for his money which, like Carnegie's, is supposed to be a perplexity to himself to know how to spend it that he may die poor.

Well, the noble lord has his idioms. Discussing the details of the little dinner already referred to a flippant but devoted critic said :

"I think he would enjoy speaking right in front of that huge fireplace. He would consider it Napoleonic."

As to the social orbit of Beaverbrook, one may suspect that it is a rather exotic atmosphere in which the sense of true human equation is lost in a jumble. A man who can entertain almost simultaneously, at his country home, financiers, politicians, authors, and actresses from his own theatre at Hammersmith, may be regarded as a shrewd social mergerist but scarcely as a subtle entertainer of congenial souls. As for the discomfort of knowing what to do with his money, Beaverbrook has never complained ; during his latest visit to Canada he was offered and he refused the purchase of two bankrupt newspapers each of which thought that the acquisition of such a side line to the *Daily Express* might enable him to do some of the good in this country which he failed to achieve while he lived here.

Estimating this man by the superficial but rather subtle qualities by which he has achieved success, it seems a sort of irony to think what he might have done and did not do for the country of his birth. What did he ever do for Canada ? Before the war—nothing He made huge fortunes here. He created mergers here. He started consolidated companies here that in time fought their way into the appreciated valuations of the stock market. He became Canada's greatest adventurer in creating a sort of "wealth" from the merging of small, sometimes decrepit, concerns under a new name and new issues of stock ; just as Mackenzie was our greatest adventurer in creating wealth from borrowed money Beaverbrook worked mainly with small groups to whom he left the task of raising most of the capital. Thus his personal gains came neither from the immediately increased earnings of companies which he amalgamated, nor directly from the pockets of the shareholders. Beaverbrook never made a dollar by defrauding a director or luring unsuspicious dollars out of the pockets of common people. That species of tactics so often practised by men who are near criminals was quite beneath him. The laboratory where he got his results was the stock market, which of course has its own codes of ethics and plays its own remorseless game of making or breaking men.

His career here had most of the elements of romance. Son of a poor parson born in a cross-roads Ontario hamlet, brilliant but erratic student at Dalhousie University, down-at-the-heels insurance agent in Halifax youthful merger of two small banks at a time when he was unable to pay for his own clothes—we have here symptoms of a career which might have turned into a character of high value in Canadian politics, public service or social reform.

But Nature thrives on migrations. Even a man sometimes takes better root when he is transplanted. The

Beaverbrook that England has is a more unusual character than the Max Aitken that Canada lost. Canada to be sure had lost enough brilliant men to other nations and imported enough able men from abroad. It was time to produce and to keep our own. There was national work for them all to do. Aitken came up in the boom time of Canada. He fitted the time. A nation's financial adversity was no occasion for him. He followed the wake and profited by the experiences of builders of railways, industries, banks and provinces. Every move forward of the country in commercial expansion was a nudge ahead for his chariot of fortune. He was the most successful "bull" factor Canada ever had. But in all probability, were he to be flung into one of the demoralized nations of democratized Europe he could make money even in disaster.

Before he was thirty-five Max Aitken had become a multi-millionaire. He worked much as clever but humbler men have invented formulae to beat bookmakers at the races. Having done all this, at so early an age, what was left ? Superficially we should have said—public life. He had the money, the talent, the leisure. Canada had the need.

But Max Aitken never so much as became a pound-keeper in Canada, not because he had not the opportunity, but because he had the shrewd sense to feel that the land where he had made "his pile" was not the land in which to serve his country. To serve a nation means as a rule to deal directly with the public. Max Aitken had never dealt with the public. Neither does he yet—except in-directly through a big daily newspaper of phenomenal circulation. On his last visit to Canada he was invited to public functions. He consistently declined; not because he shunned popularity or hated the limelight, but because he would not have felt comfortable. In one of his speeches he pointed out that the securities which he put on the market years ago were all now listed as paying ventures.

It was more comfortable to make that remark as a returned celebrity than to have made it as a citizen.

His own story of why he went to England, and stayed there, is ingenuous. He said that he went in order to do business ; that he tried to talk business ; that the public men with whom he had conference insisted on talking politics ; that he succumbed and stayed, winning a seat in the Commons, and almost before an ordinary man could have said "Jack Robinson", he was hobnobbing with men the calibre of Bonar Law, Lloyd George, Northcliffe.

Only fragmentary accounts of Beaverbrook's political history in England have as a rule drifted over here. To show what an amazing story it is, nothing can be better than to quote a curiously apt summary written for two Canadian periodicals by Arthur Baxter, who for some years now has been a sort of Boswell to Beaverbrook.

In 1910 captured the seat for Ashton-under-Lyne.

In 1912 a vigorous and successful attack on Lloyd George concerning finance matters in the House.

From 1911 to 1914 he entered parliamentary intrigue and gradually his home at Leatherhead became a Mecca for puzzled politicians.

During this time somebody made him a Knight.

The Irish situation was more than threatening ; the tariff issue was causing bitterness ; Austen Chamberlain with a minority following was fighting Walter Long to lead the Tories and on this troublesome sea Sir Max Aitken's barque bobbed up and down with the skipper's eyes keenly alert. He saw the possibilities in Bonar Law. When Chamberlain and Long created a deadlock, Beaverbrook advocated Bonar Law as leader of the Tory Party. To make his voice heard more distinctly he purchased the *Daily Express* and backed his candidate with a powerful but (then) not very profitable newspaper. Law has the reputation for modesty, but his fellow-Canadian led him to the barrier, started him off and when he stopped running he found himself leader.

For some time it had seemed as if Asquith's Coalition Government would survive the war, but late in 1917 it was obvious that the old ship was leaking badly. Carson was the first to propose scuttling the frigate. The others argued that even a sinking ship was better than no ship at all, so the Irishman went overboard and sailed away on his own raft. Bonar Law representing the good old Tory element kept on working the pumps ; Mr. Asquith kept on assuring the crew that all they needed was to "wait and see " ; and Lloyd George was wondering whether he had better take a hand at the pumps as well or throw both Asquith and Bonar Law into the sea.

At this juncture a sail was sighted. It was Max Aitken's barque that "hopped aboard" and took in the spectacle of his old Maritimian sweating at the pumps ; and noticed with a critical eye the extremely able appearance of that able-bodied politician, Lloyd George.

Beaverbrook thought the situation over—swiftly. He saw that the genial Micawber on the Bridge could not be routed as long as Bonar Law and Lloyd George stuck to him. But even if they could be persuaded to heave the skipper overboard, could they sail the ship and keep the crew loyal as well ?

He decided that Carson had to be brought back to the fold, so jumping into his little craft he scoured the political sea and returned shortly with the uncrowned king of Ireland on board.

But Lloyd George, Bonar Law and Sir Edward Carson loved each other as much as three Prima Donnas. They all agreed that Asquith was sailing to disaster, but they weren't sure that they didn't prefer disaster under the Old Chief to prolonged life in each other's company.

Beaverbrook had seen a vision and he knew that Lloyd

George was the only man in England capable of forming a ministry that would last six months. Day after day the Canadian stuck to his task and gradually the three men, all smarting from old political quarrels, agreed to send an ultimatum to the skipper that they demanded a sailing committee under the leadership of "Pincher" Lloyd George.

In other words they demanded a War Cabinet with the Welshman as Chairman.

Finally, in desperation, Lloyd George called for a mutiny. Bonar Law summoned all the Tory crew around him. They went to the bridge and told the Skipper that they were sorry to break the news to him, but it had been decided that, all things considered, he had better walk the plank.

Mr. Asquith was dismayed, blustered, then resigned— defying the mutineer Welshman to do any better. His Majesty called on Bonar Law to form a cabinet ; the Canadian declined with thanks but mentioned the name of a certain Welshman as a likely candidate for the job. The Welshman was asked—and accepted. Two days later his Cabinet was formed. Carson took over the pumps ; Bonar Law went up to the bridge and Lloyd George delegated to himself the rank of Commander and Pilot of Britain's ship of State.

And that is the story of Beaverbrook's tremendous contribution to winning the war. He secured most of the Labour Party, the Tories, and Carson for Lloyd George ; without them the Prime Minister could never have formed a government.

Sir Max Aitken wanted more than a Peerage for his work ; he had hoped for a position of tremendous power, but the Government made him a Lord and he went back to Canadian publicity.

Imagination tries to conceive of any Englishman coming over here to merge Borden, Laurier and Crerar. Imagination fails. Not even Aitken could have done it. That he succeeded in England where he must have failed in Canada must have reasons.

1. Experience in mergers.
2. Prestige as a Canadian.
3. Advantage of being—Max Aitken.

The first we understand. The second involves the Empire. Aitken was—if anything that could be labelled— a Tory. He had no trouble becoming a Unionist. His success with Bonar Law made it possible in getting rid of Asquith. He could call Carson "Edward". He could think as fast as Lloyd George. It was a time for quick thinking—and action. He had opened all the heavy doors in Montreal—and closed them upon all but those he wanted inside. He tried the same thing in England. His audacity was inspired. Something had to be done. Somebody must be the middleman. Aitken had an uncanny faculty for sizing up situations ; for manipulating men ; for interpreting ambition—because no man in England had an ambition surpassing his own. He could play political chess and absorb superficial culture at the same time. Books, plays, authors, artists, manners, accent—all were grist to his mill. He was an astute actor. He could assume a virtue; simulate anxiety; hover about closed doors on tiptoe; speak in the awed whisper; in the event of a crisis peer tragically into men's faces.

England knew she had taken a queer character to bosom ; a child who was growing up at Gargantuan speed, an *enfant terrible* of sudden and prodigious experience ; a creature who could sit up o' nights and plot and organize and cabal and next morning rub out the wrinkles at tennis, amiable if he beat his opponent, growling and savage if beaten, ready for a campaign in the afternoon, a speech in the evening and a conference at midnight Or he could plunge into polite arts, talk familiarly of literature with duchesses, undergo a surgical operation to-day and sit up for correspondence to-morrow. He has a brain whose recipe for complete rest is "change of work"! Barring Lloyd George and De Valera, he has perhaps the most unusual brain in Great Britain.

No Canadian, already a millionaire, had ever done these things. Not even Gilbert Parker had so amazingly cultivated the accent. Greenwood, diligent and talented, had been slow and determined. Aitken—opened the heavy doors. As in Canada, he was at last able to close out all but those who could play the game of the hour. This Canadian could not only talk, but act, Empire; not merely ape, but superficially assimilate, England ; and he understood the United States—because he was temperamentally something of an American.

His success on the surface is incomprehensible. The one key to it is his persistent cultivation of Bonar Law, who in the Coalition was the great prop to the Premier. Beaverbrook hugely admires Lloyd George. He reverences Bonar Law. The Premier and himself had too many points, though not characteristics, in common to become running mates. Intimately congenial to the Unionist leader, Aitken was never allowed to become indispensable to the Premier. His brief term as member of the War Cabinet terminated almost suddenly. Was it voluntary ? Or ambitious ? What did this Warwick want as reward more than the peerage which may have been designed to chloroform an electric battery ?

We are not told. Once during the second year of war he offered to raise and equip and command a battalion from New Brunswick. His offer was not accepted. He went to Sam Hughes. "Sam," he said, "I want a job in the Canadian Army !"

He got it. Aitken's work as Eye Witness to the Canadian troops and the publication of "Canada in Flanders" was the performance of a man who in the great crisis of war had found a sudden and sincere interest in his native land

R

that he had never exhibited while he was a citizen of this country. He showed a grasp of the human as well as the technical side of war. A man who could so rediscover his own nation could surely do something new in helping to co-ordinate the Empire. He has an astonishing knowledge of great public men in all countries, a thorough commercial knowledge of Europe and Asia, and—may we say a genius for a sort of secret diplomacy? His war record demonstrates most of these qualities. His Canadian War Memorials are a proof that he understands how to make his own country useful to British artists.

What then did Beaverbrook expect as reward for his political services, beyond a peerage and the sublime sense of having "done his duty" where he saw it?

Governor-Generalship of Canada?

Ambassadorship to the United States?

Secretaryship of State for the "Colonies"?

Or the Chancellorship of the Exchequer?

There is really nothing else left for an ambition like this except the Premiership of Great Britain. Brilliant, plotting, crafty and phenomenal, this young man has still the spirit of the corsair. England has not absorbed him. But there is a general election pending over there. The Coalition is not on Gibraltar. Party cleavages are rife. Labour, Liberals, Socialists, Syndicalists, Bolshevists and old-line Unionists are all pitching camps about the Premier's Verdun. When the battle really begins will Gen. Beaverbrook be in the citadel, or working in a headquarters tent to merge any three of the common enemy into a force that will haul down the Coalition flag?

"Why do you think Lloyd George will come back as powerfully as ever?" he was asked here, after his admission that for the time being the Premier was in the doldrums of unpopularity.

"Because—he always does!" was his cautious reply;

in which one almost detected the suspicion that he might not ; and if so—what ?

These are some of the unpredicables. Even the answer Beaverbrook himself might give to-day might be challenged by his action of to-morrow. But this man has always succeeded in finance when a country was prosperous, and in politics when the nation was confronted by emergency. He is still too ambitious to adjourn permanently to Leatherhead, Surrey ; too young to write his memoirs. England is a new world. And it may be—unless he has already alienated his personality from his genius—that one of its picturesque discoverers will be Lord Beaverbrook.

Meanwhile he remarks that most of his friends are in Canada. One misses at least a fumbling guess, if in the days to come he will not value those friends, whoever they may be, more than he ever did when he was making millions here or merging politicians over there. Such a man seldom moves his forces just for parade. As Aitken used this country to get himself preferment in England on account of the Empire, so it may be suspected that he has used England—not impossibly—to reclaim in this country whatever credit he lost some time before he left it.

Meanwhile until the Government of Great Britain finds some better function for this phenomenon, we recommend that he be made the official economic investigator of the Empire. Up to the present this has been a pastime for leisured travellers like Lord Southesk, Sir Charles Dilke, and Rider Haggard. A man with Beaverbrook's ability to analyze economic conditions and gain the confidence of men in high positions could be of incalculable value in getting a thorough survey of the commercial and political resources of a commonwealth which as yet nobody seems to understand. After that the Government might well make him Viceroy of India, where he might apply his talent for group-coalition to the great problem of constitutional Home Rule.

CONCLUSION

A Canadian newspaperman once flippantly asked the late W. T. Stead :

"What do you think about continentalism in North America ?"

The answer came just as flippantly :

"Every nation has a right to go to the devil in its own way. Canada should not be denied the privilege."

There was a blunt candour about the reply that even from an egotist like Stead meant infinitely more than the soothing-syrup idealism dispensed by some of the visiting prophets to this country. Stead did not mean that in establishing independence of the United States, Canada should cut the painter from the Great British Commonwealth. But he was a trifle cynical about the young nation, just as Disraeli was fifty years ago when he said that "these colonies would yet be a millstone about Britain s neck". Neither of them was more cynical about us than we usually are about ourselves, never in theory, but in practice.

Most of the men sketched in the foregoing pages, as well as hundreds of others in public life, realize that Parliament and Legislatures have a hard time to keep themselves from going to the devil, and that so far as they go along that road the nation travels with them. As an experiment in nationhood we have some peculiar and original weaknesses, as well as strengths. Belgium, for instance, could be tacked by Atlas overnight on to one of our northward coasts, or set down as an island in some of our northern waters, when only a geographer would notice the difference. Belgium has a king and two million more people than Canada. We have slightly more territory

than the United States, when New York State alone has as
many people as our whole country. We are as big as
many Britains and we have enough railway mileage to
make Britain a spider-web, when our population is about
one-fifth of hers and our ultimate authority in democratic
government comes from Downing Street. Yet there are
prophets among us who predict that we shall yet be the
pivot of the Empire.

Once you begin to speculate about the future of this
country there is no end. And the past of the nation has
rather little to do with estimating its future. We have
been a wide-open immigration country. In twenty years
we have transformed outselves by a foreign policy with
which Britain had nothing to do. Twenty years more and
we could do it again with even more disastrous results.
In 1867 the great compromise known as Confederation
tied four and a half millions of people into a political unity.
In half a century we doubled our population ; built 30,000
miles of transcontinental and branch lines of railway ; made
ourselves a race congress imitation of the United States ;
enacted a National Policy of protective tariffs that failed
to protect us from ourselves ; created an Oriental problem
on the Pacific, exaggerated a race problem on the Ottawa,
and developed an American-penetration system clear across
the country ; sent a small army to help establish a similar
government and dual problem to our own in South Africa
and a huge army to Europe to help make the world safe
for the kind of democracy of which we consider ourselves
a fair sample ; created a small army of millionaires and had
bestowed upon us about an equal number of knighthoods
as well as a number of peerages, and four years ago peti-
tioned the King through Parliament to abolish the practice;
gave a first mortgage on the country to one great transcontinental railway, and a second and a third to two more
whi h we have since nationalized into government ownership because the roads were bankrupt for the present and

built for the future, which is yet a long way off ; developed a cycle of quite remarkable big industries and federalized banks which a large element of our heterogeneous democracy now consider a menace to the nation ; and on the prairies which, shortly after Confederation, we bought for a few millions sterling from the Hudson's Bay Company, a Liberal Government, never contemplated by the Fathers of Confederation, carved out two new great Provinces which for ten years have tried to kill the Tory Party which gave the Northwest its birth, all Liberalism that does not go back to the furrow, and aims to abolish even the moderately successful economic system by which we have come to our present state of comparative prosperity.

If that is the kind of thing that Stead meant by "every nation going to the devil in its own way" it must be conceded that we have lost no time over the going We are among the forward nations, even though we are less radical than Australia. No young nation ever accomplished visibly and materially so much in so brief a period. We had the enormous scientific resources of the 20th century to give us momentum. Perhaps we were a little too fast on the down grade. We still take some inspiration from looking at the map to reflect that no other part of the British Empire occupies so strategic a position as Canada. We note that Canada is not only the natural interpreter between Britain and the United States—which it took some of our far-seeing statesmen a long while to discover—but that we are also a transformer between the power-house at Downing Street and the one at Tokio ; that we are fair on the highway of traffic and travel between London and Yokohama ; that we have room within a reasonable time for as many people as are now living in Britain, and that if we are not too awfully anxious about going to the devil we can make that population one of the most potential in the world for its size, not only in producing things to eat and wear and export, but in helping to hold the British Commonwealth steady long enough to let the old thing work out its big share of the world's salvation.

Such is the outlook. Meanwhile we have our innate defects, the first of which arises from the vastness of geography and the littleness of politicians. Little politics in Canada are pocketed away in sections. Some of our native born are the most parochial. There are groups in Canada as un-national as Eskimos who in some respects are our best citizens because they owe nothing to, and expect nothing from, any Government.

People shout about assimilation, not knowing to what pattern, if any, foreign peoples should be assimilated. The missionary goes abroad and extracts from the heathen even the nobilities of his own faith and leaves him often the miserable animosities of a creed: Political and social missionaries in Canada make the same mistake about foreigners. It is a great thing to Canadianize a race. But we ought to begin by Canadianizing some of our native-born.

Even our public men believe in political servitude. A man goes to Ottawa burning with zeal to inaugurate political liberation. Six months or a year produces sleeping-sickness. He is given a hyperdemic of conformity. He gravitates into the formula of a group. His message is muzzled. If not, it too often breaks loose in a tirade on behalf of some section littler than even any of the groups in Ottawa.

Big men do not, as is often said, go into Parliament. There is a great reason. The wonder is that the few big men we elect stay there so long. Government is supposed to be business. But the business takes a long while to do —even badly. Ottawa is the place where the national field-glasses too often get turned wrong end about.

We are seldom honest about public men. A man's own party praises, the opposite party damns him. In an old nation this intellectual strabismus is pardonable. In a young nation it is a form of political suicide. We too often wait for a man to make a great speech before admitting independent of party, that he is anything great as a man.

Because Canada is so vast, political leaders find it necessary to enunciate one doctrine here, another one there. This is an old trick ; playing the lights on stage when the spot-light is reserved for the big local issues. We are constantly besieged by "national policies". Many of them have very little to do with national citizenship. Most of them sketch out milleniums that are never realized. We are a people of extremisms. When national prosperity is the objective we tolerate, and even idolize, any man who is bold and big enough to capture the country with his special-interest programme. Then the delirium is over, heyday is done, and the nation wakes up to classify as public plunderers the very men whom it once regarded as the economic saviours of the country.

Our faculty of national criticism is not as yet strongly developed. Thank heaven, we are not cynical ; but it is better to be a hopeful cynic than a disgruntled idealist. Men will arise with specious programmes by means of which they can hypnotize a group and aim at capturing the country. Progress carries on by means of such men and such groups. But the devil himself stands behind the stage bush to prod these zealots into the limelight and the next moment to lead the claque in the gallery. We are carried away by the act, afterwards find that we have been duped and hold indignation meetings after the show is safely ten miles down the line.

Like all other nations we have had our share of "the new time coming". During the war we had all the old parties dead and buried along with patronage and race cries and public graft. But while the preacher was busy over the funeral rites a number of chief mourners were somewhere "making hay". A nation's adversity is too often some man's opportunity. In moneymaking this is even worse than in politics. It is too easy to shout and to shed tears. We deplore the past, suspect the future and work hard to make ourselves solid for the present.

Many men in Canada do not regard public life as public service. There is little or no preparation for doing the nation's business. Men are log-rolled into Parliament and pitchforked into Cabinets. The work they are expected to do has little or no relation to the work for which nature and experience intended them. It is regarded a simpler matter to administer a great State department than to manage a big industry.

Ottawa is the natural objective of all those who "want" something. When interests camp on the trail of Governments and of Parliament, the interest of the nation is going to suffer—and it always has. We are paying in taxes now for the lobbying that went on ten years ago. No Government is ever considered so patriotic and humanly powerful that it can resist the inroad of "big interests".

Bigger interests arise. In a storm of newly patented virtue they declaim against the "big" ones. They fail to admit that they merely want to usurp instead of to magnify Government. The political machine of the country is regarded as a part of the machine by which special interests prosper. In its efforts to repudiate such a connection Governments resort to the trick of clamouring on behalf of "the people".

Presently even the people lose faith in Government. They come to believe only in class-conscious groups. No nation can be big whose parties are small. No parties can be great whose platforms are for the good of a class or the veneration of what "my grandfather" used to think.

Elections are eternally war. A general election has for a sure sign the prediction on the part of the Opposition that the Government intend to "put one over" in order to grab another lease of power. Experience has taught us that the prediction is too often true. It does not teach us that it is time to abandon the expectation or the practice. Men who in party bondage have helped to win elections by redistribution after a census, and to award patronage to the victors, arise years later in Opposition to denounce such practices when carried on by the present Government. The pot usually succeeds in calling the kettle black. Hence a bad black eye to political sincerity.

The average parliamentarian knows very little about Canada ; much about his own Province, or his own constituency, or his own group. Politicians do not even travel except on business. A country of vast and variegated human interest, of wonderful charm even for scenery, without considering people at all, is the home of a large number of people burning to do national work who know little or nothing about the life of the nation, historically or otherwise.

President Harding solemnly predicts that the United States will produce a race of supermen. He does not say how. He merely observes the need. He knows that his country has gone the pace that will take generations of coming back before any superman nation can begin to be. In Canada we have not gone so far that we cannot easily come back. But we have no vision of any future for this nation except a larger instalment of what we have been.

We talk about being a nation when we ignore the very disadvantages that militate against true nationalism. We bluster about national sentiment and spend our money on paying to have ourselves Americanized. When we are tired trying to explain that, we fall back into dithyrambics on the Old Flag and the great British Empire.

But if we are ever going to be anything but a national and polyglot sandwich between the United States and Great Britain, it is time we paid some respect to the innate democracy of the British idea by developing our own national identity. Our strategic position in the Empire will be worth no more to us than our great native resources, or our bilingual nationalism, or our pioneering history, or all combined, unless we elect to make the biggest and best we have dominate our national life. This is a big country that must become a great nation if those who aim to lead it will abstain from little ways. We need more poetry in our public affairs. More imagination in Parliament. More vision in the Administration. More faith in the country. Less sectionalizing propaganda everywhere. If we rise to the measure of opportunity, we may yet prove that when the Fathers of Confederation hung our national future on a great compromise and a transcontinental railway they were not talking in their sleep ; and that when Empire statesmen look to our leaders for counsel we shall not send unto them any man who represents a class-conscious economic group instead of a nation.

It is true that Governments have always capitulated to groups. We have sacrificed a great deal for the sake of protection when that was merely a tariff to keep certain industries from obliteration. But a nation cannot be forever built upon smoke-stacks and blue-books. We can better afford to have continental free trade and spiritual freedom as a nation, than a high tariff and bondage to an industrial-financial-transportation group. But if we gobble the bait of free trade, and find ourselves on the hook of economic and national domination by the United States, our last state will surely be worse than our first.